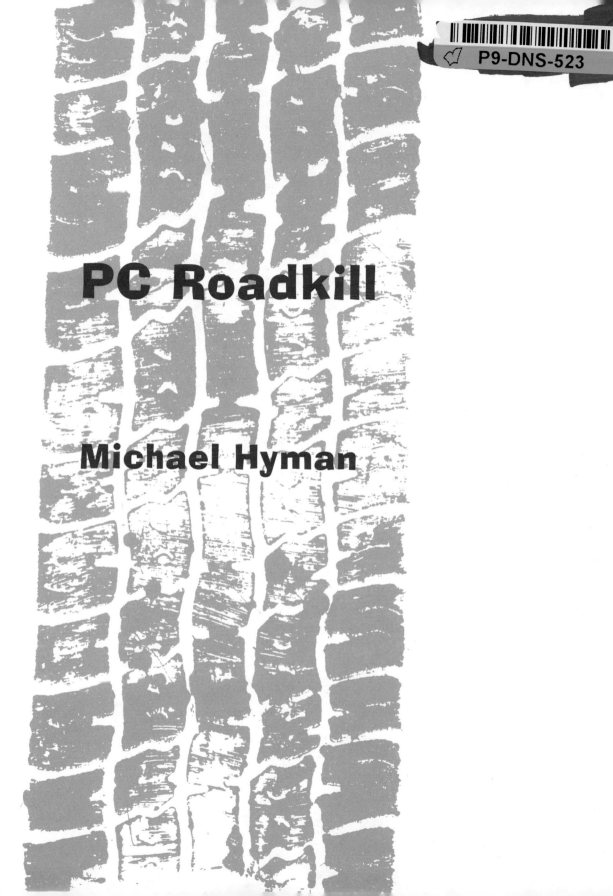

PC Roadkill

Michael Hyman

PC Roadkill

Michael Hyman

A Division of IDG Books Worldwide, Inc.
Foster City, CA • Chicago, IL • Indianapolis, IN • Braintree, MA • Dallas, TX

PC Roadkill

Published by

IDG Books Worldwide, Inc.

An International Data Group Company

919 East Hillsdale Boulevard, Suite 400

Foster City, CA 94404

Library of Congress Catalog Card No.: 95 - 79562

ISBN 1-56884-348-8

Printed in the United States of America

First Printing, September, 1995

10 9 8 7 6 5 4 3 2 1

Distributed in the United States by IDG Books Worldwide, Inc.

Published in the United States

Welcome to the world of IDG Books Worldwide.

IDG Books Worldwide, Inc. is a subsidiary of International Data Group, the world's largest publisher of computer-related information and the leading global provider of information services on information technology. IDG was founded more than 25 years ago and now employs more than 7,500 people worldwide. IDG publishes more than 235 computer publications in 67 countries (see listing below). More than fifty million people read one or more IDG publications each month.

Launched in 1990, IDG Books Worldwide is today the #1 publisher of best-selling computer books in the United States. We are proud to have received 3 awards from the Computer Press Association in recognition of editorial excellence, and our best-selling ...For Dummies™ series has more than 18 million copies in print with translations in 24 languages. IDG Books, through a recent joint venture with IDG's Hi-Tech Beijing, became the first U.S. publisher to publish a computer book in the People's Republic of China. In record time, IDG Books has become the first choice for millions of readers around the world who want to learn how to better manage their businesses.

Our mission is simple: Every IDG book is designed to bring extra value and skill-building instructions to the reader. Our books are written by experts who understand and care about our readers. The knowledge base of our editorial staff comes from years of experience in publishing, education, and journalism — experience which we use to produce books for the '90s. In short, we care about books, so we attract the best people. We devote special attention to details such as audience, interior design, use of icons, and illustrations. And because we use an efficient process of authoring, editing, and desktop publishing our books electronically, we can spend more time ensuring superior content and spend less time on the technicalities of making books.

You can count on our commitment to deliver high-quality books at competitive prices on topics consumers want to read about. At IDG, we value quality, and we have been delivering quality for more than 25 years. You'll find no better book on a subject than an IDG book

John J. Kilcullen

John Kilcullen
President and CEO
IDG Books Worldwide, Inc.

About the Author

Michael Hyman works on cool stuff at a large software company in the Northwest. He was the business-unit manager for the languages group at Borland, and cofounder of Within Technologies. He's authored eight other computer books and is a columnist for *Windows Tech Journal*.

When he's not working, Michael lavishes attention on his wife and cat, runs, bikes, and plays music far too loudly.

For More Information...

For general information on IDG Books in the U.S., including information on discounts and premiums, contact IDG Books at 800-434-3422.

For information on where to purchase IDG's books outside the U.S., contact Christina Turner at 415-655-3022.

For information on translations, contact Marc Jeffrey Mikulich, Foreign Rights Manager, at IDG Books Worldwide; fax number: 415-655-3295.

For sales inquiries and special prices for bulk quantities, contact Tony Real at 800-434-3422 or 415-655-3048.

For information on using IDG's books in the classroom and ordering examination copies, contact Jim Kelly at 800-434-2086.

PC Roadkill is distributed in Canada by Macmillan of Canada, a Division of Canada Publishing Corporation; by Computer and Technical Books in Miami, Florida, for South America and the Caribbean; by Longman Singapore in Singapore, Malaysia, Thailand, and Korea; by Toppan Co. Ltd. in Japan; by Asia Computerworld in Hong Kong; by Woodslane Pty. Ltd. in Australia and New Zealand; and by Transword Publishers Ltd. in the U.K. and Europe.

Dedication

To geeks who dream and the Not Fade Away crew.

Acknowledgments

This book would not be possible without the hard work and help of dozens of people. First, I'd like to thank my wife Sarah for her patience, understanding, and the chocolate chip cookies. A year of week ends, late nights, and early mornings disappeared into the book, despite the gorgeous weather, invites from friends, and other temptations. She knows what it is like to be a computer widow. Next, thanks to all of the friends I so quickly snubbed to finish this. I'm breathing again. (But not for long.) Thanks to my sister Betsy, off on yet another adventure, and to my parents, Richard and Roberta, who not only lent back the Microsoft Mom shirt I bought so many years ago, but gave me birth, support, and a Deodora Cedar.

Behind every book there is a team of devoted editors. Thanks to Chris Williams, with whom I brainstormed the idea over sake in a Santa Cruz restaurant. To Anne Marie Walker, who helped push it through despite all the bad jokes in Visual C++ For Dummies. To Wade Strickland, who, after being bombarded with Fed Ex packages and frantic notes about t-shirts, has decided to stick to business suits. To Tracy Brown, for relentless digging after long-vanished companies. To Audrey Anderson and Ed Tittel, who corrected many no-no's and provided valuable suggestions and information.

And finally, thanks to the many friends and acquaintences who let their stories and prized possessions become part of this work. I would love to enumerate your contributions further, but that could turn into a whole book. (Whoops, it did.) In alphabetical order: James Ableson, Dave Anderson, Robert Arnson, David Ballenger, Adam Bosworth, Brad Beitel, Eric Brown, Kevin Brown, Bruce Bruemmer, Maria Callejas, Sharon Campbell, Rod Chavez, Ives Chor, Scott Clawson, Shirley Clawson, Dale Coleman, Phil Cooper, Kim Crouse, Beth Dawson, David DeJean, Michael Dell, John Delo, Sean Dimond, John Dodge, Mark Dodge, Kevin Eagen, Peter Eden, Monty Emken, Mark Eppley, John Erickson, Susan Evans, Jim Fleming, Robert Frankenberg, Doug Franklin, Bob Frankston, Mardi Friebel, Claus Giloi, Ben GoetterMardi Friebel, Franklin Grossman, Don Hacherel, Ernest Hack, Lisa Hall, Michel Hebrant, J.D. Hildebrand, Tricia Horner, Jon Howell, Mark Hughes, Marie Huwe, David Intersimone, Tom Johnston, Kevin Jones, Bill Jordan, Mario Juarez, Philippe Kahn, Donna Keppin, F.C. Keith, Stan Krute, Carol Lamberson, Rhonda Landy, Norvin Leach, Terry Lipscomb, Keith Logan, Pearl Louie, Terry Lucas, Elliot Masie, Bob McGhee, Bob Metcalfe, Christopher Morgan, Ed Murphy, Trudy Neuhaus, Lee Newberg, Nancy Nicolaissen, David Norris, Leslie Norton, Bob O'Brien, Karen Offerman, Rick Olson, Jack Oswald, Mark Pauker, Dan Perkins, Denise Peters, Kevin Phaup, Matt Price, Vern Raburn, Lydia Schoen, Kelsey Selander, Steve Sereboff, David Sewell, Richard Hale Shaw, Hank Shiffman, Helene Shulman, Michael Shulman, Helene Shulman, Bobbi Sinyard, Ginni Swanton, Darryl Taft, Bryan Trussel, David Tuniman, Eric Vasilik, Gene Wang, David Weise, Sam Whitmore, Bryan Willman, and Lisa Wissner, Elliot x.

Thanks also to those who prefer anonymity and thus are not listed here.

Credits

Group Publisher and Vice President
Christopher J. Williams

Publishing Director
John Osborn

Senior Acquisitions Manager
Amorette Pedersen

Editorial Director
Anne Marie Walker

Editorial Assistant
Tracy Brown

Production Director
Beth A. Roberts

Project Editor
Wade Strickland

Manuscript Editor
Audrey Anderson

Technical Editor
Ed Tittel

Composition and Layout
Benchmark Productions, Inc.

Proofreader
Jeannie Smith

Indexer
Sharon Hilgenberg

Book Design
Benchmark Productions, Inc.

Cover Design
THREE 8 Creative Group

Contents

Contents

Chapter 7: The End of the Road 105

Part 2: Products 113

Chapter 8: Shhh! It's a Secret Code Name 115

Chapter 9: Riding on the Vapor Trail 147

Chapter 10: Hiding and Finding Easter Eggs 161

Chapter 11: That's Not a Bug, That's a Feature . . .197

Chapter 17: Shrink-Wrapping Blues 285

What Should We Call It, Anyway? 287
If You Are Having Problems, Just Smoke the Manual 289
And Speaking of Spelling Mistakes 289
It Won't Fit on the Shelves 290
Time Bombs 291
The World of Sex Objects 292
And Speaking of Sex 292
So Who's Counting, Anyway? 293
Getting Political 293
Control Codes 293
Viruses 294
WinDOS 294

Part 4: A Brief History of Time 297

Chapter 18: Gone but Not Forgotten 299

Early Iron 300
Birth of a Nation 302
The World Changes 306
Meanwhile, in Gotham City 307
Enter IBM 311
Store Struck 314
What Came Next 315
A History of PC Bus Architecture 315
It Even Does Windows 317
Do You Remember These Software Lines? 319

Chapter 19: An Editor Is a Nerd's Best Friend . . .323

TECO 324
vi 325
edlin 327
WordStar 327
Brief 328
WordPerfect 331

Contents

Welcome

The world of computers is a

quirky one. Groups of teenagers crash out in a sleazy hotel in Albuquerque, staying up all night, devoting their lives to writing software for a strange rectangular box with switches and blinking lights. The box is named after the destination of the Starship Enterprise on a particular episode of "Star Trek." It is built in a room that used to house a sandwich shop.

Meanwhile, a pair of bare-footed hippies sell their most prized possessions to build circuit boards in a garage. And with a starting price of $666, launch Apple Computer.

Twenty years later, the personal computer industry is a multi-billion-dollar field. The creator of the box is a doctor in a small town. And the teenagers are famous. One of them is the richest man in the world. One of them owns TicketMaster, the Portland Trailblazers, a dozen high-tech companies, and a Jimi Hendrix museum.

So the personal computer industry began. And despite its massive growth, the invasion of suits and lawyers, and the inevitable changes, it remains a fun-filled, fast-paced, around-the-clock place in which eccentric developers play tricks, race cars, calculate the number of phone booths in Manhattan, and still manage to create great hardware and software.

What's in This Book

This book takes a look at the twists and turns of the computer industry. You'll learn what it is like to work in the industry, what it is like to create products, and how many things came to be.

But most importantly, you'll learn some of the funny untold stories. Of the strange messages embedded in programs. Of mistakes like the Reeference Manual and the Softwa Reengineering sign. What happens behind the scenes at glamorous trade shows. What's on top of the Intel building. And you'll learn about the famous toga party, industry bands, and many secret code names.

If you work in the computer industry, you'll find many familiar t-shirts and office prank stories. As well as many you've never heard. You'll laugh knowingly at the trials of technical support engineers. You'll learn more computer jokes and impress your friends with trivia. And you'll see if I managed to dig up your favorite code names.

If you are an old-timer, you'll walk down memory lane, reminiscing about some of the great computers and companies of the past. You'll lust after the Altair and IMSAI emulators. And you'll lovingly look for your hole punch to double-side some diskettes.

If you are new to the industry, or just curious, you'll learn what it is like inside. The horrors of job interviews. The around-the-clock work environment. The t-shirts, the slogans, and the way things started. You'll learn about the lawsuits that have riveted the industry, and the lighthearted attitude that keeps it together.

And maybe, just maybe, you'll catch the spirit that keeps computer people glued to their keyboards beautiful day after beautiful day, in search of fame, fortune, and a few less bugs.

All Apologies

This book covers a lot. From life in the industry, to product creation, to product marketing, and industry history. From t-shirts and mugs to easter eggs and code names. Pranks and tech support stories. Hiring stories and firing stories. And even computer scenes in the movies. You'll get a pretty good taste of what computer life is like.

But by no means is this book complete. There are hundreds of stories left untold. And many more in the making.

If I've left out your favorite story about the founding of a company, or missed the best t-shirts, office pranks, or code names, let me apologize up front. Read along and laugh anyway.

And when you have finished with the book, send me some email. After all, the birds are singing, the flowers are blooming, and the blue sky peeks out from behind my monitor. I'm comfortably seated at my keyboard. Gathering stories for the next one.

Michael Hyman
tigger@nwlink.com

Walkin' the Walk, Talkin' the Talk

Do you have what it takes? Are you ready for the big time? In this section, you'll see what it is like to work in the computer industry. You'll start, of course, by walking through the door and experiencing some of the more amusing sign-in processes. Then, you'll interview and, assuming you pass, start work. Or shall we say, find your new primary residence in a high-tech office surrounded by computers where you too can read email in meetings. And send email to others in the same meeting reading their own email.

Having made it into the industry, you'll see what it is like and learn about some of the stress-relieving pranks that have been played, groove to the melody of industry bands, sweat through trade shows, and, since life isn't always a bowl of binary cherries, see what it is like to get kicked out on the streets when a company starts to plummet.

So wash down your pocket protector, stock up on your favorite caffeine-laden drinks, and get ready to jump into the strange, high-paced world of high tech.

Tune In, Turn On, & Drop By

You find yourself at the tinted, double-glass doors by the entrance of a computer company. You've already navigated past the Ferraris, Porsches, and VW vans out front. You've dodged the occasional pink flamingo, navigated through the butts in the smokers' exile area, and noticed the pirate flags hanging out the windows. Now what?

You go through the doors, of course. After all, you are trying to get a job. In front of you sits the corporate receptionist. He says, briefly glancing up from his Windows solitaire game, "Better sign in." Already you can tell you are not in an accountant's office.

You'd think that signing in to visit a company would be a simple matter. And at many companies, it is. You simply sign a log — if even that — and off you go. At other companies, however, the process is more complex:

- Many IBM offices have an elaborate security process where the entrances are completely barricaded unless you register, get a card, and are escorted at all times. This occurred even before a crazed ex-employee drove into an IBM lobby and shot several people.

- At Electronic Arts, you sign your name on a sticky-backed tag. When you leave, you place the name tag on a conveniently placed cube, sphere, or pyramid — the Electronic Arts logo — thus contributing to a large, growing sculpture created by thousands of other visitor stickers.

- At some companies, such as Starwave, the lawyers take part. The registration name tag is attached to a secrecy agreement. If you want in, you have to sign the NDA.

- At Microsoft, you fill in a name badge with the receptionist. Retired and returning employees are fond of giving fake names such as "Marilyn Monroe."

But of all the computer companies, Traveling Software — the makers of LapLink — have the best sign-in procedure. When you visit Traveling Software, you draw a picture of yourself and indicate your hobby. The bottom of the name tag warns that Traveling Software "reserves the right to refuse admittance to anyone failing to draw his/her picture properly." There are hundreds of tags preserved in their hall-of-fame books. Following are a few names you might recognize:

Figure 1-1 Here you can see Bob Metcalfe's tag. Bob was the founder of 3Com. The resemblance is amazing.

Figure 1-2 Sam Whitmore, the Editorial Director at *PC Week*, took a pause from programming VCRs to fill in this tag.

Figure 1-3 John Dodge, the Senior Executive Editor for News at *PC Week*, no longer wears a bow tie for his picture and has slightly changed his hairdo.

Figure 1-4 Vern Raburn is now the president and CEO of the Paul Allen Group. He joined Microsoft in 1979 to head Microsoft's consumer products division. He left in 1982 to be General Manager at Lotus. He then started Slate where he was the CEO. Here you can see him pretending to be an airplane.

Figure 1-5 David DeJean worked at *PC/Computing* and moonlighted as a mattress tester. He now writes for *PC Magazine*.

Figure 1-6 Kim Crouse runs a software training company and writes for *Win Tech Journal*.

Figure 1-7 Here I am, on my visit to Traveling Software in 1990.

So, You Think You Want to Work at a Computer Company?

Congratulations. You figured out how to find the entrance and you even managed to sign in. And now, feeling upbeat and energetic, you are ready to get a job. Yes, it is time to encounter the high-tech interview process.

Working at a computer company can be pretty stressful. The hours are long, the pace is grueling, and coworkers can sometimes be very opinionated. Bill Gates, for example, is fond of telling employees that their suggestion is "the dumbest idea" he has ever heard. (He is usually correct.) If Bill can say it, so can your manager and coworkers. Even if you don't work at Microsoft, you're bound to run into some heated technical criticism.

So if working in a high-tech company is fast paced, stressful, and somewhat confrontational, why should interviews be any different? The interview process varies from company to company, but regardless of the company, you can plan on an intense, all-day affair.

How to Dress

Before you interview, you need to know how to dress for success. Unfortunately, while putting on a bow tie for an interview at a legal firm might seem natural, dressing for an interview at a computer company is much trickier. Most computer companies have a very laid-back dress code. I know plenty of people who wear the same t-shirt a few days in a row, so if you come in with a clean t-shirt and jeans, that can be considered pretty fancy. If you are interviewing and nobody is wearing a suit, should you still wear one, or will you feel out of place?

If you wear a suit, you will look like a fish out of water. And if you aren't used to wearing suits, you will probably look and feel awkward. Your belt, socks, and shoes might not even go together. Plus, anyone that you run across will automatically know that you are interviewing and treat you differently. Or, they will think you are from the finance department, in which case they will avoid you altogether. On the other hand, if you don't dress up, people will think that you don't care about the interview. Either way, you lose.

The best approach is to dress up. If you make it past the first interview, come in more casually for the second. At one job, I showed up in a Hickey-Freeman suit for the first day. And beat up jeans, a Grateful Dead shirt, and a bandanna for the second. That might be regarded as slightly extreme, but I got the job. (See Figure 2-1.)

If, however, you are interviewing for a sales job instead of a programming job, dress up the best you can and follow every rule you may have learned in business school. Above all, make sure you wear the proper shoes. I can't tell you what that means, but I'm sure that there is a special course in B-school just to help you figure it out.

Some Different Styles of Interviews

Interviews vary dramatically from company to company. At some, interviews are mild. The person meets the various members of the team, they talk about past experiences, and mostly look for a superficial personality

Figure 2-1 Here I am on the first and second day of a job interview for a major computer company. Would you hire me?

and technology match. If a company is in serious trouble, interviews can be pretty easy. In fact, like selecting jurors for the OJ Simpson trial, the less you know about the company, the better the chance that you will make it through. If you fog a mirror, know what a *for loop* is, but don't seem to be worried about the ongoing gloomy prospects at the company, you have a good shot. But at other companies, the interviews are far more intense.

Apple, for example, used to have group interviews. They would bring numerous people into a large session where everyone would meet everyone else who was interviewing. Then they would have panels of up to three interviewers asking up to three interviewees questions. Some found it impersonal.

"Candidate #1, what's your favorite *hash function*?"

"Hmm, Candidate #2, can you improve on that answer?"

Welcome to Summer Camp

Microsoft hosts a summer internship program each year. Through this program, hundreds of college students get a chance to see what life in a major software corporation is like, gaining invaluable practical experience. At the same time, Microsoft gets to preview some of the top engineering talent prior to graduation.

Summer internships can be fairly intense, especially when compared to other college break activities such as dancing naked at Mardi Gras or beer guzzling at Fort Lauderdale. Each group gets to design their own t-shirt, one of which, for Uncle Bill's Summer Camp '91, is shown here.

The multi-person interview enables the 360 spin. If a few interviewers align themselves around a candidate and ask questions going around in a circle, they can get a candidate to spin around and around to face the questioners. What fun!

When I worked at Borland, I'd give candidates who passed the first round of interviews homework assignments. That provided a better chance to learn about them in depth. Of course, the poor candidate had to return to a full-time job and a full-time homework assignment just to get hired.

Microsoft is well known for providing incredibly grueling interviews, where the candidate is twisted and turned at every possible moment. The worst thing that can happen is to be perceived as being nontechnical. Even experienced people are asked random mind twisters just to see how they think. (I see you've shipped 34 products and have three Ph.Ds. So tell me, why are manholes round?) Those who survive are likely to survive in the intense work environment.

In fact, at one point there was an official, written programming test given to incoming applicants at Microsoft. Employees would get together late at night and brainstorm interview puzzlers. For a bunch of computer nerds, such problem solving and posting was a great challenge and source of entertainment while waiting for programs to compile.

Because most high-tech companies are email-centric, there is a good chance that each interviewer knows what earlier ones thought. If you do well at the beginning, that can help you build real momentum. But if you have a slow start, you might be in for a rocky ride.

Some Interviewing Stories

There are lots of amusing stories that come from interview sessions.

How to Know If You've Bombed

Here are a few telltale signs that let you know you probably aren't in for an offer.

1. **The interviewer keeps yawning while you talk.**

2. **The interviewer starts reading email.**

3. **Half way through an interview, the interviewer says he's really sorry but he has a meeting to attend, and drops you off in the lobby.**

4. **All of your afternoon interviews get canceled.**

5. **You get a number of suggestions about other companies you might want to apply to.**

Unfortunately, most involve cutting down interview candidates, so I won't repeat those. But here are some that I've found entertaining.

Exaggerated Résumé

One programmer had prepared a general résumé while looking for programming jobs. He was mostly applying to local businesses, but applied to Microsoft as well. Because he had been doing some Assembly language programming, he put down that he was an expert in Assembly and DOS. That was a fatal mistake. Never claim you are an expert in something when you are interviewing at a company such as Apple, Lotus, or Microsoft unless you really are an expert. Especially if you say you are an expert in a product that the company ships. In this case, the candidate spent much of the day with the people who wrote DOS. And they spent much of the candidate's miserable day proving that he wasn't an expert.

Interviewer:	"Aha, I see that you are an expert in DOS."
Candidate (about to be trashed):	"(Gulp) Yes, I've done a lot of DOS programming."
Interviewer:	"Me, too. I wrote part of it. Tell me, why does INT 25h have a different call stack return than INT 21h?"

Don't Cut in Line

A senior manager from a software company told me this story. He was interviewing with a competitor, and things were going very well. He was excited about the job, and the hiring manager clearly indicated that my acquaintance would be offered the position, as long as the Senior Vice President approved. Late that night, the senior manager received a phone call at his hotel room:

"The VP says you interviewed here a few months ago. Is that true?"

"No — I didn't, and I haven't seen the VP in years. That's strange."

"Yeah, I thought so. He says he interviewed someone with a similar title a few months ago, but that the person was a complete no hire. I seemed to remember the person's name was Saul, though. Do you know him?"

"Saul? Oh my gosh, that's my manager!"

"Aha — great! Well, looks like he didn't do so well when he interviewed here. I'll call the VP right away and get it straightened out."

Not only did the guy interviewing find out that his boss had interviewed just a bit ago while ostensibly on vacation, but he almost didn't get hired because of it. Giving notice had an extra pleasure.

Faking It

Melinda was interviewing for a job with a computer company that made several products, including the programming language called Modula-2. She didn't know much about Modula-2, but she had some friends at the company who said, "Just put down you know it on your résumé. They love Modula-2 and will call anyone who has it there." She did, and was quickly called in for an interview. She even saw Modula-2 circled in red on her résumé during her first interview. She was panicked the whole time, how-ever, that they would call her bluff, and had prepared a dozen stories to explain why she didn't even know the basics of Modula-2. She ended up getting the job, but to this day still doesn't know Modula-2.

Pardon My Engine

One Borland executive was a car fanatic. He had a huge house with sev-eral sports cars and kept an engine block from a Ferrari in his office. When candidates would come in, they'd have to avoid the oil puddles on the floor and put up with the oil stench.

Headhunters at the Gate

Finding highly qualified technical people can be a challenge. To overcome this, companies hire headhunters to find the names of the hot-shot folks at the competition, get their résumés, and entice them in for an interview. Getting called by one or two headhunters is flattering except they usually come in droves, never stop calling, and quickly become a pain.

You can tell you've been called by a headhunter when you get a message such as

- Hi, this is Mary calling on behalf of John. It is very important that you call him as soon as possible. (In this case, if you know Mary and John, it is probably not a headhunter and you should call John. If you've never heard of them, and it sounds like a long-distance call, chances are it is a headhunter and not a wrong number.)

- Hi, I'm conducting some research. Can you please call me? (This means they are researching for names of people to hire. You, in particular.)

- This is Sally. I'm doing an executive search and was wondering if you knew anyone who might qualify for a position. (This means, would you be interested in switching jobs? Do you have any friends? Do you want to give away the names of your team members so that they can be hired away?)

Headhunters use all types of tricks to find the names of people at companies. At Microsoft, a number of people on the OLE team received calls from someone saying they were organizing a conference and needed speakers — who else on the team might be qualified? The developers caught on when the person refused to leave a number and had no details on the conference. Other people have received calls from "facilities" saying they were trying to confirm the person's title, responsibilities, and manager — even though the call was from an outside line and their name didn't check out on the company roster.

Another popular trick is to send headhunters after anyone who attends a technical conference. In a related incident, the president of a communications software producer, Hilgraeve, got a call asking for the names of the company's Windows programmers so that they all could receive free passes to a technical seminar from Microsoft. Instead of getting free passes, they got headhunter calls — from Borland.

A typical way to deal with headhunters is to give them the names of key executives at the competition:

> "No, I'm not particularly interested in switching jobs. In fact, I like my job very much. But you might try this guy named Jim Manzi..."

If the person at the competition switches, you've done well. If they don't switch, they just received a harrassing phone call. And if the job the headhunter was trying to fill was a real loser, they just got insulted in the process. Such fun.

Now It's Your Turn

OK. So you've read about a few interviewing stories. Now its your turn to answer some typical interview questions and see whether you'll get the job. The following questions are all from real interviews. The answers are at the end of the chapter.

Before you start, get yourself in the right mind-set. Imagine that you just flew into a strange city the night before and maybe you are slightly jet lagged. You've been up for a couple of hours pacing in your hotel room, ironing your clothes, and drinking way too much coffee. You've gone through an easy introductory interview with the HR department. And now you are ready for the real thing.

A man in his late twenties, wearing blue jeans and a Ren and Stimpy t-shirt picks you up in the lobby. He offers you some coffee as he takes you back to his office. You sit down in a seat facing his desk, which is covered with two computers, one with the top off; three mouse pads; several stacks of technical papers; and a few Diet Coke cans. A toy robot whirs in circles in the corner. The blinds are half shut. He leans back, smiles, and without much of an introduction, starts in on the questions. Good luck:

1. Why are manhole covers round?

2. Suppose you have a rectangular cake. From this cake you cut a rectangular slice of cake, which you promptly eat. Come up with an approach whereby you can slice the remaining cake once, and end up with two pieces of equal area. (See Figure 2-2.)

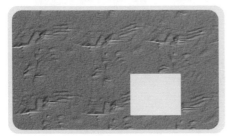

Figure 2-2 Here is an arbitrary rectangular cake with an arbitrary rectangle cut out of it.

3. How many phone booths are there in New York City?

4. This one comes from "Car Talk," a great source of high-tech interview questions. Two men are walking in a railroad tunnel. It's a really thin tunnel, so they know if they hear a whistle they have to run to get out. After they have made it a fifth of the way through, they hear a whistle. One runs towards the train and makes it out of the tunnel just as the train is about to come in. The other runs away from the train, and just makes it out of the tunnel as well. Both men run at 15 mph. How fast is the train going?

5. What's your favorite color?

6. You have two buckets, each filled with 100 ping pong balls. Bucket A contains red balls. Bucket B contains blue balls. You take N balls out of bucket A, place them in bucket B, and mix them thoroughly. You then select N balls from bucket B, and put them back into bucket A. What is the ratio of blue balls in bucket A as compared to red balls in bucket B? How does this change as N approaches 100?

7. What's wrong with this code?:

```
while (*s = *t)
        ;
```

Answers on Next Page

Answers

1. If manhole covers were any other shape, they could fall into the hole. For example, suppose the cover were square. If you twisted it, the shortest side of the cover would be smaller than the diagonal of the manhole. You would then drop it in. (See Figure 2-3.) Another acceptable answer is because manholes are round. But that reply is only good for stalling time.

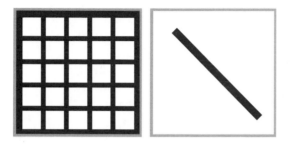

Figure 2-3 If you rotate a square manhole cover 45 degrees and put it on the side, it will fall through a square manhole.

2. Find the midpoint of the cake and the midpoint of the piece that was removed. Cut the cake along a line formed by the two midpoints. (See Figure 2-4.) Why does this work? Any line drawn through the midpoint of a rectangle will bisect the rectangle. (See Figure 2-5.) This can be proven with equilateral triangles created by using the side-angle-side theorem. Looking at the figure, side A is the same size as side B, by the definition of a rectangle. Side C is shared by the upper and lower triangles, so it is the same size in both. Angle D is also the same as Angle E. Thus, the upper and lower triangles are the same.

   Now let's apply this to the cake problem. If you slice through the midpoint of the cake and of the removed piece, you will be guaranteed of an equal amount of cake and missing cake on each side of the slice. That's because you have cut both the cake and the not-cake into two equal halves. If you still don't believe it, try it out yourself. Another answer is to turn the cake on its side and slice down the middle. That's usually regarded as cheating, but what's wrong with that?

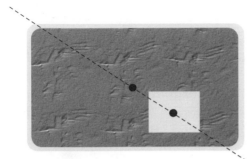

Figure 2-4 Find the midpoints of the two sections and cut a line that connects the two. The cake will be evenly divided.

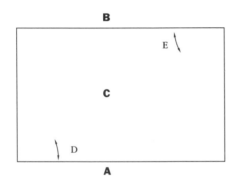

Figure 2-5 Any line through the center of a rectangle will bisect the rectangle.

3. Here, the actual answer doesn't really matter. The thing being tested is they way you think. So, you might say, well, I don't know, but I figure there are an average of 3 phone booths per corner. And there are about 100 streets up, and about 20 across. So that would make 6,000 phone booths.

4. The tricky part about this puzzle is that you aren't told how far away the train is when the men hear the whistle, and you also don't know the length of the tunnel. There are two ways to solve this puzzle. The first is by solving a series of simultaneous equations. The other is a little easier. Since you know both men run at the same speed, when the first man makes it out, he has run through ⅕ of the tunnel. Thus, the other man is now ⅖ through, leaving ⅗ of the tunnel for him to run through. It takes the same amount of time for the train to travel through the whole tunnel as it does for the man to travel through the

remaining ⅗ of the tunnel. Thus the train is going ⅘ times the speed of the man, or 25 mph.

5. This is really a culture check. Computer people love movies. Science fiction movies and Monty Python are favorites. If you are asked this question, you should instantly yell, "Blue, no red, aaaaah" or any other variation that lets the interviewer know that you have seen *Monty Python and the Holy Grail*. You might even get into a discussion about whether the knights who say "nih" are really the knights who say "nicht." A related question might begin "You are walking through a desert. You come across a tortoise on its back," which is from a particularly violent interview scene in *Bladerunner*.

6. This is another fun logic problem. The number of balls is fixed. That is, there are always 100 red balls and 100 blue balls. After you are finished mixing up the balls, there are still 100 balls in each bucket. If M red balls remain in bucket A, that means there are M blue balls in bucket B. So the ratio of red to blue in bucket A will always be the same as the ratio of blue to red in bucket B. The ratio remains the same regardless of N. Don't believe me? Try it. I've shown this with a bowl of grapes and cherries at the dinner table.

7. This is actually a very easy problem. Far more difficult programming problems are usually given, relating to *hash* tables, sorting arrays, and walking through lists backwards, but they can be a little harder to explain. Of course, if everyone just buys *Borland C++ For Dummies* or *Visual C++ For Dummies*, I can let you in on some better mind twisters. In this case, there is a very high chance that this program will cause an endless loop. Endless loops are bad.

"Help! Help! We're being held prisoner in a system software factory!"

— quote embedded in data fork of Macintosh System 7.0

That Ain't Workin'

Congratulations! You made it through interviews. You negotiated your salary as best you could. (And you even calculated how at a typical, 80-hour work week, your hourly wage will be far less than that of a plumber.) It's time to say good-bye to your family and friends because, after all, you won't be seeing them too often. With the advent of portable computers, 28.8 modems, and beepers, even coming home after 16 hours at the office is no excuse for staying off email.

What are work hours really like? Well, you can be guaranteed that if your company is good, there will be lights on at all hours, day or night. *Flextime* means the ability to choose which 12-16 hours of a day you'll work. And *vacation time* is often defined as "you can choose which weekend of the year you won't work." Even if you aren't on a tight deadline for shipping a product, 8-hour days are unheard of in most places. And start-up companies are even worse. It is no wonder that Microsoft and companies like it are called "velvet sweatshops."

In this chapter we'll take a look at what it is like to work at a high-tech company with lots of perks, but little free time.

Family

Family life? Forget it. You'd better hope your family is tolerant of long, strange hours and ready to play intensely should you get an odd afternoon or weekend off. Here's an excerpt from an essay written by a programmer's spouse.

To properly coexist with a techie, you must first understand three basic premises on which his view of the world is based.

1. There is a proper order in the universe. Computers come first; significant others somewhere thereafter.

2. Programmers, while reluctantly admitting (subsequent to intense pressure) that they are not God, are however, equal to God.

3. Computer illiterate people are complete morons.

These three premises result in techies having a drastically different way of thinking as compared to the average person. This unique approach to life will be exhibited on a daily basis in many subtle ways.

TOPIC	WHAT YOU'RE THINKING	WHAT HE'S THINKING
Ideal Vacation	Tahiti	Las Vegas—during Comdex
Shopping Trip	New wardrobe	Computer bookstore
Eating Out	Chez Romantic	Vending machine at the office
Fun Weekend	Picnic in the mountains	Nonstop programming
6 A.M.	Romantic sunrise	Late night of programming
Shared Housework	50/50	Refrain from complaining that Pepsi isn't restocked

It is true that techies rarely subscribe to *GQ* magazine but, in all fairness, let's dispense with the slide-rule, taped glasses, white button-down shirt stereotype. They no longer wear slide-rules; laptops are in. Taped glasses—well, OK, sometimes. White shirts have been replaced by t-shirts and flowered Hawaiian atrocities. "Dressing up" for a special occasion entails putting on jeans and a wrinkled shirt with a collar. If you happen to be domestically inclined, don't bother ironing shirts (or if you're not, don't bother feeling guilty about *not* ironing them) because pressed shirts are simply not a priority in a techie's life and neither he nor any of his contemporaries will notice that the shirt he's wearing looks like it's been trapped between his mattress and box spring for a year.

Material possessions are of vital importance to the techie. Of paramount importance is the Car. The cost of this is directly proportional to the size of the Ego. There are two types of vehicles owned by techies: 1966 station wagons with deteriorating wood on the sides *or* the most expensive vehicle income will allow. (Neither category of car owner would be caught dead, however, driving a car with a Mary Kay bumper sticker attached.) Single techies can be identified by their dumpy apartments, frayed clothing, and impeccably maintained Ferraris.

Techies with vehicles in the second category assemble their machines for the annual Testosterone 500. Grown men gather at an area racetrack, spend 90 percent of the day walking around bragging about their car to anyone who will listen, and devote the balance of the time tearing around on a track, hoping they won't kill themselves. What we are witnessing is *not* simply a car race, but rather a battle of the egos. This same group of techies has also mastered the art of maneuvering discussion of *THE CAR* into every conversation.

The home computer system is another source of competition. Our family of four (techie, significant other, eight- and two-year-old) is the proud owner of six computers, seven monitors, three laser printers, two dot matrix printers, two scanners, two optical disk drives, a CD ROM drive, and four boxes of cables that "might come in handy someday." Most appalling of all is that the two-year-old is limited to a 286 with an EGA! Horrors! Special effort is made to explain to visiting techies that we are in the process of upgrading the two-year-old's system.

Other elaborate electronic devices run a close second to the "home computer competition." Techies must always have the latest and the best of any electronic device on the market, and they *must* be the first in their group to own one. We have established true superiority with our home PBX phone system with the capacity to handle ten incoming lines, conference calls, 45 auto-dial numbers, and best of all, music on hold. Oh, and our answering machine has voice mail capabilities, can receive fax transmissions, and makes dinner.

As you've probably already noticed, dating a techie has special challenges and rewards. Although your social hours are restricted to 11:00 P.M. to 3:00 A.M., you do have the opportunity to meet other significant others who, like you, are hanging around the office waiting for "just one more compile." A techie's estimate of "fifteen more minutes" generally means he will appear an hour or two later having absolutely no clue that more than fifteen minutes have passed.

If you do manage to convince your techie to take a vacation, plan on his inspecting the computer system at every hotel, gas station, restaurant, car rental agency, and airline. Expect him to make suggestions for improvements to busboys, valets, maids, and waiters, none of whom have the remotest interest in their establishment's computer system, much less any influence in this arena. Keep in mind also that no matter where you go, techies will find each other. The first trip I, my sweetie, and his portable computer took together was to Europe. I was one of the lucky few to be dating a man who owned one of the first portable computers manufactured, which of course automatically entitled us to first class service everywhere. He no sooner had placed the computer on the airline tray table than six fellow techies leaped to his side to discuss the merits of the computer. Personal conversation with my traveling companion totaled ten minutes out of a six-hour flight.

Lunching with a group of techies is comparable to being dropped into a remote village in central Albania, with one major difference: Sign language is completely useless. The techies are speaking a foreign language and they are completely oblivious to this fact. My suggestion: Don't bother going. No one will notice that you were there anyway, including your techie.

Parties dominated by techies are truly exciting experiences. Techies have never developed the art of smalltalk (their computers don't require this attribute) so don't expect to see a techie talking to a non-techie. If a techie was forced to bring his significant other, he will feel obligated, however, to forego technical discussions for at least the first ten minutes.

If you are unfortunate enough to be a significant other with a "real job," you will encounter additional difficulties. The techie cannot fathom anyone going to work earlier than 10:00 A.M. He will tell you to simply inform your boss that you won't be starting until then.

Techies are very well read. They devour books and articles on such exciting topics as memory management, VXDs, and debugging, but give them a book on relationships and watch the panic spread across their faces. Mention a couples workshop you think both of you should attend and watch those deadlines move up.

At some point in their relationship, the significant other must reveal to the techie that a romantic holiday does not entail bringing along a portable computer, stacks of computer magazines, and a trunkload of listings. The techie will be expected to spend an entire weekend without his computer! If you make it through this traumatic experience, a marriage or move-in-together proposal may be in the air. Expect any proposal to be very practical. Important issues such as what kind of dog you will get, how much money will be allotted to ego-related purchases, and how much space will be allocated for the special, hands-off place for his computers in your future home must be settled before a techie will even

29

consider a permanent relationship. (Critical tip: This allotted space will double in size within six months, often spewing out into other areas of your home if you have not planned ahead.) Your wedding date will be arranged around development conferences, COMDEX, and technical crises.

If, at some point in your relationship, you decide to have children, you will have to fit baby-making in between compiles. If you do manage to conceive, take a few photographs of your techie to tape over the baby's crib so your child will recognize your techie's face as well as his back.

On a personal level, the techie is very supportive of his significant other. When I decided to diet, my techie stood by me and agreed to diet with me; as long as he didn't have to give up Pepsi and Twinkies. When I determined that I needed a new look, he promised not to laugh when I came back with a new hairdo and agreed to unlimited funding for purchases made at lingerie shops.

The techie is also an accomplished gift giver. Just last month, for my birthday, my techie gave me a Bug Zapper. (You know, one of those things that vaporizes the bugs flying around on your patio.) It seems he "heard me mention that we should get one." Guess he missed the references to the diamond necklace and pearl earrings. Last Christmas, I was the proud recipient of a portable toolkit — it's a beaut.

Well, I'd better close now. I'm due for my 10:43 appointment to review the 1991 COMDEX floor plan with you-know-who. Never a dull moment...

Philippe Kahn, President of Borland, was proud of calling Borland employees "barbarians." It exemplified the idea of working hard to create great software and breaking rules that got in the way. The furry purple creature riding the burro represents Philippe.

Your Home Away from Home

The office is your second home. (Or is it your first home? Hmm.) Offices vary dramatically from computer company to computer company. In many, such as Apple, Borland, and Microsoft, the offices are modeled after university campuses. There are libraries, ponds, gyms, and running paths. IBM, by contrast, tends to have much more formal offices and elaborate security measures.

Startups have two types of offices: the VC-funded office and the not-funded office. The former tends to be plush, using someone else's money to make an impact on customers. The latter can be a place where the rent is cheap, the power is grounded, and with any luck, there is an all-night junk food store or a pizza joint nearby.

For example, Borland was started in a room over a garage. Apple began inside a garage. Dell started in a dorm room. The MITS offices were in what used to be a restaurant. Within Technologies (later bought by Computer Associates) was run in a basement. Everyone in the company as well as their families lived in the same house, which was always under construction. The startup company run by Nathan Myhrvold (and subsequently bought by Microsoft, where he is now a Senior Vice President) ran out of a Victorian house. They were even visited by police one night because of strange lights in the attic. (The lights were from programmers working through the night.) Still other startup companies have worked out of warehouses, bedrooms, and condemned buildings.

Did You Know?

Can We Switch That Time to 6:00, Bill?
When Microsoft was smaller, many people would make dinner reservations using Bill Gates's name, figuring that it might get them better seating. This worked fine, until some restaurants started calling back to confirm the reservations.

But with success comes the fancy campus. At Microsoft, everyone gets an office. Though sometimes that means an office shared with one or two other people (who may or may not shower, wear shoes, or practice other elements of personal hygiene), six computers, and stacks of manuals. And each employee gets all the milk, juice, soda, and coffee they can drink. (Apparently the free drink policy, which keeps programmers buzzed with caffeine and means there is never a reason to leave campus, is now one of the ten most expensive benefits at Microsoft.) Each building is filled with art from local artists. Although the buildings are given boring numbers, the storage rooms are called things such as "Fortress of Solitude" (named after Superman's hangout) and "Object Store" (a pun on an OLE programming term).

Borland has a similarly fancy corporate office. During its design, Philippe was said to have wanted to build a campus even more elaborate than Microsoft's. Borland features a built-in gym, spa, swimming pool, coi pond, and running trails. The campus is a three-story building with a pecking order. Programmers and lawyers get the third floor, with the more senior people getting window offices. QA and Doc people are on the second floor, mostly in cubicles. And marketing and sales round out the least desirable bottom floor, again mostly in cubicles.

Apple was famous not only for attractive office buildings in sunny California, but for providing free popcorn and free video game machines. There was even a Kurzweil synthesizer in one of the buildings, ready for playing.

At ConnectSoft, a small email company run by ex-Microsoft programmers, every new employee is given a stereo, complete with CD player. And encouraged to play it loudly. (The semi-official excuse is that employees need speakers for their multimedia computers.) All the meeting rooms have a "Star Trek" theme, such as 10 Forward and The Bridge.

At Think, an early Macintosh development house that was bought by Symantec, programmers were famous for blasting music, painting their offices black, and playing ping pong through the night.

Amusingly, despite the fancy campuses and attractive window offices, you'll find many shut blinds, or windows covered by cardboard, blankets, or tin foil. All to prevent glare on monitors. Such treatment often infuriates those without windows, who view it as a squandered privilege.

Dress for Success

Another great attraction of high-tech companies is the usual lack of a dress code. At most high-tech companies, you'll find far more t-shirts than you will dress shirts, suits, and skirts. In fact, wearing a suit or leather shoes is often a sign that you are a marketing person — that is, a "suit" — and thus not technical. Some programmers, however, wear a tie just to be counter cultural. For example, Stewart Konzen, a longtime Microsoft employee, wore a tie every day during the 14 years he worked there before retiring.

The tie avoidance policy extends beyond the corporate campus. When making presentations to technical user groups, many companies find the talks are much better received when the speakers wear t-shirts instead of dressing up.

The lack of a dress code is sometimes taken to an extreme. One person I knew at Microsoft programmed in the nude. He would arrive at work, walk into his office, and strip. His token gesture to decency was to keep his keyboard in his lap when visitors came in. Or, at least, he would usually do this.

Lake BillG

Microsoft's campus is a set of over 25 buildings located in Redmond, Washington. Many offices in the suite of modern buildings feature views of the Cascade Mountains. The buildings are all numbered, with 1–4 the original set of buildings for that site. Between these four is a man-made pond that is the favored hang-out for jugglers and unicycle riders on the few days that it doesn't rain. The lake is now called Lake Bill (after Bill Gates), but was originally known as Lake BillG (pronounced "bilge," and named after Bill's email name.)

There is no Building 7, because employees protested that too many trees would be cut to build it. So Microsoft went immediately to 8 and 9, which were in a slightly different location.

Treehenge

Borland had an amateur astronomy club. They designed a portion of Borland's new, $160 million dollar headquarters. Behind the building, between the outside auditorium and the swimming pool, sits a ring of trees with stone blocks reminiscent of Stonehenge. The trees are planted in a pattern akin to the stones at Stonehenge. If you look at them during the proper time of day from the proper angle, they form a sundial of sorts that tells the ship dates of various Borland products.

IBM, by contrast, had a very formal dress policy. (And I've never heard of nudity at IBM buildings.) Dark suits, starched white shirts, and dull ties were the norm. While this wasn't an official, written policy, it was an understood, unofficial way of life. From time to time, a rebellious employee would sneak in wearing a bright tie. In February 1995 that changed, with IBM officially announcing that a dress code was no longer required. The only requirement was that employees should not be poorly dressed when meeting customers.

Who says you can't be nerdy and stylish at the same time? This shirt features a detailed, small print listing of the various key functions in the C runtime libraries. It is conveniently printed upside down so that you can read the reference with out having to take the shirt off.

Work Standards Are a Joke!

The letter on the next page appeared in a Microsoft newspaper. It was met by strong reactions from programmers who were very happy with the existing work environment.

When I look at our workplace, I am appalled. Isn't it time for Microsoft to adopt the mainstream business standards of corporate America? How much longer must we alienate this vital market segment, responsible for the majority of our earnings, with the sophomoric trappings of our so-called "Corporate" Campus? More importantly, how much longer must we pay the price in quality, in ever-escalating bug counts and product support costs, that these pretensions exact?

A walk down the halls of any of the product groups reveals employees missing shoes or wearing ill-fitting, printed t-shirts, bandannas, and worse. These same employees' offices display a disorder that certainly spills into their work habits. Does not software — a body of rules abiding by a precise order and internal discipline — mandate an orderly and disciplined environment for its correct construction? Of course it does! And our shortcomings here drive up defect rates, break schedules, and ultimately yield dissatisfied customers.

In the workplace, correct attention to dress indicates corresponding attention to detail. Conversely, sloppy clothes suggest sloppy code. Every untucked shirttail reflects an unchecked error condition. Only by adopting and enforcing proper codes of personal grooming and dress can we ensure an environment that fosters quality in our products.

The standards of renowned companies such as Intel or IBM (the old IBM — back when the *B* truly stood for "Business") stemmed from the discipline they imposed on their workplace; if we really seek quality, our product groups must do likewise. Let's clean up our act.

Only those who knew the Microsoft programmer who wrote this knew that the letter was a joke — a last gesture before retiring at the age of 30 to live a life of leisure. Flames poured in — to the newspaper and to the author personally. While a few respondents figured that he was joking, most took the letter as a serious attack at one of the basic tenets of life at Microsoft. Some wrote very polite letters in reply. Most did not.

One respondent commented that Einstein and the Buddha didn't have a great dress code. One person asked if it was OK that he parked his '63 Ford truck outside. Many strongly suggested that the writer take a job at IBM. While yet another letter suggested that HR should adopt a new policy of recruiting programmers from the *GQ* magazine models. The flames and dialog kept going long after the employee was happily retired and spending his days at the gym.

Great Quotes: Richie Rich

"Let's say the stock dropped in half or a third. Big deal...I have an infinite amount of money. I would still order the same hamburger" — Bill Gates, when asked about the hammering Microsoft stock was taking when the FTC announced they were investigating Microsoft for possible monopolistic practices.

Keeping Them Happy

Some of the top industry executives receive gigantic salaries and bonuses. For example, Eckehard Pfieffer (of Compaq) received over $3,000,000 in 1994. But most people never come close to such salaries. Rather, other things are used to keep programmers happy:

- The chance to work on great products. This is often the reward for hard work. Do a project well, and you get to work on the hottest product in the company. Perform poorly, and you may find yourself supporting old DOS versions or sorting decks of punch cards.

- Getting paid for hacking on computers and hanging out with nerds. Hey, it's what we like doing. Isn't it amazing that we get paid for it?

- Stock options. These are the golden handcuffs that make it possible to sacrifice one's life for the hope that a startup will go public, or that a public company's fortunes will soar. Thousands of the early programmers at Microsoft are now multimillionaires from being at the right place at the right time. On the other hand, when a company hits bad times, stock options become a disincentive and a source of complaint.

These incentives, while enough to attract most any programmer, aren't always enough to get through the incredible ordeal of shipping a product. That's when extras come in to play.

Many companies offer free dinner to developers who stay late working during ship cycles. That works well for a while, because many programmers will do anything for a free meal, but after a bit people just shift their work schedules. They still get free dinner, but since they arrive at noon that doesn't mean that they spend more time at the office. When Microsoft was getting ready to ship NT, it provided lunch every weekend as an extra incentive for programmers to work full-time seven days a week. There is a story that one worker, pressured by coworkers because he spent the weekends with his family instead of at the office, sat in the parking lot outside the NT building one Saturday from 8 in the morning until 5 at night. He carefully noted who came in when, and concluded that most people were just coming in for a free lunch.

In the early days at Lotus, certain programmers had unlimited nighttime accounts at a nearby deli and at Steve's Ice Cream.

Pizza is a favorite method of squeezing out extra performance. When the first boards for the Macintosh came in, the team rushed to get them in the machines. They got the boards in late that Friday afternoon, and Steve Jobs said, "Well, if you get these done before midnight, we'll take you for pizza." According to Andy Hertzfeld, a key member of the team who later left Apple to cofound General Magic, "We stayed there... not because we wanted the pizza, but because we wanted to see the board working." In addition to supplying pizza, Steve Jobs would also walk around the Macintosh team once a month. If someone had done an outstanding job, he would give them an envelope filled with cash as a reward.

On its way to shipping OS/2, Microsoft brought masseuses in three times a week to help relieve stress.

At Think, programmers were often put up in hotel rooms so they could work all day and night, without having to worry about driving, cooking, or cleaning. Mail or other necessities would be slipped under the door on occasion.

Did You Know?

Steve Jobs's Motorcycle

Steve Jobs used to park his BMW motorcycle in the lobby of the Macintosh building.

Microsoft places red, asset-tracking tags on all of its computers so that it can keep tabs on the millions of dollars of equipment it owns. The tags look similar to that shown in this t-shirt. Of course, if you read the shirt quickly...

Making Fools of Themselves

Financial incentives and free food aren't the only things that get computer people fired up and working hard. Sometimes t-shirts are given out, such as the Zero Bug t-shirts given out to NT team members who knocked out all their bugs. In other cases, executives pitch in to give additional challenges.

For example, a manager in the networking group in NT bet a manager from a different group that his team would finish their code on time. If they didn't, he said he would put on a woman's swimsuit and swim across Lake BillG. He lost, but postponed his cross-dressing swim by raising the stakes and saying his whole team would swim if they didn't make a later date.

Fortunately for the team, they made this later date, and thus were spared from swimming in the goose-infested waters of Lake BillG. Not everyone who made such bets was lucky enough to escape. Steve Ballmer and Mike Maples once made a bet where the loser would have to swim across Lake BillG. Somehow they tied, so both of them had to make the swim. It was a rather cold day, but just to be sure that the water was not pleasant, a group of programmers got together and placed several large chunks of dry ice in the lake before the two vice presidents began.

In a slightly different boast, Steve Ballmer once challenged IBM, at that time an arch enemy in the Windows versus OS/2 wars. To show how certain he was that IBM wouldn't deliver on its OS/2 promises, Steve publicly stated that he would eat a floppy disk if IBM shipped OS/2 2.0 by the 1991 Fall Comdex. IBM missed the date. Steve stuck to his favorite snack of popcorn.

Shipping Rewards

The big rewards, however, come when products ship. Sometimes companies celebrate such events with parties. These can range from a group of sleep-deprived programmers hanging around outside with a few beers, to extremely elaborate, catered celebrations complete with bands. Most team members prefer shipping bonuses to parties, which at some companies can be several thousand

Nerd Humor:

The Frog and the Programmer

A computer programmer came across a frog in a road. The frog could speak and said, "I'm really a beautiful princess and if you kiss me, I'll turn back into a princess, and I'll allow myself to be seen with you." The programmer shrugged his shoulders and put the frog in his pocket.

A few minutes later, the programmer heard the frog again, so he took it out of his pocket. The frog said, "OK, OK, if you kiss me, I'll turn into a beautiful princess, and I'll have sex with you." The programmer nodded and put the frog back in his pocket.

A few minutes later, he heard a noise again and the frog said, "Turn me back into a princess and I'll give you great sex for a whole year!" The programmer smiled and walked on.

Finally, the frog said, "What's wrong with you? I've promised you great sex for a year from a beautiful princess and you won't even kiss a frog?"

"I'm a programmer," the programmer replied. "I don't have time for sex. But a talking frog, now that's cool."

dollars or several thousand additional options. For some reason, money seems to get most a little more excited than free food.

And sometimes, the rewards are even more extravagant. At Borland, Philippe Kahn promised a swimming pool when the millionth copy of Quattro Pro shipped. And thus there is a swimming pool at the new building. When C++ met a major sales milestone, Borland added a hot tub to the plans.

At Microsoft, when OS/2 1.1 shipped, everyone from the team and a guest got a week-long, all-expenses-paid trip to Hawaii. The promise of this trip encouraged many to work insane hours to meet the deadline. Morale-building contests along the way kept the team moving. One such event was a Hawaiian spirit contest. The winner (who happened to be me) dressed in the brightest and most tackiest Hawaiian clothes available in the continental U.S. — so loud that they would make Mitch Kapor jealous — plastered himself with tropical oil, and then tracked sand wherever he walked.

As the event neared, the excitement intensified. Many team members, mostly male, got together to discuss dating strategy. After all, since they got to bring a guest, it could in fact be the first time many of them would successfully get a date. Lists of the women in the company were poured over, people racked their brains for women they knew from college who might attend, while others got up the courage to try barhopping. Despite the grand efforts and the Hawaiian trip prize, many couldn't find dates and ended up traveling alone.

Getting a Real Tan

Hundreds of programmers devoted years of their life to creating OS/2. The final push for version 1.1 was particularly strenuous, with Microsoft programmers working around the clock to meet deadlines. As an incentive, Microsoft promised a free trip to Hawaii if the product shipped by Halloween. Team leaders gave out this Club Mauisoft shirt as a reminder of the reward at the end of the tunnel.

Borland, among much controversy, also sent part of its team to Hawaii when Quattro Pro for Windows shipped. Strangely enough, there seems to be a correlation between such trips and product lifetime. Within two years Microsoft was completely divorced from OS/2 development, and within a year Borland sold Quattro Pro to Novell.

This 1984 picture shows Bob Needham, the president of Sage Computer Technology. Sage was an early computer maker. Demand for computers constantly exceeded inventory, so as soon as Bob got a PC, someone would take it and ship it to a customer. Bob decided this was a hassle, so he took a Sage II computer out of its case and bolted it to the side of his desk. The power supply and disk drives sat in one of the desk drawers.

Coi Death

Borland was very proud of the coi pond it installed at its new campus. The coi pond started in the lobby, in a sunken pond carefully protected from raccoons and the outside world by a Plexiglas shield. The water flowed out into a stream that traversed the length of the campus, leading to a waterfall by the outdoor seating for the cafeteria. Borland had received a special exemption from the drought-prone region to use 400,000 gallons of water for the stream. Yet, soon after the fish arrived, they started dying.

It turned out that no one had realized that the chemicals put in the water to keep algae off the rocks would poison the fish. They had to drain the stream and clean the chemicals from the rocks before they could bring the fish in again.

The coi pond also caused other problems — employees occasionally fell into the part that was in the lobby. In one of the more amusing incidents, a direct-mail marketing manager was hurrying to a meeting. She, as was often her habit, was dressed very nicely and had her leather briefcase with her. She stopped to talk to some employees in the lobby, backed up, and soon was flat on her back in the pond, the items from her briefcase scattered and soaked. That lent a bit of levity to the meeting.

Culture Clash

Not all computer companies have the laid-back attitude discussed here. And when laid-back and uptight companies work together, many amusing culture clashes arise. Some of the largest, ongoing clashes occurred when Microsoft and IBM worked together to create OS/2. Microsoft had no dress code. IBM required white shirts, except on Fridays. Microsoft was very open. IBM required security passes. Here is what the result was, as told by various Microsoft employees:

- IBM had a very strict policy on keeping documents secure. Confidential documents could only be sent back and forth to Microsoft using certain approved carriers. Thus, if a programmer visited IBM for a technical meeting, he couldn't take back any IBM specifications with him on the airplane. The specs had to be sent by separate courier, even if the programmer was carrying a Microsoft version of the same document. At one point, we planned to photocopy the title page of a spec (which just said "IBM Confidential") and leave it around at various points at the airport nearest to IBM's Boca Raton offices. We wouldn't have revealed anything confidential, but we sure would have freaked out anyone from IBM who came across the documents.

- All visitors had to be escorted through the hallways at IBM. The escort, who was always the person we were visiting, could get in trouble (and even fired), if he or she let a visitor walk anywhere unescorted. When traveling in twos, we often threatened to run in different directions.

- Any desk drawer or cabinet had to be made secure before an office was left unattended. Once this process was complete (essentially, locking all drawers and removing any papers from the desk), a sign was placed on the desk. These signs said "Secure" on one side and "Not Secure" on the other. We used to steal them from the desks, or turn them around.

- The main place we visited while working on OS/2 was the IBM Boca Raton office. Being in Florida, the weather was often considerably warmer and sunnier than that in Washington State. At one point, a Microsoft programmer went to the IBM front lawn, took off his shirt, and sunbathed with a reflector. This caused a huge stink at IBM, as it was a severe violation of dress and conduct codes. But they couldn't say anything, since the programmer didn't work for them. They made an emergency call to Microsoft headquarters, so that the developer's manager could request he not suntan at IBM.

- IBM had a very strict policy against alcohol at work. Not only could you not drink at the office (which is a reasonable policy except at parties), but you couldn't have bottles in your trash. We were a lot rowdier, and since we were working 16 to 20 hours a day, compared to the 8 hours a day many of our IBM cohorts were putting in, we felt we could run our office block the way we wanted. One Saturday night we had a few beers. A security guard found them, and collected them as evidence to report to a senior manager at IBM. We just barely avoided being kicked out for good. Which in retrospect might not have been such a bad thing after all.

Many speculate that similar clashes will occur now that IBM has bought Lotus. There are numerous jokes about this, including one that IBM bought Lotus just so it could force the Lotus programmers to wear shoes when they come to the office.

Great Quotes:

Working With IBM

"Our efforts to work with IBM on software definitely come to mind as one of the more painful experiences we've had." — Bill Gates

These mugs are part of the general fanfare celebrating Microsoft OS/2 development. The one on the left is for the abandoned Microsoft OS/2 2.0, while the one on the right is from the earlier OS/2 1.1 days.

Change Comes Slowly

It took a while for IBM to leave its mainframe mentality behind when marketing OS/2. The first several OS/2 marketing campaigns were very tame, and the product was undermarketed. The boxes were bland and the little text they had was filled with IBM-speak. Instead of saying technical support was available, the boxes would talk about things such as zero-defect events monitored by service center representatives. At one point a Borland marketing manager suggested to an IBM Vice President that he spend some time looking at pornographic movie boxes, which seemed to get more of a message across with even fewer words. The Vice President did not seem amused.

Eventually IBM woke up and came out with a new look and a concerted effort to attract software developers to the OS/2 platform. As this shift began, a senior marketing manager tried to launch an aggressive campaign to increase awareness of OS/2 among programmers. Thus, he planned a campaign that placed ads in several magazines, including *Byte* and *Dr. Dobb's*. His plan was shot down, with a message that "IBM does not advertise in medical journals." They didn't realize that *Dr. Dobb's* was one of the largest circulation programming magazines, not a medical magazine.

Letting Out Steam

There are many other amusing stories of life in high-tech companies, as are told in Chapter 4, "April Fools." Programmers, being at the top of the barrel in most high-tech companies, feel compelled to express their individuality. In many cases this is expressed through office sports. For example, Microsoft applications developers ran a golf tournament through the building hallways for many years. This group would hold their event on a scheduled floor of a scheduled building every Friday.

Other groups were very fond of juggling, an important tradition among engineers and programmers. During the summer you can often find jugglers riding around Lake BillG on unicycles while passing balls back and forth to each other. Juggling was also popular inside hallways. At one point, Bill Gates was taking a group of key Japanese businessmen on a tour through Microsoft. One hallway was clogged with jugglers, giving a bit of an unprofessional look to the company. A dictate soon followed: no more juggling in the hallways. So they juggled in their offices, passing balls and pins to each other across the hallways, resulting in quite the sight for those traveling through.

Another hallway sport was "hoser ball". For this event empty soda cans would be lined up much like bowling pins, and a tennis ball weighted with pennies would be rolled to knock them down.

Keeping this free-form lifestyle was very important to Microsoft employees. It was part of what set them apart from other companies and made working the insane hours so much fun. It is no surprise that employees reacted harshly to any attempts to curtail such freedom. When Microsoft first introduced card keys to prevent unwanted visitors, there was a rumor that they planned to track the hours employees were working. Gordon

Letwin, one of the first Microsoft employees, and his wife were not happy about this "big company" attitude. So they got in their car and drove back and forth from one end of the building to the other, running Gordon's card key through the door locks. They eventually overflowed the software that tracked key usage. The security folks got the message and never tracked key usage.

Activities such as these are by no means unique to Microsoft. For example, in August 1989 all 280 employees of Adobe got together for a large water fight in celebration of shipping a product.

Did You Know?

Pirate Flags

The Macintosh development team regarded itself as a rebel group and flew a Jolly Roger flag outside of its building. Borland's debugger group also hung Jolly Roger flags throughout its work area.

And Now for Something Completely Different

Not all software companies have the same relaxed attitudes as those exemplified by Microsoft. MetaWare, a producer of C++ compilers, is known for being a very religiously oriented company. Which is somewhat amusing given that it is headquartered about a mile away from the Santa Cruz beach, a hangout of hippies, surfers, and subject to occasional visits from locals such as Lady Bo, Neil Young, and Carlos Santana.

In fact, MetaWare is said to hold opening prayers before beginning meetings and ships books from the New Testament with their products. Their business cards stress their focus clearly, as shown in Figure 3-1.

An ex-employee of MetaWare told me that an emergency meeting was once called by a senior executive to discuss a very troubling piece of news. Apparently, he was concerned about evolution being taught in schools and railed against discussions of dinosaurs, which were clearly evil animals brought about by satanic scientists.

Figure 3-1 The back of a business card from a senior executive at MetaWare shows their Christian orientation. This is something of an anomaly for software companies.

Did You Know?

Would You Turn It Down?

Don Estridge was one of the fundamental drivers behind IBM's personal computer presence, having run the team that released the IBM PC. In 1983, he was the VP of Worldwide Manufacturing and was making $250,000 a year in salary and bonuses. Steve Jobs wanted to hire Estridge to be president of Apple and offered him $1,000,000 per year in salary, a $1,000,000 sign-on bonus, and a $2,000,000 loan to buy a house. Estridge turned him down. Some say this was because he felt IBM was an institution, whereas Apple was just a company.

After Estridge turned down the offer, Jobs offered the same deal to John Sculley, who left PepsiCo to take it.

The Graz

Apple had a reputation for paying huge sign-on bonuses to attract top talent. This was especially important to the company during its many bouts with ill fortune. In 1990, John Sculley hired Joe Graziano back from Sun to be Apple's CFO. He paid Joe a $1.5 million sign-on bonus. Allegedly, news of this spread though the company, and the term "one Graz" turned into jargon meaning $1.5 million. So if you sold $3 million worth of products, you would say you sold two Graz's.

Making It to the Top

Bob Frankenberg was chatting with Ray Noorda one day when Ray asked who Bob thought would make a good replacement for Ray when he chose to retire from Novell. Jokingly, Bob (then at Hewlett-Packard) answered, "I always thought I would be a good candidate." The next day Bob got a call from the executive search committee, and after a series of interviews, ended up becoming the new President of Novell.

"We thought they would have more of a sense of humor."

— President of Delrina
After Berkeley Software sued Delrina
over the flying toaster screensaver

April Fools

You have now learned (and may very well know from firsthand experience) that people in the computer industry work hard. In fact, many programmers and engineers pride themselves on how long they work. It is a test of endurance. A way to prove one's man (or woman) hood. Drive around any major software company in the middle of the night, and you are bound to see people still working. In fact, it is not uncommon for people to pull all-nighters while trying to ship a product. When I was at a startup, I often worked from 4AM until midnight — seven days a week. And I wasn't alone.

This isn't unique to startups. Around larger companies such as Borland, Microsoft, and Apple you'll find that people move couches or futons into their offices so that they can sleep there. One developer (who happens to be a close friend of mine) was quoted in the book *Showstoppers* as saying that despite having a beautiful waterfront home, he felt homeless because he spent so many nights sleeping on the floor of his office when trying to ship Windows NT. Another friend crammed bookshelves, cooking equipment, a hammock, and even a bed for his dog inside a small office so that he could work uninterrupted. Yet another brought in a sleeping bag and didn't go home for weeks at a time.

Any time a ship date looms, there is bound to be some late-night activity of one type or another. For example, while working on shipping the Amiga, developers would dance to stay awake during late-night development sessions. In fact, there is a hidden message in the Amiga OS 1.2, saying "Moral Support: Joe Pillow and the Dancing Fools."

So what do you do when you spend more time with your coworkers than your family? When your only chance of getting a tan is from the radiation from your monitor? When you have formed an incredible bond of camaraderie with a bunch of nerds as you struggle to meet insurmountable goals? And when you have no means of releasing stress, because there is no time for exercise, movies, or simply relaxing? You fall back on past experience. And for many programmers, this means returning to college

Nerd Humor: Monopoly Compiler

FORTRAN is a programming language that was quite popular for writing scientific applications. The following two lines of FORTRAN code create an endless loop.

```
10      assign 10 to jail
        goto jail
```

If you compile this program with the FORTRAN compiler for the CP-V OS on Xerox Sigma computers, you'll get the following diagnostic message:

Go directly to jail. Do not pass Go. Do not collect $200.

habits. After all, that is another place where you pull all-nighters, wear sweat pants and t-shirts, and spend inordinate amounts of time working on intellectual problems with people of the same age. When not spending time complaining about the lack of dates, engineers and programmers in college play practical jokes (sometimes called *hacks*) to relieve stress.

Many fine engineering institutions, such as MIT and CalTech, have a long tradition of practical jokes. MIT is known for cars occasionally showing up on dorm roofs and for pranks pulled at the nearby Harvard/Yale game. In a famous story, MIT students planted electric wires under the playing field so that they could burn the words "Go MIT" into the field at halftime. While they were setting this up, a suspicious security guard searched them and found that they were carrying a large number of batteries to the field. The guards called the Dean of the Engineering School. When he arrived, the guard complained that he thought the students were up to no good. The Dean calmly opened up his jacket to reveal that it too was lined with batteries. "We're from MIT," he explained.

CalTech is known for a hazing practice in which students barricade their rooms to prevent the next year's class from getting into the dorm. The students then have to face a time limit to gain the right to enter their rooms. Various tricks are used to keep the returning students out, from bricking doors to the use of elaborate electronic locks on them, to leaving complex mathematical problems, or creating treasure hunts snaking across the country. (In fact, in one famous treasure hunt, at the very end the student came to a hotel room. Inside was a naked woman holding the dorm key. He could either grab the key and speed back to make the deadline, or spend some time with a naked woman — an opportunity undoubtedly rare for him. He dutifully grabbed the key.)

It is no wonder that once students leave this environment to work in the computer field, some of these habits carry over. And when you combine the eccentric nature of these computer people with a little bit of discretionary income, you never know what might happen.

Most often corporate pranks relate to "office decorating." And once the word gets out about a particular prank, others try to out do it. Pranks are rarely malicious. Instead, they are timed as birthday presents, or welcome back messages for those who have managed to take vacations. In the following section, some hackers share their stories.

Figure 4-1 Every April Fools' Day Microsoft puts out a joke issue of its company newsletter, *The MicroNews*. The 1995 issue featured many fake stories and pictures, including this one, of a giant cat using the Microsoft beach volleyball court as a litter box. (Photo courtesy of *The MicroNews*.)

A Greener Carpet

We knew Bob wasn't working over the weekend. So we decided to play a little trick on him. First we moved out all of his office furniture, his computers, and anything else in the room. Then we sodded the floor. Completely. And put everything back the way it was. When he came in Monday he had grass on the floor instead of a carpet. It was pretty funny. Of course, it did start to smell after a few weeks.

A Birthday Surprise

Our administrative assistant's birthday was coming up. We wanted to give her a surprise she would remember. So we began gathering Styrofoam packing peanuts. Every time a package came, we would save the peanuts and take them to our homes. We would go through every building over the weekends looking for corporate supply rooms that were open so we could take bigger packages. And we even told her that one of us was moving so that she would help us gather the peanuts. The night before her birthday we brought bag after bag of these to her office. We went to the neighboring office so that we could go through the ceiling to fill her office — that way we could get it quite full without having to figure out a way to get the door closed. Unfortunately, it turned out that her office had at one point stored an early prototype of a PC from IBM. And thus it had been outfitted to be secure. The whole ceiling was blocked off and covered with wire mesh, so we couldn't get through that way. It was just as well, because although we had gathered at least 30 cubic feet of peanuts, we didn't have enough to fill the office completely. We ended up filling a cone behind the window to her office so it would look like it was filled floor to ceiling from the outside. We then created another cone filled with the remaining peanuts and attached it to the door. That way, once the door was open, tons of peanuts would cascade out. It was certainly a birthday she remembered.

Another Birthday Surprise

Not surprisingly, birthdays are often singled out as days to play pranks. A friend of ours, Michelle, worked in the HR department at Microsoft. Like most recruiters at Microsoft, she was attractive, overworked, and stressed out. As her birthday neared, she was convinced no one had remembered it and was quite depressed that she would spend it slaving away all day at work. Several of us got together to plan a grand event. We made sure that none of her friends let on that they knew it was her birthday. One of Michelle's jobs was doing the introductory interviews for candidates. They would come in, meet with her for a bit, and then she would make sure that they met all the appropriate interviewers. We found out who she would be meeting at 10:00 on her birthday, and secretly had a different recruiter meet that candidate. Meanwhile, we hired a stripper and gave him a rough description of who he needed to be — a college student studying computers at the University of Chicago. Sure enough, when 10:00 arrived Michelle's candidate was ushered to her office. She thought it was a little funny that the guy carried a Harley-Davidson briefcase, but then, who knows with programmers. Meanwhile, Michelle's friends crowded around the outside of her office and jammed against the windows of other offices where they could look in. Unfortunately, the stripper forgot all of the lines we had so carefully scripted for him. When Michelle indicated an engineer would take him to lunch, he kept requesting that she take him instead. And then he asked if she would meet him for dinner. Shortly, he reached behind the door, turned on some music, and began his routine. She was thoroughly embarrassed, but had a birthday she would never forget.

False Advertising

Sometimes pranksters take aim at a larger target than an unsuspecting co-worker and go right after their company. Figures 4-2 and 4-3 are examples of two ads — one genuine and one a fake — created to promote MS OS/2.

Figure 4-2 In the early days, programming for Windows and OS/2 was expensive. There were few tools, the operating system was more complex than anything else on the market, and the manuals were a few thousand pages thicker than those for DOS. Not only were these systems hard to learn, it cost $3,000 just to get the development kit, as shown in this 1987 ad. Within four years, such kits would drop dramatically in price, first to a few hundred dollars, and then to free, as they became included with compilers and other development tools.

For those software developers who won't pay lots of money to get started on MS OS/2.

If you don't have the money or think that $3000 is just too much bread to pay for paper, ink and magnetic oxide, here's what you can get for $25:

A subscription to PC Week, including frequent references to Microsoft Operating System/2 and the Windows presentation manager.

A copy of Kernighan and Ritchie's C book.

Three feet of coaxial cable.

A coupon for 20 cents off the inevitable SAMS book on OS/2.

Continual invoices for $25, right up until you pay.

A pair of BVD's for superior product support.

And most importantly, a seat at Ed Begley's "How to turn a million dollars of real estate into five dollars, overnight!" seminar in Seattle, or Tacoma if it's more convenient.

Everything you need to get a real head start in producing new applications that might run under MS OS/2.

That's the good news.

The bad news is that we've only got 15 feet of coaxial cable. So it's first come, first served.

And if you don't sign up before May 1st, you're S.O.L.

$25

THE MS OS/2 CHEAP DEVELOPMENT KIT/TRAINING SEMINAR.

Please send me...MS OS/2 Cheap Software Development Kit(s)/Training Seminar Registration(s) at $25 each. I understand that these kits are probably worthless and will likely not work at all. I agree that I will not use the software at all and that, if I do, Microsoft is not responsible for anything that might happen to my hard disk.

Signature of Licensee: _____

Name _____

Address _____

Where you leave your spare key

I would like to attend the following seminar (check one):
☐ Seattle, June 31, 1987.   ☐   Tacoma, July 4, 1987.

Note: There is a limited attendance to the seminar. It is strictly most pay, first served, and although every effort will be made, we cannot guarantee your location preference. Others will receive a VHS video tape of "Benji Come Home". The tape is not available seperately or as a choice.

I enclose $_____ in cash (including sales tax , if applicable). California residents please add 6%, Washington State residents, add 8.1%. Please charge to my VISA/MC/MACY's card.
No:_____ Exp. date_____ Signature_____
(No company BOs, no telephone orders, no nothing)

Send to: Microsoft Corporation, Dept. MO OS/2 CSDK, 16011 N.E. 36th Way, Box 97017, Redmond, WA 98073-9717. Please allow 6-8 weeks for us to collect interest on your money

Microsoft

Figure 4-3 Not everyone at Microsoft thought $3,000 was a good price for the OS/2 development kit. This hilarious advertisement is an internally created spoof of the real OS/2 ad.

Size Does Matter

We often had discussions about office size, and whether all offices were the same size. One person on the team was very concerned about his office size and wanted to make sure that, if there were bigger offices, he would get one. We came in one weekend, moved out all of his furniture, and took down the whiteboard from his back wall. We then brought in a carpenter who laid a new sheet of drywall on the back wall of the office — only it was two feet in from where it used to be. We put everything back the way it was. So it looked like it did on Friday, only now it was two feet shorter than it used to be. For about six weeks he kept wondering why other people's offices felt bigger. Finally he measured it.

Removing an Office

Joe went away for a week-long vacation. To show how much we missed him, we hired a carpenter to come in, take down his door, and put drywall across it. When the carpenter was finished, there was no sign that there was ever an office there. Just a long blank wall. When Joe came back he was very confused.

Flame Mail from the Top

Carl was getting a bit cockier than usual, so we decided to take him down a notch. We pulled together some fake email from Bill Gates and forwarded it on to Carl:

```
From: xxxxx
To: yyyy
Subject: FW: RE: proposal
xxxx —
I ran your idea past bill. thought you might
like to hear what he had to say

From: billg
To: xxxxx
Subject: RE: proposal
That is the stupidest thing I have ever heard
```

Of course, we typed the message from Bill ourselves, and just filled in the header so it would look like it was real mail. Bill wasn't involved with the proposal at that point, but it sure freaked Carl out for a bit.

Getting a Roommate

Tom was in Europe working for two weeks. We had been hiring a lot of people, and it was almost time for the summer interns to show up, so everyone was worried about getting an office mate. (Which, by the way, is generally considered a bad thing. And a sign of low status.) A few days before Tom returned, we gave him an office mate. Not only that, since Tom was very shy, we gave him a female office mate. We brought in an extra bookshelf, desk, telephone, email terminal, computer, and corkboard. These things were really hard to find. We put books on the bookshelf, papers in the desk, and various family photographs on the corkboard. We hacked the email system so that there would be mail from Tom's manager to the group welcoming the new person and saying she would be sharing Tom's office. We sent out additional email to Tom saying that his office mate's phone wouldn't be ready for a few days, did he mind taking messages. And we left some phone messages on the line. We got a name plate for this person. We then hacked Tom's electronic phone list, so that if he checked where the person belonged it would say his office. Tom was really shocked when he got back.

Actually, though, it turned out the joke was more on us. Tom routinely ran a program when he booted his computer that checked if the time stamp on his phone list was changed. So he pretty quickly knew something was up, and just went along with the joke to please us. Why anyone would write such a program was kind of amazing, but when you hang out with computer nerds, not too much is surprising.

Gift Wrapped

Todd's birthday was coming up. So the night before, about five of us got together. We went through Todd's office item by item, wrapping things in newspaper. And I mean everything. We took every single book off his bookshelf and wrapped it in newspaper, and then put it back on in the exact same spot. We wrapped his monitor, his keyboard, his desk, his shoes, even his Frisbees. And put everything back in the exact same position.

More Gift Wrap

We didn't want our manager to think that she was less special than Todd, so we decided to outdo the group that hacked his office. Before our manager's birthday, we pretty much did the same thing. We took everything out and wrapped it in papier-mâché. Only we wrapped it in paper mache. So she had one heck of a surprise for her birthday. I can't say she was particularly happy, because it took a long time to get her office back to normal, but at least she knew someone cared.

Here Comes the Union

The memo in Figure 4-4 was photocopied and placed in all Microsoft mailboxes one night. It generated a lot of interesting email.

Married Name

I went away for a week-long honeymoon after I got married. When I got back, everything was normal. Which was a big relief. But I couldn't figure out why people I didn't know — interns and people new to the group — kept calling me by my wife's last name. About two months later, I realized that someone had changed the name plate on my door to have my wife's last name instead of mine.

Moving Yet Again

We had just moved offices for the third time in a few weeks. It was driving me crazy. Not only did I have to pack up my office, but I had to pack up all of the legal files for the whole department. And then unpack them. It wasn't like the moves were for a good reason, either. They were just the typical computer industry moves. Someone reorganized a department, so everyone would switch offices. And here it was the beginning of April. I had just unpacked. And there was a memo from Philippe Kahn saying that it was time to move again. Legal would go where shipping was, and shipping would go where legal was. Further, legal would now have to be non-smoking. I was furious. I called up Phillippe, screaming. After I had ranted for about five minutes, he said, "What is today?" I had just made a complete fool of myself to the company president, and only then realized it was April Fools' Day.

Microsoft Memo

TO: All Development Staff

FROM: Jon Shirley

DATE: June 21, 1989

RE: Unionization of Microsoft Development Staff

It has come to our attention that various outside organizers, in conjunction with a few Microsoft employees, are attempting to unionize Microsoft development staff. Many of you have already been contacted about your interest in joining such a union.

Under the National Labor Relations Act of 1946, it is illegal for Microsoft to use intimidation or threatening tactics to hinder the formation of a labor union. Nevertheless, the Board of Directors and I feel that all development staff members should know the official position of the company and understand the issues involved.

It is not at all clear that Microsoft would be legally required to negotiate with or even recognize such a union. As stated in a recent California Supreme Court decision concerning the rights of engineers at a software company to unionize: "Employees of a corporation which gives its employees a significant stake in the company's future by means of stock options or profit sharing are considered to have certain fiduciary responsibilities which prevent them from forming a union for the purpose of collective bargaining with the company without a conflict of interest, dude." We are currently having the Legal Department research these issues fully.

Legal considerations aside, we strongly believe that Microsoft is very generous with its exempt employees regarding benefits and work incentives, and that an adversarial stance between management and development would harm the company's unique relationship with all of its employees. We urge you to consider carefully what the union would offer you and compare it to what you currently receive from Microsoft.

We do ask that you please refrain from speaking of this matter with outsiders, particularly members of the press. Should you wish to discuss further any of the topics mentioned above, please contact Jim Hoffa or Carl Marks of the Legal Department.

Figure 4-4 This memo suggests that Microsoft was about to unionize. It seems pretty real until you see whom to contact for more information.

The Nearest Bathroom

As a joke, we built a bathroom in Carl's office. A complete bathroom. We moved in a toilet, a toilet paper holder complete with toilet paper, a shower curtain, and a towel rod. Carl kept it there for a couple of weeks. It was pretty funny to see the look on people's faces when they went by.

More Bathroom Humor

Toilet papering a house is nothing compared to what caring coworkers did to Microsoft's James Ableson. He was minding his own business, so to speak, when his office got turned into an elaborate wooden outhouse, complete with a door with moon cut away, toilet seats, and toilet paper rolls. (See Figure 4-5.) James worked in the outhouse for a week before taking it down. He says, "I knew something was coming...I just never imagined they would take the time and effort to build a fully furnished outhouse. The payback is planned and ready for execution, I am just waiting for the right time."

Figure 4-5 James Ableson surveys his new throne.

A Really Important Meeting

Philippe Kahn's administrative assistant got an urgent call on his direct phone line. Lou Gerstner — recently elected Chairman of IBM — had to talk with Philippe right away about Borland's OS/2 products. Philippe was out of the office, so his administrative assistant immediately contacted his personal assistant. And his personal assistant frantically searched everywhere for him. After all, Mr. Gerstner insisted on holding, and said that he couldn't be called back. Eventually they found Philippe and patched him in. Lou asked a couple of questions about how OS/2 was going, and then insisted that Philippe fly out to IBM's headquarters in New York right away to discuss urgent business. Philippe suggested meeting somewhere halfway, such as Chicago. But Mr. Gerstner insisted. Philippe thought something was fishy, so asked a few times if it really was Lou. And Mr. Gerstner insisted it was he and that he felt insulted. Finally Philippe asked him a technical detail. That's when the guy confessed he was really a DJ and was live on the air playing a prank. Kind of like the Howard Stern show. So even people outside of the industry get into the spirit of things.

Sorry about Your Car

We were locked in bitter competition with Microsoft. One guy in particular was driving us crazy. He was bragging about how nice his new car was, how great it was to work at Microsoft, and so forth. So we found the name of a woman who worked a few buildings away from him. We then called him up, long distance, and had someone in our group leave him a message about how sorry she was that she bumped into his car in the parking lot, but that she had a boyfriend that she was sure could fix it, just give her a call if there were any questions. He actually did call her, but figured out pretty quickly that it was us.

Tired of the Same Old Thing

At trade shows, presenters say the same thing over and over again. Many companies hire professional entertainers who repeat the same lines over and over, amplified enough to annoy anyone except customers who get to pass through once and move on to the next act. One of these staged events in Borland's booth at Spring Comdex involved a faked, lively discussion between a professional MC and product managers for the various software being shown. Afterwards, the MC would ask a set of questions, accompanied by background slides, and those who could answer would win prizes. The MC, named Scotty, would go through the same slides with the same questions every 30 minutes. During the next-to-last presentation, we switched slides on Scotty. Now, Scotty had just gotten new, fancy leather shoes that he was very proud of. They had a strange, mottled look to them. So we made one of the questions "Why are Scotty's shoes so ugly?" We had a couple of other joke slides in there, too. Scotty burst out laughing in front of the whole audience. You should have seen how nervous he was during his last presentation.

Internet Jokes

April Fools' Day is often a big event on the Internet. In 1994, a user in Holland sent out a fake press release announcing that McDonald's was about to head on-line. "Every highway needs restaurants," it proclaimed.

Ten years before, someone hacked an account so that it said Konstantin Chernenko, the Soviet leader at the time, and sent out greetings to the on-line world. Apparently he received many replies welcoming him and congratulating him for an openness uncharacteristic of the Soviets at the time.

Keeping Away Headhunters

Microsoft used to distribute employee phone lists on a regular basis. The lists were considered highly confidential, because if they got into the hands of a headhunter, they could lead to trouble. As a result, there were many reminders to keep them secure.

This led to the prank newsletter shown in Figure 4-6, written by a guy whom we'll call David, for convenience. Part of the memo discusses a program on a fake network share that would allegedly shred documents. Of course, this was complete nonsense, as deleting a file would get rid of it, and shredding a computer file is pretty meaningless.

That night, David's manager created a network location with the fake name and wrote a program called netshred.exe, as was discussed in the memo. The next morning he marched into David's office, described net-shred to him — exactly as was outlined in the memo — and assigned David the task of maintaining it.

MICROSOFT® MEMO

TO   Building 2, Second Floor

FROM   Facilities

DATE   April 16, 1986

RE   New Shredder Policy

CC   Richardg, Danl, Steveb

Level 2

To ease use of the new shredder without sacrificing security, it is asked that people follow the guidelines promulgated in this memorandum. Documents will now be classified by security level, and shredder access will be allocated on the basis of this level. Higher classification jobs will be given preferential shredder access and be shredded more times. Classification numbers will range from Level 0 (duplicate before disposal) to Level 5 (shred before reading). In addition, queuing at the shredder should follow this hierarchy. For example: Bill has a Level 1 document, Joan has a Level 3 document, and Sam has a Level 2 document. The order of use of the shredder should then be Joan, Sam, and finally Bill. If, however, Sally comes to use the shredder with last month's phonelist, a Level 5 document, she would immediately move to the head of the line. A document should be shredded the number of times equal to its classification -- an automatic chaff refeeder will be attached to the shredder, allowing the user to merely enter the number of times a document is to be shredded. The chaff from the shredded document will be recycled through the shredder until the document has been shredded the number of times specified.

The second major change in shredder usage is the new network shredding capability. Files may now be sent directly to the shredder from both DOS and Xenix machines, using the Ungerman-Bass network. To use this from a DOS machine, copy the file \\TOOLSRV\NEWTOOLS\BIN\NETSHRED.EXE to your machine. On Xenix machines, netshred will be found in the /usr/bin directory. The syntax of NETSHRED is as follows:

netshred file1 [file2 file3. . .] [/P=priority (or for Xenix) -p priority]

The default priority is 1, and if no files are specified on the command line, NETSHRED will read from standard input. NETSHRED on DOS supports wildcards on the command line. Interactive shredding jobs will be boosted two priority levels for purposes of comparison with network jobs, to avoid long lines at the shredder.

Please help these guidelines to work. Be sure to specify the Security Level of any mail or memorandum you write, whether paper or electronic, to aid the recipients in its eventual disposal. Obey the queuing hierarchy at the shredder, and don't falsely claim higher priority for the documents you are shredding. If you have any questions about shredder policy or use, ask your group assistant, who will have received training for the new shredders.

Figure 4-6 This fake memo outlines a new shredder policy designed to keep phone lists out of the hands of the enemy.

Nerd Humor:

The Press Releases Keep On Coming

Apple introduces new AppleSquawk networking system

CUPERTINO, California—April 1, 1991—Apple Computer, Inc., today announced that its newest networking product, AppleSquawk, will be shown to the public for its first demonstration within the next week. The AppleSquawk software is a bold new networking concept, using sound to transfer data between computers rather than traditional, cable-based systems.

AppleSquawk uses the built-in speaker port on Macintosh computers to transmit a carefully chosen set of 16 sound packets. At a rate of 8 packets per second (later versions are expected to achieve 64), AppleSquawk can handle data transfers at a rate of 0.0039 KB/sec. While slower than competing network products, AppleSquawk is designed to require no (Macintosh IIsi installations) or minimal (other Macintosh models) additional hardware, reducing its price and mainte-nance needs.

Other products increasing AppleSquawk's utility include the new Apple/Kawai Macintosh External Speaker, a self-contained sound sys-tem increasing the range of an AppleSquawk installation as well as Macintosh system sound output quality; and the AppleSquawk HandsOff system, software to allow a trained user to control a Macintosh without typing or using the mouse, simply using mostly whistled sounds to per-form simple actions such as pointing and clicking. HandsOff, expected to ship with AppleSquawk, will come with a training tape and guide, and the software has an instruction mode to ease learning how to use it.

Software developers in the Apple Developers Program can expect the AppleSquawk development package to ship in the next week. Final ver-sions are planned to be released on the market in early summer.

Yet Another Birthday Present

For Dave Cutler's fiftieth birthday, an employee named Rob Short bought a Vax 780 — an old DEC machine — and reassembled the 5 × 8 computer in Cutler's house as a surprise. Because it required special power to run, Short embedded a MicroVax inside the system and connected the terminal to that, making it appear to be on and running. This was particularly amusing because Cutler had designed the operating system that ran on the machine.

What Is That Noise?

Builders in the NT lab often listened to loud music, sometimes playing the same album over and over. Dave Cutler often hung out there. One day, he brought in the worst albums he and his companion/girlfriend could find — a "Gomer Pyle" cast member singing gospel tunes and a Chipmunks album. Dave insisted on playing the former over and over. Eventually the build team hid the album.

Fix the Reception

Steve Wozniak was famous for pranks. In high school he put an electronic metronome in a friend's locker. Instead of his friend finding it, the principal did, assumed it was a bomb, and ran with it outside of the building to save the school. Wozniak got suspended for two days as a result.

At college, Wozniak created a device to jam TV reception. He would turn it on and then instruct hall mates to climb on the roof and adjust the antenna. Once these people were in a very awkward position, Wozniak would turn off the jammer, congratulate them on their efforts, and make them stay in position until the show was over.

Wozniak also pulled a prank on Jobs when they launched the Apple II at the West Coast Computer Faire. Wozniak made a brochure about a fake MITS computer called the Zaltair, with a comparison chart to the Apple II. Of course, it was all a fake, but it fooled Jobs, who was relieved to see the Apple II performed better than the Zaltair.

What Suit Is That Card?

When companies fall on hard times, competitors often recruit away their top talent. This happened to Borland. After a string of losses and layoffs, many of the top programmers and marketers went to Microsoft. As a result of this, a group of poker players found their game disrupted. The group was made up of several marketers, one of the top lawyers, a vice president, and an ex-Borland employee regarded as one of the top database consultants in the country.

After the second poker player left for Microsoft, the lawyer decided to play a practical joke. He drafted up a threatening letter and promptly sent it to the recently departed employee, care of Microsoft. He even included Judge Sporkin — then involved in the government's investigation of Microsoft — on the fake CC line.

Ventricles in the Frammistan

It's a well-known fact that very few computer salespeople understand what they are talking about. After all, marketing extremely technical products to an extremely technical audience is difficult if you don't have an extremely technical background. And most salespeople don't.

Jerry Pournelle, a famous science fiction writer and long-time *Byte* columnist, used this fact to play a joke on a salesman at the 1983 West Coast Computer Faire. The salesman had been using a lot of jargon that he clearly didn't understand, and although he didn't understand some of Jerry's questions, gave fake answers anyway.

Jerry then said, "I've noticed that some of the competition has ventricles. Do you have them?"

"Yes, we have the most features of any portable machine on the market," answered the salesman. Of course, there is no such thing as a ventricle on a computer, at least not as of the writing of this book.

Jerry then said, "Do you have them in the frammistan where they belong?"

The salesman answered yes, and then, embarrassed, realized Jerry was pulling his leg.

Nerd Humor

Q: What's the difference between a computer salesperson and a used car salesperson?

A: Car salespeople know when they are lying.

Learn How to Type

This classic prank was pulled by Robert Hummel, Jeff Prosise, and Charles Petzold on the executive editor of *PC Magazine,* Paul Somerson. (Paul is now at *PC Computing*.)

These three guys wrote a program that hooked the keyboard interrupt on Paul's machine. They cleverly disguised the program via a hook in COMMAND.COM so that there'd be no tell-tale evidence in AUTOEXEC.BAT or CONFIG.SYS. (By the way, modifying COMMAND.COM like this is a technique that became popular among virus writers.)

Hooking the keyboard interrupt lets you see keystrokes before they are passed on to applications. This was commonly done by programs to create TSRs — pop-up programs such as Sidekick — and to provide keyboard macros — such as those provided by the program SuperKey. In other words, you can create a small program that looks for a particular keystroke combination, such as a Ctrl+F1, and then act on that, even if a program is running.

What Robert, Jeff, and Charles cooked up wasn't so benign. The program watched each keystroke. When Paul typed slowly, it just passed the keystrokes on. But when Paul typed quickly, it would spit out an adjacent key instead of the real one. For example, if he quickly typed "Hello", the program might translate that to "jr;;p". The faster Paul typed, the more often the program would spit out incorrect keys. But if he slowed down and looked at each key as he typed, the correct letters would appear. As a result, it would seem as if he were a lousy speed typist.

Listening outside, the three pranksters heard Paul cuss up a storm. When they later confessed, Paul was relieved, saying, "I thought I was going crazy."

Where Men Are Men and Sheep Are Scared

Hewlett-Packard has offices around the world. Once one group was entertaining some visitors from the Boise, Idaho, branch of HP. They rented a sheep and dressed it in lingerie and black stockings, so as to make their Idaho visitors "feel at home."

Into the Jungle

Michel Hebrant of Microsoft returned to his office one day to find it had turned into a tropical paradise. (See Figure 4-7.) Despite the suddenly cramped conditions, he left the decorations intact for a week.

The Old Lobby Trick

Rick Olson of Microsoft came back to work from a morning dentist appointment only to find that his office had been moved into a lobby area. (See Figure 4-8.) Here's what he had to say: "What were my reactions? Denial, shock, laughter. When I arrived at work, I passed one of the testers from my group in the parking garage. When he walked up to my car and said, 'I had nothing to do with it,' I wasn't sure what to think. I took the elevator up to the third floor and started walking towards my office, when I noticed that there was a meeting in the lobby area. A couch and jacket just like mine were located in the back corner. During the next 25 seconds as I walked to my office, I was in serious denial, thinking 'There's no way they would have moved that stuff out of my office.' When I rounded the corner and noticed that my office was empty, except for a phone, I couldn't stop laughing. I went back to the meeting in the lobby, which was just breaking up. They thanked me for the use of my office and I noticed that my Rubik's cube and a few other puzzles had helped people pass the time. Not only had they moved my office and all four computers, but they had me up and running on the Net, hooked up my stereo, and had music playing on my favorite station. I rather enjoyed the larger space and diverse selection of couches.

As it turns out, this is not the first time my office has been targeted. Previously, they managed to cover it in little orange dots and post a measles warning sign. I still occasionally find an orange sticker in the pages of some manuals."

Figure 4-7 Michel Hebrant poses before his jungle lair. (Photo courtesy of *The MicroNews.*)

Figure 4-8 Rick Olson has a little trouble adjusting to his new public office space. (Photo courtesy of *The MicroNews.*)

King Kong

One April Fools' Day in Texas, a group of 20 Dell Computer employees put a 20-foot gorilla on top of the company's 9-story headquarters.

A Sunny Beginning of April

There is a long-standing tradition at Sun Microsystems to play pranks on the founders and other key executives every April Fools'. Here are some of the things that have happened:

- 1985 — Eric Schmidt's office was moved outside, complete with a working phone and Ethernet connection.

- 1986 — A Volkswagon Bug was assembled inside Eric Schmidt's office.

- 1987 — Bill Joy's Ferrari was put into the middle of the pond behind the Sun building.

- 1988 — Scott McNealy and Bernie Lacroute's offices got turned into a golf course. At the same time, another office got turned into a bird sanctuary, and a manager's office was moved into an elevator, also complete with a working phone and Ethernet connection.

- 1989 — In a drive to get all the bugs out of Sun products, Building 14 was covered in plastic and fumigated. A crane was parked outside with a giant, foam high-five hand with a "No Bugs" logo pointing at the building.

- 1990 — A giant arrow was placed sticking out of the headquarters. Scott McNealy's window was removed and replaced with a Plexiglas sheet through which the arrow exited.

- 1991 — In a pun on Sun's SPARCstation, Wayne Rosing was taken to the nearby Steinhart Aquarium, where an office with a SPARCstation was set up in the shark tank. Wayne went to work on this SHARKstation in his SCUBA gear.

- 1992 — In another pun on sharks vs. SPARCs, a hockey game was arranged between Scott McNealy and other company members and the San Jose Sharks. The Sharks were on strike at the time, so this was a particularly good hack. The Zamboni machine was decked out to look like a SPARCstation.

- 1993 — More shark jokes. Andy Bechtolsheim's Porsche was moved into his office, with a fish tank containing a small, live shark placed on top. A SPARCstation was also put in the fish tank, running one of Sun's 3D demo programs that happened to show a fish tank. A hockey puck in the tank was an allusion to the previous year's joke.

- 1994 — Scott McNealy's office was turned into a daycare center.

Did You Know?

US and US2

In something of a Woodstock revival, Steve Wozniak produced two rock festivals. Combined, these lost close to twenty-five million dollars.

Join Together with the Band

You've learned about interviews, the work environment, and how bit-heads often relieve work stress through pranks. Another popular stress relief is music. Music permeates the computer industry. Most computer people like music. And most computer people like shopping for things that plug into the wall. Such as stereos. Not only do successful computer people have incredibly fancy stereo equipment at home, you will often find very loud stereo equipment at work as well. Come into an office building late at night or early in the morning, and you are bound to hear music blasting. Some companies, such as ConnectSoft, even supply all employees with stereos.

In addition to playing loud music, computer people often make their own loud music. In the early days of Microsoft, a group of programmers used to convene on the building roof with electric guitars and hold stress-relieving jam sessions. On more than a few occasions they narrowly escaped the local police and the building security guards. Likewise, a row of Microsoft's OS/2 programmers all kept electric guitars in their offices just in case a need for them arose. At any industry convention, you're bound to come across press, executives, and programmers jamming together.

Here are a few industry figures and the instruments they play:

- Al Stevens — piano
- Bob Frankenberg — trombone and piano
- Dave Duffield — guitar
- Gen Kiyooka — guitar
- Gene Wang — saxophone
- J.D. Hildebrand — piano, ukelele, anything you blow into
- Jim McCarthy — drums
- Jon Erickson — piano
- Michael Dell — piano
- Michael Hyman — digiridoo (OK, call this a gratuitous insert, but how many digiridoo players do you know?)
- Paul Allen — guitar
- Peter Eden — piano
- Philippe Kahn — saxophone, flute
- Richard Hale Shaw — bass
- Rob Dickerson — bass
- Steve Jobs — piano
- Todd Rundgren — famous for his band Utopia, Rundgren is also a fanatic Mac programmer

Not only are there many individuals who play, but there are many industry bands as well. Such bands tend to have amusing, computer-oriented names, as you can see in the list that follows:

- DEC Big Band — Digital Equipment
- Deth Specula — Santa Cruz Operation
- Flame and the Outer Joins — Informix

- Kludge — *Information Week*
- Microsoft Orchestra — a 30-member orchestra composed of Microsoft employees
- Microtones — Microsoft
- Raving Daves — PeopleSoft, named after the company CEO, Dave Duffield
- Threads — Paul Allen's band
- The BMC Brothers — BMC
- The Propeller Heads — Data General
- Tightly Integrated — Unix Technology Group
- Turbo Jazz — Borland
- Turbo Rock — Borland

Despite the lack of free time for most people who work in the computer industry (after all, if you have free time, you probably don't have enough work to do), computer companies are also a breeding ground for local bands. For example, the following bands, which I'm sure you will want to catch next time you visit the Redmond, Washington, club scene, are all predominantly filled by Microsoft employees:

- Spike — this rock band has a CD called *Whelmed*
- Springchamber — a sabre-toothed multi-pop band (hah, do you know what that means?) with a CD out called *Brightface*
- True Human — a rock band
- Planet Couch — a band that plays heavy, melodic, moody, groove music
- Xebec — a mellow jazz band with a CD called *Urban Christmas*
- Amaranth — rock
- Wicked Ash — rock
- Lucy's Fishing Trip — a Seattle-style rock band
- Random Brothers — retro rock and roll
- Susan Evans — a solo pianist with two Cds out, called *Up Until Now* and *Feel This*

Turbo Jazz

Borland is probably the only computer company that has produced music compact discs made by its executives. (By contrast, the Bill Gates *Unplugged* CD does not feature Bill playing music. It was given out at COMDEX one year following a keynote he gave, though.) Pictured here, the three CDs were given out to customers for holiday presents and featured some top-notch musicians, such as John Abercrombie, in addition to Philippe Kahn.

Philippe's first Borland band was called Pecan and the Nuts, a subtle pun on Philippe's name — P. Kahn. The band had its first gig at the first COMDEX Borland attended, providing the entertainment for the famous toga party. Pecan and the Nuts quickly became Turbo Jazz, which has played at major Borland events ever since. The band does have a bit of a reputation for clearing off the dance floor.

Philippe's musical career gave him much press in Borland's heyday, and he was featured in numerous magazines and newspapers holding his saxophone. Once Borland hit financial troubles, however, it was revealed that the company paid $300,000 to produce the Turbo Jazz CDs. Shareholders did not take kindly to that, and there was quite an uproar in the press. Philippe did reimburse Borland for the expense, though.

The Turbo Jazz albums contain a mix of songs, including covers of songs such as "Walking on the Moon," and many originals. For the most part, the songs are a spacey jazz style. Other songs, such as "Turbo Disturbo," have a rap beat.

In case you don't have these albums, I've excerpted some of the lyrics from the song "Turbo Disturbo" off the album *Pacific High*. The song starts with a modem squelch and the following rap lyrics:

> *They're coming man,*
>
> *Start running man,*
>
> *Scram, skedadle, jump for your saddle,*
>
> *Hide, hide, hide in your huts,*
>
> *Here comes Pecan and the Nuts.*

Did You Know?

Tetris

The creators of Tetris once offered the product to Philippe Kahn. He turned them down because Borland didn't sell games. It went on to become a huge market success.

Paul Allen and the Jimi Hendrix Museum

In addition to being an avid guitar player, the head of numerous software companies, and a co-founder of Microsoft, Paul Allen is a big Jimi Hendrix fan. In fact, he is pulling together an elaborate Jimi Hendrix museum, featuring all types of Hendrix memorabilia as well as an extensive collection of items related to the NorthWest musical scene. The museum, called the Experience Music Project, will occupy a 100,000-square-foot building near the Space Needle in Seattle, Washington. It will feature a multimedia library, a "Jamnasium" where visitors can get together to create music on their own, and a broad collection of musical gear.

Some of the NorthWest music items in the collection include

- A guitar played and smashed by Kurt Cobain
- Ray Charles' debut recording, *Confession Blues*, which was recorded in Seattle around 1949
- The original sheet music for "Louie, Louie," which is not only one of the most duplicated songs ever, but the unofficial rock song of Washington State
- Thousands of jazz, rock, punk, and alternative concert posters
- Over 3,000 recordings of Jimi Hendrix
- The guitars Jimi played at Woodstock and the Monterey International Pop Festival
- The mixer from Jimi's Electric Lady Studio
- And much more

Did You Know?

Whistling Dixie

Exploiting the way the Altair gave off radio interference, an engineer named Steve Dompier wrote a program that played "Fool on the Hill" and "A Bicycle Built for Two." It was perhaps the first PC multimedia program.

There were lots of other strange ways to make music with a computer. Commodore 64 programmers used to program the floppy drive stepper motor so as to make music. This was called "Drive Music."

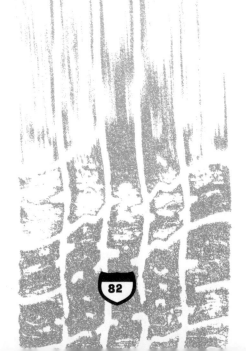

"I don't like them . . . those brain-sucked, slot-faced pinheads."

— Drew Major, Chief Scientist, Novell

Novell holds a developers' conference each year called Brainshare. In 1995, it featured mascots named Bob and Tina, whose twenty-foot statues adorned the main presentation stage. Drew Major found them somewhat less than awe-inspiring.

A Vacation in Las Vegas with 150,000 Friends

Many employees in the high-tech community stay put at the corporate headquarters, focusing their time on creating and supporting products and playing the occassional practical joke. Those in marketing, sales, and evangelism, however, need to make sure that news about the company products spreads, so as to build excitement and, most of all, make money. So what happens when you've cranked out a new product that you want to turn into an overnight success? How do you get the word out, excite customers, and mingle with the press? By going to trade shows, of course.

Trade shows sound like glamorous things. Travel to interesting places, such as Dallas, Las Vegas, and San Diego. All on company business, where you can dine at fancy restaurants, meet important people, and explore the latest technology.

Unfortunately, the reality is a little different. While you do get to travel to some interesting places, you also get to spend your weekends in Trenton, Boise, and other travel hot spots. In Las Vegas, you get to see the tackiest hotels known to man. And that fine cuisine you lust for is often peanuts from the airplane or hotel room pizza.

Trade shows are one of the curses of the industry. They started in the mid-70s with the Altair conference and the West Coast Computer Faire — energetic gatherings of hobbyists joined together by a common love — and have turned into multimillion-dollar extravaganzas filled with as much showmanship as technology.

Admittedly, trade shows are fun to attend as a spectator, and they are even fun for exhibitors the first couple of times. But the charm wears off quickly. After all, imagine having to be enthusiastic about giving the same presentation over and over and over again. Especially when you know you have yet another trade show to go to the following week. To make it worse, you have to hear the same neighboring exhibitor's faked enthusiasm over and over and over. Once the guests are kicked out, you'll often hear exhibitors parodying their own presentations or that of their nearest neighbor.

There are a few constants about trade shows:

- Of the first two visitors to a booth, at least one will ask what is being given away.

- People will stand in a 50-person-long line just to receive a free hat.

- People will stand in a 200-person-long line just to get the signature from a scantily clad model.

- The goal is to gather as many t-shirts as you can.

- No matter how long or hard you plan, something will go wrong.

- The real action happens at the parties.

- A stale bagel will cost 5 times what it is worth.

84

Did You Know?
Comdex

Comdex stands for COMputer Dealers' EXposition.

Comdex and CeBit :
The King of Shows

Of the hundreds of computer trade shows that place every year, there are two that stand out: CeBit and Comdex. CeBit is the largest computer trade show in the world. It attracts as many as 300,000 visitors. It takes place in Hanover, Germany, in a gigantic compound. So many people arrive for the show that the town is overwhelmed. There are not enough hotels, so many guests and exhibitors stay with residents who lease rooms in their home.

CeBit is a very serious computer fair. There is little glitz or glamour on the showroom floor. Many of the exhibits are permanent. The larger vendors, such as IBM, build multistory structures inside of the CeBit compound and never take them down. They are only used for CeBit, year after year.

As soon as the show hours end, the exhibitors haul beer and bands to the show floor.

Comdex is the largest computer show in the U.S. It is held twice a year. In the winter it is held in Las Vegas. In the spring, it is held typically in Atlanta or Chicago. The Las Vegas show is the big one, with as many as 180,000 attendees.

Unlike CeBit, Comdex is all glitz and glamour. It is held in the convention centers of the various casinos in downtown Las Vegas. Surrounded by slot machines, fake volcanoes and pyramids, and advertisements for cultural extravaganzas such as *Nudes On Ice*, it is no wonder that the show itself tends to be a bit flashy. The multimedia wing is famous for pornographic displays (which are now banned, at least in theory). Scantily clad women hawk all types of computer products. And there are noise, sound, and giveaways everywhere.

Sometimes attending Comdex can be a bit surreal. Picture a town in the middle of a desert, made green by water piped in from neighboring California. A place where casinos air-condition the sidewalks, even during 100 degree weather. Where the light from the top of one casino — the Luxor — can be seen from the moon.

Add to this mix prostitution and gambling. A flock of retirees and honeymooners. All-you-can-eat buffets for $4. And 180,000 nerds.

The mix is overwhelming. Walking to the Comdex exhibit halls — which you may as well do, since cab lines can take over an hour to get through and traffic is horrendous — you will run across casinos, pawn shops, statues of Elvis, advertisements for night clubs and "services" strewn across the sidewalk, houses, and abandoned buildings. Gigantic theme hotels. And finally, you near the show. There are two signals. First, traffic becomes very intense. And second, there are a lot of people on the street handing you literature. The very first set you meet will hand you brochures for striptease shows. The second set will hand you information about OS/2. It is a strange combination indeed.

Once you make it through the show crowds, you will find booths for just about everything, ranging from the latest in graphics cards, to software, to disk-manufacturing kits.

And you will also run into every type of promotion imaginable. Philippe Kahn doing stunts in his biplane. Huge banners hung from the sides of hotels. Blimps. Even the cab drivers get involved. One year, the cab drivers all wore Microsoft hats. Apparently they were told if they were wearing the hats and gave a Microsoft person a ride, they might be given an instant $1,000 tip. (Fat chance.) I once was in a cab with a Borland salesperson who gave the driver $20 to throw the hat out the window. This message quickly transmitted through the dispatcher, with cheers from drivers across the city as they chucked their hats at pedestrians.

Comdex is also home to some of the most extravagant computer parties, such as the Chili Cookoff, the *PC Computing* MVP awards, and the Spencer the Katt party, all discussed later in this chapter.

Handy Tips

Here are some things to remember when attending Comdex:

- Make your room reservations 1–2 years in advance. If you try to "just show up," you better be willing to gamble large sums of money, stay in a roach-infested hotel whose room rates just went up by $100 a night, or drive 100 miles or more each day.

- Eat at the casino buffets. The food is lousy, but cheap and better than an airplane.

- Only gamble if you know what you are doing. Casinos don't afford to air-condition the sidewalks because the odds are in your favor.

Software companies aren't the only ones who create t-shirts. Trade shows get into the act too, as shown in these three trade show t-shirts, which range from the simple Object World t-shirt to the fancy Windows World Open polo shirt.

Getting Ready for a Trade Show

So what is it like if you are a vendor getting ready for a big trade show? Anticipate a very hectic pace several months as you prepare. First, you need to choose booth space. This is often done a year in advance. The vendors who have exhibited the longest and spent the most money get first choice. Choosing the right spot can mean the difference between a great show and a terrible show. For example, if you choose a spot by Microsoft, you are guaranteed to have a lot of foot traffic. But you'll also have to compete with a lot of noise and flash. If you are in an obscure exhibit hall along with vendors who supply circuit board vacuum cleaners, you probably won't have as much traffic. In fact, you won't have very much traffic at all. Since a tiny exhibit may run $50K once all is said and done, and larger vendors spend several million dollars for their exhibits and presentations, you want to be sure to choose carefully.

Next you have to decide what your messages and themes will be. Since Comdex is such a glitzy show, just showing technology often isn't enough. You need some coherent theme that ties together your presentation and generates publicity. After all, you are at the show to spread a message, ding your competition, and get sales leads.

Next you figure out what products to show. With any luck, the products you have under development will proceed according to schedule so you can show brand new products at the show. Quite often, things don't work out that way. That's why Comdex is such a great place to see beta software. After a vendor has spent huge amounts of money to be at a show, they aren't going to waste the money by showing yesterday's products.

Of course, figuring out what to show is often a tedious process. Someone has to determine exactly what products to show. And what features to show for each product. And how to explain them. Then a training plan is pulled together so that the various people who man the show floor know what to show and how. Then they get trained. And so on.

Not only do you need to determine what everyone will say, you need to find people to staff the show floor. You need to line up press meetings and customer meetings, and coordinate everybody's schedules. You also need to make sure everyone is trained on the latest spin. The last thing you want is for a person who's representing the company for the first time to tell the raw truth. For example, suppose someone asks when a product is going to ship. You don't want someone saying, "Well, we just found some killer bugs in it. You see, I'm in the test group, and most of the other testers are morons, so they didn't find a bunch of problems. It probably will be a few more months." The desired answer is probably, "We're still on schedule, but of course we will only ship quality products."

There are lots of other mechanics to worry about. Such as how to get marketing material to the booth. And how to get the booth to the booth spot. Some people will need to show up several days in advance to coordinate all of the deliveries. And to work with the various union personnel to make sure that things are set up properly. Sometimes this means providing lots of "bribes." If you want your booth to be set up in a hurry, you may find that you are not allowed to carry anything in yourself. You need to get someone from one union. And then to set it up, someone from another

Did You Know?
Dressed Executives

At a 1991 Microsoft party, Bill Gates came dressed as Spock, Gary Gigot (VP of Marketing at the time, now at Shapeware) as the Joker, and Michael Hallman as John Wayne.

At a Borland sales conference, people dressed as *Star Wars* characters, including one product marketing manager who was forced to wear a wookie suit.

At a product launch, various Symantec executives dressed as *Star Trek* figures.

And Lotus executive Michael Landry descended on the stage dressed in a Spiderman costume at one launch, only to become caught in his own web.

union. And then to get the power run, someone from another union. It can be a good season for receiving tips.

But the most important part of show planning is determining what you will give away. After all, that is what will really drive people to your exhibit. For many years, WordPerfect gave away hats and had comedians. Microsoft often ran training sessions with row after row of portable computers, and gave away various hats and shirts. One year Borland gave away $10,000 each day. That was pretty insane, but cheaper than a product launch or advertising. By the second day, word had gotten out and the booth was mobbed with record crowds. I had the pleasure of drawing the name of the winner each day. The one time a winner was present in the audience was very exciting. He immediately called his wife, who told him to stop lying and to stay away from the casinos. She was really angry at him. We had to send a telegram so that she believed him.

Other times, giveaways can be pretty funny. I once brought a bunch of leather samples to a show and handed them out as leather mini-mouse pads, perfect for airplane travel. They were gobbled up. For all I know, someone could now be starting a traveling mouse-pad business.

Great Quotes:

If at First You Don't Succeed

Lou Gerstner had this to say at an IBM pep rally, when describing why it would win: "It's like walking on the beach and the prevailing wind is in your face. We've had it in our face for the last three to four years. . . If we keep pushing, momentum is going to be at our back."

A Day in the Life

Exhibiting at a trade show is grueling. Let's see what it is like:

6:00 AM   What the hell is that noise? Huh? An alarm. Oh my gosh, I'm in a hotel. This is not my beautiful hotel. What am I doing? How did I get here?

6:30 AM   Damn. These wake-up calls are persistent. It's 3:30 AM at home. Time to get up.

7:30 AM   How many boxes of powdered eggs and powdered potatoes do these casinos really use each day?

8:00 AM   Group rah-rah meeting. Spend an hour listening to the marketing folks repeat the messages from the night before. Pretty boring, but the new t-shirt is cool.

9:00 AM   Time to meet the first customers.

10:00 AM   Time to meet the next client. Tell them the same thing as the first one.

11:00 AM   Booth duty. Sit in front of the computer repeating the same speech every 20 minutes. Answer questions. No, I'm not giving away the computer. The bathroom is to the left. I'm sorry, I can't help you debug your program right now, but our tech support number is 510-555-1212. It's always busy? Oh, that can't be. The price is $99.95. No, I'm sorry, I ran out of business cards.

12:30 PM   Eat a stale donut. Could have bought a dozen at home for this price.

1:00 PM   More booth duty. Gotta smile.

2:00 PM   Press meeting. An hour-long gig explaining features of upcoming products to the press. At least they ask good questions, and there is free pop in the press room.

3:00 PM   Press meeting. Same thing as before.

4:00 PM   Press meeting. Same thing as before.

5:00 PM   Press meeting. I can do this with my eyes closed. Maybe I *will* do this with my eyes closed.

6:00 PM   Wrap-up meeting and dinner. Lousy food. More rah rah.

7:00 PM   The first party. This one is from a client. Lots of people in suits. Plenty of hors d'oeuvres. Drink a beer.

8:30 PM   The next party. Now it is for a magazine, so it is a lot more fun. Lots of bigwigs to hobnob with, or at least to stare at. I think Penn and Teller are performing at the party tomorrow night. Can't wait until that.

11:00 PM   The last party for the night. And it is a good one — Spencer the Katt. Wait in line to get in. Sure glad I got an invitation. Smirk at the people without invitations trying to con their way in. Hah. I must be important. Push through the crowd. Gosh it is hot in here. Steve — great to see you buddy. How's business at NeXT? Huh, you don't remember me?

1:30 AM   Stagger back to the hotel room. Watch the high rollers for a bit.

2:30 AM   Hello, operator? Can you give me a wake-up call for 6:00 AM please? Thanks.

Countdown to the Launch

Trade shows are also a popular place to launch — that is, *introduce* — new products. Among other products, Microsoft introduced Windows NT and Access at Comdex. Borland, Microsoft, and Symantec have a tradition of launching new programming tools at the Software Development conference. The list goes on and on.

Launching a product just doubles the stress of a trade show. In addition to worrying about everything else, you need to make sure that all of the equipment for the launch arrives, the audio-visual equipment works, and that any key company executives remember to show up. But the biggest headache, of course, is getting the demo to work. Typically, products are launched before they ship. Sometimes products are launched long in advance of shipping. So there are usually some unexpected bugs — uh, *features*, that's what they are — that show up. The buggier the product, the more exciting it can be to be on stage demonstrating it to hundreds or thousands of people.

Companies sometimes go to elaborate steps to get around this. Microsoft kicked off one of their C++ launches with a live orchestra, followed by all types of speeches. Then they started their demo, which went beautifully. Everything worked according to plan. What the audience didn't know was that there were several computers behind the projection screen, each manned by someone mimicking every action of the presenter. If the product blew, they'd seamlessly switch to one of the backup machines and continue on as if nothing happened.

Philippe Kahn had a simpler technique. He'd wrap the computer power cord around his leg. If something bad happened, he'd just walk a little bit farther away from the computer, knocking out the power. Damn, tripped on the power cord! How clumsy of me. Let's start this again.

Preparing all the hardware, speeches, and demo software can be quite an ordeal. Something always goes wrong. At one product launch I did, I needed four separate machines to show Windows, OS/2, and Windows 95 programs as well as the talk slides. After flying from California to Florida, we arrived in the hotel and got ready to set up for the launch two days later. But none of the machines were there. We frantically called back and forth, trying to track down the shipper. But the shipper no longer had a listed phone number. No one at the front desk had seen them. A day before the show, they turned up. A bellboy who was subbing for someone put them underneath a desk in a back room. Phew.

Launch preparations can get even more ridiculous than this For example, I helped Borland launch Borland C++ for OS/2 in the beginning of 1993. Compilers aren't always the most exciting thing to demo, so compiler vendors often add some multimedia fun to their demonstrations. We needed a fancy multimedia computer to demonstrate the product. But at the time, OS/2 multimedia programs would only run on special IBM hardware. So Borland asked IBM for the fastest multimedia machine they could spare. And a few weeks later we received what was supposed to be a loaded 486.

For some reason, though, the machine kept crashing every time the debugger ran. While this is bad in general, it was particularly bad in this case, since we planned to demonstrate the debugger. Borland checked the video driver, the compiler, the OS version — and everything checked out. Then, someone decided to check the inside of the computer. The hot 486 was really a 386 with very little memory. In fact, the machine was so slow that it kept crashing every time someone typed in the debugger, because the keyboard interrupts couldn't be processed fast enough.

So Borland begged for a new machine. Finally, the Saturday before the launch (which was happening on a Monday night), IBM overnighted a 486 to my house. We anxiously assembled the 486/50, booted it, and lo and behold, nothing but a numeric error message appeared on the screen. Having gone without sleep for a few days, this was not what we wanted to see. Some swearing ensued.

There were no manuals in the box, so we figured the hard drive was locked. But there were no keys for opening the computer. We brought over a locksmith, but he couldn't open it because IBM made its machines with a high level of security, and the round keys are almost impossible to pick.

Panicked, we called around looking for a store that carried the machine. But no one had them or knew anything about them. They we called the IBM 800 number. But no one there had heard of the machine, either. In

desperation, I said, "Look, we are a key partner and we need this to work."
Key partner seemed to have been a magic term, because I instantly got
sent to a different phone queue. And 30 minutes later, an IBM service representative made an hour-long trek up the Pacific Coast to my house, formatted the disk (which was the problem — it was unformatted), and
helped install enough of OS/2 to get the beta version we needed installed
from CD-ROM.

Now we had it running, but there still wasn't enough memory to get the
performance we needed. And to do that, we needed to open the box,
which was still protected by the C-2 security-level lock. Surprising what a
crowbar can do.

Great Quotes:

DOS vs. OS/2

At a sneak preview of OS/2 given at a programmers' conference,
Gordon Letwin, one of Microsoft's early employees and an OS/2 architect, described the difference between DOS and OS/2. He said something along the lines of "One of the primary differences between
MS-DOS and OS/2 is that OS/2 is multitasking, and MS-DOS is serially
multitasking."

Have It Your Way

Exhibiting at trade shows is expensive, so when you are a startup company, finding a way to get your message across can be quite an ordeal.
Philippe Kahn went through some interesting hoops at his first Comdex.
In the fall of 1983, he was ready to hold the first Borland press conference. He arrived in Las Vegas and managed to corner Shelly Adelson, the
guy who ran Comdex. Borland had no money, so Philippe tried to get a
press conference room on credit. Shelly wasn't amused and after ten minutes of Philippe's begging, said, "If you can't afford my place, just go to

McDonald's." That's exactly what Philippe did. He held Borland's very first press conference at McDonald's. Six journalists showed up and Borland got five reviews, launching the company into the public's eye.

Spencer the Katt

Few animals strike dread into the hearts of computer executives faster than Spencer the Katt. Spencer the Katt is the pseudonym for a number of gossip reporters at *PC Week*. The Spencer the Katt column appears every week on the last page of PC Week and contains the latest in rumors and embarrassing anecdotes.

Like his counterpart, Mac the Knife from *MacWeek* (see Figure 6-1), Spencer often offers prizes to those who turn in good rumors or stories. If you see a co-worker at the gym with a Spencer the Katt gym bag, you know you better watch what secrets you pass along. (Figure 6-2)

At each Comdex, there is a Spencer the Katt party. One of the many "invitation-only" parties, this originally was a very small party for only those on the inside of the industry. You could find Bill Gates in one room, Michael Miller in another, and a roomful of programmers watching porno movies on *PC Week*'s room tab in a third. Many venture capitalists are said to have hooked up with new companies at the Spencer the Katt party.

In recent years, though, the Spencer parties have become quite large and have gone from intimate suite parties to huge, nightclub events. You'll less and less find the movers and shakers, and more and more people that somehow scammed tickets. In general, the later you go, the more likely you are to find interesting people. If you have trouble finding the really famous, just look for the huge crowds. They undoubtedly follow the big names or the free beer. Either is a fine thing to seek.

The crowds, however, do sometimes lead to amusing incidents. At one crowded Spencer party in Atlanta, I was speaking with Bill Gates when an attractive woman shoved ahead of me. "Hello," she said to Bill in a soft Southern drawl. "You must be someone famous. Do you work at IBM?"

Figure 6-1 If you turn in some MacSecrets, you may be lucky enough to get a mug such as this.

Figure 6-2 There are all types of great things you can get from Spencer the Katt parties and from turning in secrets to *PC Week*. Here you can see a Spencer the Katt doll, deck of cards, and clock. Think I'll tell you how I got all this great stuff?

The Parties

There are many other parties besides the Spencer the Katt party. In fact, for major shows, there is even a party list maintained and sent out electronically by Karen Thomas, a trained opera singer who runs a PR agency mostly handling new software companies. For example, there is the ShadowRam party, *Byte* awards ceremonies, various vendor bashes, bashes for advertisers, general bashes, and so on.

There are really lousy parties, such as the Microsoft Geek Fest, which is held at Software Development. This party is known for cold pizza, warm beer, and rows of computers where you can check out Microsoft products.

There are strange parties, such as the *Compute* magazine parties. *Compute* is owned by Bob Guccione, who also owns *Omni* and *Penthouse*. He sometimes holds parties in his palatial house in Manhattan. There you will find an indoor swimming pool, priceless Quattrocento and Baroque art scattered on the walls and the floors (for example, there is a gorgeous Botticelli on one wall), and a movie theater. In to this, throw the glitterati from the New York art scene and a bunch of computer nerds, all feeling awkward, wondering about Bob's platform shoes, and whispering, "Where are the babes? Where are the babes?" It is a true example of an oil and water party. But a great one, nonetheless. And in case you are wondering, nude models do not appear at the party.

There are parties held at fancy hotels, at Liberace's house, and in hotel suites. Figure 6-3 shows a souvenir from one of those parties.

And there are lavish ballroom parties. For example, the *PC Computing* MVP awards party, held at Comdex in Las Vegas, is a fancy event, complete with lavish; stop-action; video bite films; roaring sound tracks; and performances by Penn and Teller. (Penn writes a column in *PC Computing*.) One year, they put an audience member in a box, sawed it in half, and out came Philippe Kahn. (The same year they pulled a rabbit out of a hat and tossed it into a mulcher. Comedy isn't pretty.)

Another famous Comdex party is the Chili Cookoff. This is a fund-raiser for the National Center for Missing and Exploited Children. Tickets are $50 apiece. Various companies sponsor it and set up teams of people who cook chili. The guests walk around, sample the various chilis, and vote for their favorites using wooden tokens. Companies do all types of things to try to get the most tokens to win a prize. In addition, the party features armadillo races — where various

Figure 6-3 This apron was given out at a *PC Magazine* party held at Liberace's house.

computer executives blow on an armadillo's butt to try to get it to win in a race (see Figure 6-4). Paul Grayson, who with his brother George founded MicroGrafx, organizes this event. One year he brought in Scott Page from Pink Floyd, Jon Anderson, Peter Gabriel, Cirque du Soleil, and all types of additional great musicians, bands, and performers.

Figure 6-4 The Chili Cookoff, held each year during Fall Comdex, raises money for National Center for Missing and Exploited Children. Vendors line the UNLV basketball stadium with chili booths. Partiers then roam through the building, drinking beer and trying the different chilis. They vote for their favorite chili by placing wooden tokens or money into a bin. Several vendors make t-shirts just for this event, either for the booth staffers or as giveaways to encourage attendees to vote for their chili. This t-shirt alludes to the armadillo races also held at the Chili Cookoff.

One of the most exclusive Comdex parties is John Dvorak's party. Held in a secret location, those in the know have invites leading them to an obscure hotel suite. Others get misleading invitations, leading them and their followers onto locations in the middle of the desert.

The computer industry is a close-knit industry with regular turnover, so conferences are also a great place to catch up with old friends. After Borland bought Ashton-Tate, many Ashton-Tate, employees got laid off. They organized a FATE party at Comdex— which stands for Former Ashton-Tate Employee. Since there is a group of ex-Borlanders at Microsoft called the Dead Borlander's Society, perhaps there will be future FATE/DBS parties for those doubly honored.

Toga! Toga! Toga!

Of all the parties that have happened in the industry, few stories have spread and become exaggerated as much as those about the infamous

Borland toga party, often called "The Toga Party." It was rumored to be an elaborate Bacchanalian festival, complete with a drunken orgy of top computer executives. It kind of was — here's the real story. Borland was exhibiting at the West Coast Computer Faire in 1984. They had just gotten the company off the ground and were putting the finishing touches on SideKick, their second product. Being in a great mood, they decided to throw a party. But they didn't have much money. Fortunately for them, a company that had rented the Gift Center didn't show up. So there was a vacant room available. Borland told the Gift Center they'd rent the room for $2,500 and throw a party. They then announced a "Costumed Toga Party" featuring "Pecan and the Nuts" playing Turbo Jazz. This, of course, was Philippe's band.

The party was a last-minute thing, so of course there was no beforehand planning. The Borland employees ran to the nearest Safeway and bought everything that they could find. They expected that 200 people would show up. But 2,000 did. People just kept on bringing food and drinks at an amazing rate, and Borland quickly lost control of the event. All types of people were there — IBM executives, Apple executives, Borland executives — all wrapped in togas and totally smashed.

Drinking with the Enemy

Vendors regularly hold conferences to brief key customers on upcoming products and strategies. Typically these events are held in resort towns. For example, Borland held a Paradox conference in Palm Springs, California, to brief key beta testers on an upcoming release (you can see the official t-shirt in figure 6-5). Industry influencers and corporate managers flew in from across the country for the meeting. Having arrived early, the Borland team wandered out to the swimming pool for some much-needed relaxation. And who should they run across, but the PR manager for Microsoft's Access team. She said she just happened to be on vacation and had always heard that Palm Springs was beautiful. It turned out that several people from the Access team happened to be on

Figure 6-5 This shirt celebrates Borland's Paradox conference in Palm Springs.

101

vacation, too, at the same resort. And, surprisingly enough, once they found that several key Borland customers were in town — who happened to be key Microsoft customers as well — they figured they should throw a dinner party, conveniently timed to be after Borland's first day of in-depth technical presentations. The Borland crowd heard about this party and deduced that it was a ploy to pump attendees for secret information. So, they held a surprise cocktail party in return, making sure that all attendees were royally pickled. Apparently, the strategy worked. Many attendees were too drunk to talk about software, and rather concentrated on singing and running up Microsoft's bar tab. Which would perhaps make up for the time when the Microsoft Visual Basic team drank several hundred dollars' worth of booze on Borland's tab. But, that's a different story...

"We need to swallow the bitter pill whole this year."

— Rich Thoman, IBM Personal Computer Co.

Regarding planned reorganizations after just being appointed Senior Vice President.

The End of the Road

Unfortunately, while working in the computer industry is a blast, its fast-pace brings rapid ups and downs. When things go well, companies become quite extravagant. For example, Borland built a $160 million dollar building, bought hundreds of acres of land, and had a private plane just for Philippe, only to hit hard times and have their stock drop from over $80 to under $8. Other companies have rented lavish workplaces, only to find the income didn't cover rent.

When things go bad, the inevitable occurs. The company executives — who often make several hundred thousand dollars or even several million dollars a year — go through the difficult task of firing people. In most cases, the folks who get axed aren't the high-paid executives, but the people who are doing the real work down in the trenches.

Nerd Humor:

Executive Wisdom

After a mixed year, the vice president of the products division left for a different company. He appointed his most senior manager to take his place and said, "Bob, things at the company are tight. You may run into a few roadblocks. But I want you to succeed. So I've prepared three envelopes with tips I've learned through the years. Open them in dire straits."

Bob was thrilled. He now was a vice president. He got a big office and could afford a fancy new car. And things were wonderful. At least for a few months. Then sales started dropping. The company president put a lot of pressure on Bob and employees were restless. So Bob opened the first envelope. "Blame the previous management — after all, it is long gone," it said. The next day Bob called an emergency, all-hands meeting. "Do not worry about our troubles," Bob said. "I've discovered some accounting irregularities with the previous management. But fortunately, Jim is gone. We're going to get the situation under control. It will be a bit rough adjusting from the horrible state Jim put us in, but we'll pull through."

The president eased up. Everyone felt good. But the troubles persisted. Two months later, Bob opened the second envelope. "Blame the organization," it said. So Bob called another meeting, said the organization no longer met the changing needs of the company, and announced an immediate reshuffling of staff. The business units would be broken up. Functional units would be formed. Matrix management would keep the groups focused, but in synch.

A few months later, sales were still plummeting. Customers were loosing faith. Key employees were starting to loiter around the fax machines in the early morning. Bob opened the last envelope. It said: "Prepare three envelopes..."

Before layoffs occur, the the rumor mill begins. Instead of working, people focus on who they think will be fired, what, if any, the severance package will hold, when the layoff will occur, and so on.

Here are five sure signs that a lay-off is forthcoming:

- There is a line at the fax machine in the morning.

- Even though earnings are bad, the company executives take off on a mysterious weekend company retreat.

- Senior management circulates stories about how the previous management messed up.

- There are a lot of hushed, hallway discussions.

- Dilbert cartoons appear everywhere, overnight (Note that Dilbert cartoons might already be everywhere. That doesn't mean a layoff is happening. It's when there weren't any before, and all of a sudden they appear.)

The day of the layoff can be very surreal. Especially if the company has timed it to be right before a major holiday, such as Christmas. Which companies often do. The company will say, "It is only kind to the employee, so that they don't spend too much on gifts they can't afford." This usually means, "Why should we pay vacation time for an employee we are about to fire?" Many times, employees are given a few hours notice to clear out. Sometimes they are even escorted out of the building by armed security guards. Here arc a few telltale signs that D day is about to hit:

- There are a lot more security guards than normal (or in some cases, there are security guards, where normally there were not.)

- Your card key no longer works.

- You can no longer get into the parking garage.

- You can't log on to your email account.

- The network is shut down (this keeps people from downloading or tampering with files).

- Your manager arrives to work early.

- You arrive to work late, and there is a stream of cars leaving.

Firing people, of course, is embarrassing. And no company wants to be embarrassed. So they come up with euphemisms to describe what is happening. Instead of firing people, things such as the following happen:

- We are restructuring for success. (This translates to "We are firing indiscriminately.")

- We are refocusing on our key areas. (This translates to "We are firing whole divisions.")

- We are downsizing to be competitive. (This translates to "We are getting our butts kicked by the competition.")

- We are incorporating that technology into other product lines. (This translates to "We are shelving the product and firing the staff, but we don't want customers to be upset.")

- We are outsourcing our marketing. (This translates to "We are firing all of our marketing staff and looking for consultants so we don't have to pay benefits.")

Nerd Humor:

How Do You Make a $200,000,000 Business?

This is a joke that is told over and over. Just substitute the company or executive name with that of anyone who is down on their luck. I've seen it used with Philippe Kahn and Ed Esber, as well as with Media Vision.

Q: How do you make a 200-million-dollar multimedia business?

A: Give Media Vision a 400-million-dollar multimedia business.

Great Quotes in Times of Trouble:

Amnesia

After the Lotus-Novell merger collapsed, there were rumors that IBM and Novell would merge. Jim Manzi, President of Lotus, said, "There is now talk of an alliance between IBM and a networking company in Provo, Utah, whose name I no longer remember."

You Call That a Loss?

Regarding Lotus' 1994 earnings report showing a 1994 net loss of $20.9 million, Jim Manzi said, "We never really lost money."

Let's Be Specific Here

When asked how well Newtons were selling, an Apple official answered in January 1995, "We don't think a numbers game is a valid measure of our success."

Management Style

Ashton-Tate's chief scientist had this to say of former company president Ed Esber's management style: "Esber thought management of a development group meant going over the phone bills and accusing us of making too many long-distance calls."

Here are a few real-world examples of how companies handle firings in this industry:

- Microsoft cut out a number of people from an international division. They kept it very quiet and simply said that various people were transferred. What they didn't mention was that the people were transferred out of the company.

- After buying Ashton-Tate, Philippe Kahn told reporters that a certain amount of "staff consolidation" would occur. This meant a major layoff.

- When IBM began to hit financial troubles and needed to reduce its workforce, it introduced an Individual Transition Program. This was a fancy way of saying if you left voluntarily, IBM would pay eight weeks' salary as severance.

- After IBM laid off 35,000 employees, Lou Gerstner wanted to assure employees that IBM was heading for better times. During a satellite broadcast to IBM employees, he held up two fingers pinched together and said: "We're that close to having this job-security thing behind us."

- Lotus laid off a number of employees in mid-1995. Jim Manzi referred to this as "adjusting our expense base." He also suggested that employees who didn't think Lotus should win might want to look for new jobs, saying, "If you can't be happy getting on board, I urge you to leave the company."

- When Asymetrix was about to lay off a large percentage of its employees, its President, Vern Raburn, described the upcoming firing with classic layoff language: "During the past year, Asymetrix has been very successful in meeting its key goals... However, it is clear that in order for Asymetrix to achieve its long-term business and financial goals, we need to focus our resources in those areas that provide the most opportunity for growth."

- At Symantec, the Q&A project was said to be going fine despite the loss of "a small group of people." Which apparently was the whole team.

- When New Leaf — a joint venture between IBM and Blockbuster — ran into hard times and broke up the company, they said: "We aren't disbanding, we're evolving as the business has evolved."

As you can see, there is no shortage of ways to say someone's job is about to go.

The End of the Road

PART 2

Products

In the first section you learned a bit about what it is like to find a job and work in the industry. In this section it is time to learn about what it takes to ship a product. Shipping products is a delicate art, requiring balancing engineering's desires for perfection with marketing's lust after money. There are many books about how to manage this process, as well as books on software design and marketing fundamentals.

That's not what this section will cover. Rather, it will cover some of the realities of the development cycle, starting with the all-important beginning step of choosing a code name. Next, you'll learn about inevitable delays, hidden screens, the unfortunate hidden features (that is, *bugs*) often left in products, and the horror stories from the trenches of technical support.

If you've ever shipped a product, some of this may seem painfully familiar. Otherwise, hang on and prepare to learn about the strange underside of the product development process.

"We're probably not going to have a contest this time because our marketing team has their own specific ideas."

— Howard High, Intel

On choosing a name for the P6. The name for the previous chip, the Pentium, was chosen from an employee contest. I guess the marketing department was clueless at that point.

Shhh!
It's a Secret
Code Name

Sometimes it can be very hard to understand what computer people are talking about, especially if you are an outsider. Partly, that's because computer people are shy, mumble, and tend to fill their sentences with technical terms. So instead of saying, "I tried to call you, but no one answered," they will say, "My attempts to establish a secure asynchronous communications line timed out." Partly it's because computer people frequently use acronyms. So, you can hear discussions of TSR hooks to BIOS, or TCP/IP issues, or whether there are good V.32 PCMCIA cards. And finally, computer people often speak with code names. Instead of saying, "That will be in Windows 95," they will say, "That will be in Chicago." You need to know that Chicago is the code name for Windows 95.

A code name is simply a special name made up for a product so that others won't know what you are talking about. A good code name won't indicate to someone what the product is. For example, suppose you want a code name for the next version of Visual C++. If you called it Visual D, it would be pretty easy to guess what you were talking about. If you called it Barracuda, it would be a lot harder. That way, if someone overheard you saying, "Barracuda won't ship until May," they wouldn't get nearly the same amount of information as they would hearing, "Visual C++ won't ship until May." A good code name will also make a team feel excited to work on a secret project. After all, if it has a code name, it must be special.

Code names serve a very simple purpose. They keep future products secret. That's important, because to maintain competitive advantage, you don't want your competitors to know what you are working on. Otherwise, your strategies for making money by attacking competitors or taking the world by surprise are at risk.

Code names are necessary because there are lots of people who work hard to find out about future products. Not only do competitors scour magazines, trade shows, and likely beta users for information, but so does the press. Weekly magazines such as *InfoWorld*, *PC Week*, and *Computer Reseller News* pride themselves on finding out about future products. It's kind of like finding out about affairs among movie stars.

Code names aren't the only measure companies use to keep product information secret. In fact, there are several other techniques companies use. One is to tightly control who in the company knows about future developments. Second is to make sure that any outside people who have the product sign a Non Disclosure Agreement (NDA)

Nerd Humor

Merger Rumor

Before Novell bought WordPerfect, there were numerous rumors that WordPerfect and Borland would merge. The proposed name of the combined company was PerfectBore.

guaranteeing that they won't talk about it. Unfortunately, a lot of times employees and outside folks forget not to talk. After all, they can gain stature by showing others that they know about upcoming secret products. And sometimes when you've been working on a product for a long time, it is hard to believe that everyone outside the company hasn't heard of it.

When to Pick One

Creating code names is a hallowed part of software and hardware development, often leading to more debate than feature definition and sales forecasting. Development teams particularly enjoy code names that have some hidden joke in them, such as Wanda (see "Ten All-Time Great Code Names," page 121). It is often an honor when a developer's code name suggestion is selected for a product. Sometimes the importance of a person is measured by the number of code names they know.

Ten Techniques for Learning about Secret Products

There are lots of techniques that companies and the press use to

Code name selection usually occurs very early in a product cycle. Theoretically, product development proceeds in an orderly fashion:

1. Get a product idea
2. Perform market research
3. Plan the product
4. Create the product
5. Test the product
6. Ship the product
7. Sell the product

Realistically, though, it is more in this order:

1. Get a product idea
2. Choose a code name
3. Plan the product
4. Begin implementation
5. Test it
6. Rewrite the plan so that it matches what was created
7. Ship it
8. Perform market research
9. Figure out how to make it sell or who to blame

As you can see, getting the code name is absolutely critical.

determine what secret products are under development. Here are a few you'll see in use over and over if you watch the industry carefully. By the way, kids, these are the tricks of trained professionals. Don't try them out at home:

1. You are attending a trade show and notice that a group of people from Company X are standing together, chatting. Someone from Company X's competition innocently walks behind them and pauses to tie his shoe, listening the whole time.

2. Telephones at trade shows are jammed. Sometimes attendees are simply arranging their return flights or trying to make reservations at fancy restaurants while on company expense. But most of the time, they are busy reporting gossip about competitors, reactions from key meetings with press and clients, or other juicy tidbits. You'll occasionally see someone hanging out in the phone booth doing a lot more listening than talking.

3. Most trade shows have special rooms reserved for the press where they can work on deadline stories, call the office, or meet vendors. Press people will occasionally spy on each other at such locations. More importantly, you'll sometimes find vendors walking through to try to overhear gossip about their competition.

4. A favorite technique of companies and reporters is the take-advantage-of-the-sales-dude technique. Salespeople love to sell things. That's how they make money. I've heard many stories of vendors who call the competition's local salesperson. They pretend to be deciding between product x (their own product) and product y (the competing product). A dialog might go something like this, where the vendor wants to know if the competition is going to put a particular feature in their next version: "Hey, Bill, this is Ted, I'm with Boeing, and I'm trying to figure out whether I should switch from Excel 98 to IBM 1-2-3, Version 6." "Why, of course you should, Ted." "Well, you know Excel 98 has IntelliDynamicRecalc, and that sure sounds useful. Is Version 6 going to have that?" "Well, I can't really tell you that, Ted." "That's a shame Bill, looks like I'll have to buy 2,000 Excel 98s instead." "Well, I tell you what, Ted, I'm not really supposed to tell you this, but you sure can expect to see that in Version 6 — in fact, it is in the beta right now. Say, what's your number, I'll come by and show it to you." Click.

5. A similar technique to #4 is used on beta testers or the press. Here, the vendor calls someone who they know has seen the next version of a competing product. In a casual, all-knowing voice, they disdainfully say, "I can't believe they don't have feature x." When the beta tester snickers or asks why you think that feature isn't there, the vendor can guess that the feature probably is there.

6. Many, if not most, trade shows have technical talks in addition to general exhibit areas. Sometimes vendors give talks about upcoming technology, and protect themselves by asking attendees to sign an NDA. Every now and then, competing vendors will try to sneak in or will try to talk their way in without signing an NDA. While the talks themselves are good sources of information, so are the papers and lecture notes handed out at the talks. Presenters sometimes think it is beneath them to clean up trash left in a room, and many times confidential documents are left behind.

7. Vendors often put on their own trade shows. For example, Novell has a show called BrainShare. Borland has a trade show called BIC. Competitors often try to crash such conferences, signing up with their home address and phone numbers. Some even go so far as to bring in fake business cards. I've kicked a few people out of confidential talks who had fake names and businesses on their badges. It is pretty embarrassing when you are caught. Borland used to give neon badges to competitors who attended BIC. Instead of having their name in big letters, it would have their company name in big letters. That way presenters and attendees could be extra careful around them. It also was a humorous competitive jab.

8. Another great source of information is the Internet and electronic bulletin boards. Here customers, beta testers, vendor representatives, and the competition interchange ideas and questions, all with electronic anonymity. Sometimes vendors accidentally give information about upcoming products. Sometimes hackers illegally post beta copies of future products.

9. Before vendors release a product, they usually brief the weekly press, giving names of beta testers for the weeklies to contact. In fact, many of the stories where "unnamed sources" reveal information about upcoming products are really plants from the vendors themselves. One of the risks of such intentional leaks is that it is embarrassing if

the product slips. Another risk is that the competition can then call up the beta testers to pry for information. If the beta tester happens to be a major account, it also gives a good in for the sales team from the competition.

10. Vendors sometimes take beta testers or employees from the competition out to dinner. After a lot of drinks, interesting information flows. (See the related story on page 101.)

Stupid Code Name Tricks

Code names are also used to track leaks. That is, suppose you know that someone is leaking secrets to the press. You want to narrow down who it might be. To help, you create many different code names. So when you see a write-up in the press using a name, you have a much better idea who leaked it. This is very similar to the technique of switching your middle initial when you order products from catalogs so that you can track how you got on various junk mail lists.

For example, Borland had a secret product under the development code named Delphi. The code name itself was top secret. So some people were told its code name was Delmar. Others Delaware. And so forth. If the press wrote about Delmar, it would be pretty clear who leaked. In this case, however, Philippe Kahn, President of Borland at the time, used the name Delphi in the press and later discussed it at a users' group. Thus the code name and general product information spread widely. Eventually, Borland used the code name as the final product name.

Another trick is to change code names midway in the development cycle. This often happens after a key executive has left a company or after a lay-off. The goal is to prevent past employees from knowing what current employees are talking about, even if it relates to products that the past employees had worked on. In other cases, code names are switched so executives can truthfully deny that a product is under development. For example, the first code name for Quattro Pro 1.0 was Mark Twain. A rumor about it leaked, and Philippe needed to swear that there was no such product under development. So the code name was switched to Palm Springs.

Sometimes, however, there are so many names for a particular product that no one can keep track of them anymore. In such a case, the code name and real product name are often used in the same sentence, thereby removing all benefits of using code names in the first place. For example, you might see mention of "Windows NT 3.5, known as Daytona, is reported to have gone to manufacturing."

A final trick is to invent spurious code names. This can get the press and competition chasing down false trails and, with any luck, have them quite confused.

At one point when I was in the languages group at Borland, disgruntled (or recently laid-off) employees leaked code name after code name to the press. I planned to use swear words for all future products. That way they couldn't get printed in the magazines, thus keeping them secret. It would also lead to amusing interchanges:

Reporter: "What's your next compiler called?"

Employee: "Fudge off."

Ten All-Time Great Code Names

Now that you know what a code name is for, lets look at some. In fact, this chapter lists over 350 code names for products, ranging from all-time greats to categories such as animals, places, and cartoon characters. While there are hundreds more that I haven't mentioned, this should give you a pretty good idea of what code names are all about.

We'll start with some of the all-time greats.

10. Ansa — Code name for the first version of Paradox (and the name of the company that created Paradox). Came from "Ask me a question and I'll give you an ansa." (Ansa)

9. Wanda — ATM switch. In other words, it was a switch named Wanda — a pun on the movie of similar title. (Adaptive Corp.)

8. Pandora — The first code name for Microsoft's set top box (TV) operating system. Thus, it was Pandora's Set Top Box. The project later got renamed to Amazon. (Microsoft)

7. Phoenix — A code name frequently used for products that were killed and then revived

Ten All Time Great Code Names

continued

from the ashes. For example, it was the name for the dBASE Compiler and ObjectVision at various points in their life (and regained life) cycles. There are at least ten different products with this code name, coming from multiple vendors.

6. Pigeon — This is reportedly the name of one of the servers at Microsoft where interim builds of Windows 95 were stored. Many interim builds are created prior to an official beta release, so that internal testers can check new features and new bug fixes. Such releases are often called *drops*. Thus, this is the server containing pigeon droppings. (Microsoft)

5. Honeymooners — This was the code name for a computer at Dell. The team was falling behind, and Michael Dell, the President of Dell, was about to get married. He organized a tough meeting that pulled the team back on track and, in honor of his upcoming disappearance for his honeymoon, they gave it this code name. (Dell Computer Corp.)

4. Road Pizza — QuickTime. This has to be one of the stranger code names. There are lots of other fun names you'll see too, such as Next Big Fish and CyberDog, but Road Pizza is pretty far out. Of course, pizza is one of the basic nerd food groups. (Apple)

3. Visine — This is the name for a Microsoft tool that converts from NetWare to NT. NetWare is network software from Novell, and is a competitor in many ways to Windows NT. Novell's logo and company colors are red. So the idea is to use Visine to get the red out. (See also page 280.) (Microsoft)

2. Buddha — This was a code name for Quattro Pro, a spreadsheet that competed with Lotus 1-2-3. Buddha often sits in the lotus position, so the code name was chosen with the goal of assuming the Lotus 1-2-3 position in the marketplace. At the time, Lotus was the leading software spreadsheet. (Borland)

1. Thong — A point release of Borland C++ 4.0. A small number of fixes for embarrassing problems were made — just enough to barely cover the engineers' butts. Thus, it was named after the underwear style. (Borland)

Code Name Adventures

Sometimes choosing a code name may have undesired side effects. Even though code names are humorous and meant for internal use, not everyone appreciates their humor. The following code names all resulted in lawsuits or threats of litigation:

Butt Head Astronomer (BHA)

The original code name for the PowerMac 7100/66 product was Sagan, named after the astronomer Carl Sagan. Apple may have hoped to sell billions and billions of these machines. However, Apple was sued by Carl Sagan, who was seeking damages for copyright violation, unfair competition, and unrequested rights to publicity. Sagan lost the case, with the judge ruling: "The temporary use of the name reduced the likelihood that consumers expected to purchase a Carl Sagan–endorsed computer." Apple changed the name to BHA, which stood for Butt Head Astronomer. Sagan sued once more, saying the name subjected him to "hatred, contempt and ridicule." This was also rejected, with a ruling that Butt Head Astronomer is a generic term.

Dylan

An object-oriented scripting language from Apple. Bob Dylan sued saying Apple used "the names of famous individuals including Newton, Carl Sagan and now Dylan in conjunction with Apple's products in a deliberate attempt to unlawfully capitalize on the goodwill associated with these famous individuals." Apple claims the name is short for *dynamic language*. Maybe they will rename the product to Butt Head Musician.

Marvel

This was the code name for the Microsoft Network. Apparently, Marvel Comics sent a threatening note to Microsoft, indicating that it infringed on their company name

Code Name Themes

Code names often fall into groups of related themes. Sometimes this is to show the relations among products from a single company. Novell is particularly fond of naming products after related themes. For example, UnixWare projects are named after ski resorts such as Alta and Snowbird. NetWare projects are named after places in Utah, such as Moab and Arches. In a similar approach, Hewlett-Packard's PA-RISC program was code-named Spectrum, and the projects within it were named after colors such as Red, Indigo, and Violet. DEC named a series of products after lasers: Laser, Neon, and Ruby. And of course, there are Amstel and Rolling Rock from Go.

Aggressive Names

In many cases, companies naturally gravitate towards a variety of themes. In fact, you'll find the same code names in use by several companies. For example, this chapter lists three different products named Project X, two named Capone, and four named Tsunami, among others.

One of the most common themes for code names is aggressive names. That's because no one wants to get stuck working on a wimpy product. You will rarely see code names like "Buttercup," "Puffball," or "Wuss." Instead, you'll find testosterone-laden names such as these:

Barracuda: Microsoft Visual C++ 1.0. (Microsoft)

Bladerunner: dBase for Windows. (Borland)

Capone: Mail engine for Windows 95. Capone is a popular code name for Windows 95 products because the code name for Windows 95 was Chicago, a home of Al Capone. (Microsoft)

Capone: A Borland C++ version designed for Windows 95. (Borland)

Conan: Lotus 1-2-3, Release 2.3. This was named Conan because it was designed to compete with Philippe Kahn's Quattro Pro. Philippe often called himself a software barbarian. Thus, Conan the Barbarian would defeat Philippe the Barbarian. (See also *Crom*, under "Mythological and Magical Gods and Figures," page 136. Lotus)

Derringer: One of the Mac PowerBook versions. (Apple)

Nitro: Mac version. (Apple)

Operation DOS Storm: a crackdown on DOS counterfeiters, named after U.S. military Operation Desert Storm. (Microsoft)

Predator: Borland C++ 4.0. (Borland)

Raptor: Lotus 1-2-3, Version 4.1. (Lotus)

Raptor: Turbo C++ for Windows 4.5. (Borland)

Road Warrior: Saros Document Manager Local Library. (Saros)

Samurai: Multimedia workstation. Apricot Computers (PLC)

Spike: Pentium competitor from Cyrix. (Cyrix)

Spitfire: OS/2-based messaging server. Cancelled, to later become Exchange. (Microsoft)

Starfighter: SQL Server 6.0. (Microsoft)

TailGun: Aldus FreeHand. (Adobe)

Thruster: framegrabber for PhotoShop. (Radius)

TNT: PowerPC. (Apple)

Viking: SuperSPARC. (Texas Instruments)

Nerd Humor

Nabisco's PDA

This joke circulated around the time **Apple** announced the **Newton**: Nabisco is mad at Apple for announcing a product called Newton. In retaliation, they're coming out with a computer called **Fig**. It's for regular people who want to stay that way.

Nature and Natural Phenomena

When you are holed up in the office working day in and day out on a product, sometimes the closest you get to nature is the code name for your product. Natural code names usually evoke the idea of solidity, sense, and power:

Bedrock: Cross-platform application framework developed by Apple and Symantec. The name is chosen both as where the Flintstones live, as well as the earth's foundation, since the framework was to be the foundation of cross-platform applications. After much hoopla and hype, the product was scaled back and essentially shelved. (Symantec)

Blue Lightning: 100 MHz 486 chip from IBM. (IBM)

Cirrus: Access 1.0. (Microsoft)

Cirrus: VAX 3,000 ft. Not only is Cirrus a high cloud layer, but it is also the name of a vendor that supplies computer equipment to IBM. (DEC)

Cyclone: PowerMac. (Apple)

Earth: ObjectVision 3.0. Cancelled, but then revived as Phoenix, and then cancelled again. (Borland)

Hilltop: Sidekick for Windows. (Borland)

Iceberg: RAID system. (Storage Technology)

Iceberg: Microsoft's interactive television operating system. (Microsoft)

Lightning: HP LaserJet IV. (Hewlett-Packard)

Magma: OWL for AppWare. This was to compete with Bedrock, so it was the hot stuff that is under bedrock. Plus, it is the name of a German pornographic movie company. (Borland)

Planet: Multimedia project. (IBM)

Rainbow: Symantec C++ 8.0 for Power Macintosh. (Symantec)

Spring: Object-oriented operating system. (Sun)

Storm: BA350 modular storage enclosure. (DEC)

Storm: End-user data access tools. (Informix)

Thunder: Visual Basic 1.0. (Microsoft)

Tornado: OpenView 4.0. (Hewlett-Packard)

Tsunami: Paradox for Windows 1.0. (Borland)

Tsunami: PowerPC 604-based Power Mac. (Apple)

Tsunami: MicroSparc. (Sun)

Tsunami: NewWave, with a clear pun on the meaning of Tsunami. (Hewlett-Packard)

Whirlwind: Q/Media for Windows. (Q/Media)

White Water: Mainframe accounting package. Allegedly after spending $100 million to develop, it was shelved. Given President Clinton's trouble with White Water, this name is even more amusing. (IBM)

OS/2 Boat Names

When Microsoft and IBM were jointly developing OS/2, they started off with Mercedes-Benz code names. These were just numbers, changed frequently, and never got anywhere. Next, they switched to naming the various releases after boats. Unfortunately (at least in some people's opinions) the boats sunk.

Sloop: Version 1.2 of OS/2. (IBM and Microsoft)

Cruiser: OS/2, version 2.0. Never shipped. Microsoft went on to create NT, and IBM to create their own version 2.0. (See the Cruiser sweatshirt in figure 8-1 — IBM and Microsoft)

Hydroplane: Set of features planned to improve Cruiser prior to Yawl. Ended up turning into OS/2 2.0 from IBM. (Microsoft)

Yawl: OS/2 3.0 from Microsoft; never shipped. (IBM and Microsoft)

Outrigger: Borland C++ for OS/2 1.5. Amusingly enough, Borland ended up with a boat name for their OS/2 product, completely without knowledge of the IBM naming scheme. (Borland)

Figure 8-1 This is the official team sweatshirt for the Microsoft OS/2 2.0 team. It is a collector's item since the project was canceled after Microsoft and IBM had a falling out over operating systems. The product's code name, "Cruiser," shows clearly on the back of the sweatshirt.

IBM and Others Get Hip with "Star Trek" Names

Once IBM took over OS/2 development fully, they favored "Star Trek" names:

Borg: OS/2, version 2.1, interim release. (IBM)

Ferengi: OS/2 for Windows. (IBM)

Tricord: Operating system for IBM PowerPC-based PDA. (IBM)

Q: Motorola 68060. On the other hand, if this is just a plain old letter Q, it should go in the "Code Names That Suck" category with most of the other CPU names. (Motorola)

Q: Future MessagePad hand-held computer. (Apple)

Warp: OS/2 Warp 3.0. Amusingly enough, the head of the division liked the code name so much, he wanted to call it OS/2 Warp. The marketing people liked OS/2, version 3.0, because it made it very clear what version it was. They compromised and called it OS/2 Warp 3.0. (See also "Code names that Stuck," page 139.)

Shakespeare and Borland

Romeo: Borland Visual Solutions Pack 1.0. (Borland)

Juliet: Borland Visual Solutions Pack 2.0. (Borland)

Go Corporation and Beer

Beer is one of the basic food groups for programmers, along with pizza, chocolate, and coffee. It is a wonder that there aren't far more code names based on beer names.

Amstel: PenPoint 2.0 for Intel. (Go Corporation)

Amstel: Lotus 1-2-3/W. This was developed unofficially at Lotus, because Manzi didn't want to support Windows in order to hurt Microsoft. Eventually it became critical to support Windows, and this underground effort turned into Lotus 1-2-3/W. (Lotus)

Rolling Rock: PenPoint for Hobbit. (Go Corporation)

Starfish and Sushi Names

In a slightly cannibalistic twist, all code names at Starfish (the company founded by Philippe Kahn after leaving his role of running Borland) are sushi names.

Uni: Dashboard 95. (Starfish)

Dynamite: Sidekick 95. Note that this is a type of spicy tuna roll. (Starfish)

Windows City Names

All of these products had code names named after cities in the U.S. Originally, Daytona was code-named Champaign. This was because Chicago, Cairo, and Champaign were all cities along Interstate 57 in Illinois.

Cairo: Windows NT 4.0. (Microsoft)

Champaign: Windows NT 3.5. (Microsoft)

Chicago: Windows 95. The ultimate windy, er, Windows city. (Microsoft)

Clevelend: Windows 4.1. (Microsoft)

Daytona: Windows NT 3.5. (See figure 8-2 — Microsoft)

Memphis: A version of Windows after Wndows 96. (Microsoft)

Nashville: A version of NT after Cairo. (Microsoft)

Sparta: Windows for Workgroups. (Microsoft)

Tukwilla: a release between NT 3.5 and Cairo. (Microsoft)

Figure 8-2 Daytona was the code name for Windows NT 3.1. In this shirt you can see NT scooting ahead of the competition on the racetrack, edging out Sun and Novell. Meanwhile, in the back, OS/2 crashes and turns over. In addition to the code name reference, there is a further inside joke to the shirt. Dave Cutler and many key engineers on the project raced cars for fun, often taking classes at the Laguna Seca racetrack in Monterey, California.

Place Names

In the 1970s and 1980s there were a slew of bands named after places: Kansas, Boston, and Chicago are but a few. Development teams often do the same for products, naming them after interesting cities, nearby places, or areas of historical significance. For example, Arcada named its software after tropical islands. NetWare products were often named after places in Utah.

Aspen: CA Visual Objects. (Computer Associates)

Back Bay: Lotus Improv. (Lotus)

Brazil: Performa 600CD. (Apple)

Cayman: Backup software. (Arcada Software)

DeNali: A visual development environment for creating OpenDoc parts. (Apple and IBM)

Durango: An early code name for ObjectVision 3.0. Later turned into Phoenix. (Borland)

Everest: SCO OpenServer, Release 5. (Santa Cruz Operations)

Fiji: Backup software. (Arcada Software)

Golden Gate: Future version of eWorld. (Apple)

Hawaii: Backup software. (Arcada Software)

Huron: Application development environment. (Amdahl Corporation)

Long Beach: dBase for Windows. (Borland)

Kitty Hawk: 1.3-inch disk drive. (Hewlett-Packard)

Iowa: User interface building tool. (UserLand Software Inc.)

Manhattan: Games SDK for Windows 95. (Microsoft)

Mississippi: 486 chip for notebooks. (Texas Instruments)

New Zealand: Windows requestor for Office Vision. (IBM)

Nile: Object Linking and Embedding–based data-access and query model. (Microsoft)

Normandy: WebAuthor for Word for Windows 6.0. (Quarterdeck Office Systems)

Palm Springs: second code name for Quattro Pro. (Borland)

Potomac: 486 chip for notebooks. (Texas Instruments)

Rio Grande: 486 chip for notebooks. (Texas Instruments)

Silverlake: AS/400. This is named after a small lake in Rochester, Minnesota. (IBM)

Superior: The second series of AS/400 minicomputers. Named after the Great Lake, though the obvious other meaning of the word is clearly intentional. (IBM)

Surrey: Series of mainframes. (ICL Incorporated)

Trinidad: First code name for dBase for Windows. Later changed to Jah and then Bladerunner. (Borland)

Female Names

Nerds are notoriously socially handicapped, so sometimes female code names are as close as the developers ever get to spending copious amounts of time with someone/thing with a female name. Sometimes products are named after famous women; other times they are named after the girlfriend or wife of someone on the team.

Charlotte: 100 MHz Pentium multiprocessor server. (DEC)

Clare: Server performance testing tool. (IBM)

Golda Meir: dBase Compiler. Later changed to Long Beach. And then to Amber. (Borland)

Maxine: Personal DECstation. (DEC)

Sara: Apple III. (Apple)

Artists, Musicians, and Actors

There are many stereotypes about nerds. One is that they are socially inept. This is true. Another is that they are not athletic and don't know how to color-coordinate. This is usually true. But contrary to some beliefs, nerds are not culturally illiterate. In fact, most nerds are extremely well read. (While others in high school were dating, nerds were at home studying, reading, listening to music, or watching obscure videos.) The love of the arts shows through in code names. Many such code names leverage the essence of the artist. For example, Apple Search was code-named Bogart: an actor who often played a detective. QuickDraw, a drawing API, had artist code names.

Bogart: AppleSearch. (Apple)

Brooks: PowerBook 160. (Apple)

Copland: System 8. (Apple)

Dante: Newton Intelligence 2.0 operating system. (Apple)

Escher: VB for DOS. (Microsoft)

Escher: QuickDraw 3D. (Apple)

Gershwin: future Mac OS. (Apple)

Harpo: MacroModeler for Windows. (Macromind)

Houdini: DOS compatibility card. (Apple)

Jackson Pollock: 32-bit QuickDraw. (Apple)

Jaws: PowerLine 450DE/2 DGX. So, maybe this one should really be listed in the "Animals" section. Or maybe the "Aggressive Names" section. But if it were Lassie or Benji, it would go here, right? (Dell Computer Corp.)

Mark Twain: The first code name for Quattro Pro 1.0. Abruptly renamed to Palm Springs so that Borland executives could deny they were working on a product named Mark Twain. (Borland)

Monet: Freelance Graphics 2.0 for OS/2 2.0. (Lotus)

Picasso: A word processor program. Cancelled. (Borland)

Shamu: Graphical front end to CompuServe. (CompuServe, Inc.)

Socrates: Network management software. (Hewlett-Packard)

Zappa: PCI motherboard for 90 and 120 MHz Pentiums. (Intel)

Zeppo: MacroModel for Macintosh. See also, Harpo. What happened to Groucho? (Macromind)

Nerd Humor:

Alternative Microsoft Bob Personas

Microsoft Bob is a product that provides a friendly, home-like environment for interacting with applications. One of the features of Bob is built-in characters who help guide you through computer operations. The following circulated on the Net shortly after Bob's release. It provides a list of personalities that didn't quite make it into Bob:

Fritz the Ferret: Alternately helpful and asleep behind the furniture. Poops in the corners of your windows. Drags program icons under the couch when you're not using them.

Hunter Bob Thompson: Provides "gonzo" style wizard for the letter writer. Behavior is erratic. Protests loudly that there are purple lizards hiding in your system and tries to eradicate them with a scoped, .44 Magnum handgun.

G. Bob Liddy: Steals your files and emails them to the FBI. Seeks to impress female users by scorching his hand over a candle in the living room scene and demonstrating 704 ways to kill someone with a 3.5" disk. Keeps trying to catch and eat "Scratch," the rat.

Bob & Butt-head: Sit on the couch in the living room and complain that "this sytem sucks." Use all the system resources surfing the Internet and filling the hard drive with downloaded files from alt.binaires.pictures.erotica.blondes and alt.sounds.gwar.

Rush LimBob: Continuously offers advice based on uninformed or incomplete analysis of user activity. If you ignore the LimBob's advice, repeatedly chastises you with "See, I told you so!" Uses the CrankFax™ Wizard to fax complaints about Department of Justice harassment of Microsoft to Congress and the White House. Sends self-promoting emails and faxes to everyone in your Address Book, then bills you for them.

Animals

Lots of products are named after animals. For example, the HP Workstation program was called Snakes, and all projects within it were named after various snakes, such as Rattler, Asp, and King. Some names, such as Blackbird, Tiger, and Viper are very popular, and you will see them used by many different companies. Note that some of the code names listed in "Aggressive Names," such as as Raptor and Barracuda, could have just as easily appeared here.

Blackbird: PowerBook 540c. Of course, some would argue that all of the Blackbird names are really named after the SR-71 stealth plane. (Apple)

Blowfish: Nantucket's code name for a future version of Clipper, most features of which were canned after CA bought them. (Computer Associates)

Blue Marlin: Lotus Improv. (Lotus)

Bluefish: ATM system. (WellFleet)

Brahma: 486 clone from AMD. (AMD)

Butterfly: ThinkPad 701C. Some say it got this name not only because it is a lightweight machine, but also because the keyboard unfolds like butterfly wings. (IBM)

Calimari: Access Node. Perhaps chosen for the various "arms" coming out from the hub. (Bay Networks)

Cobra: DEC 4000 Model 600 server. (DEC)

CyberDog: A framework for browsing the Internet and other networks. Truly a great code name. (Apple)

Eagle: Distributed storage management system. (Sterling Software)

Falcon: OLE component coordinator. (Microsoft)

Ferret: The social user interface for Novell's experimental desktop operating system, also known as Corsair. (Novell)

Flamingo: DEC Alpha deskside workstation with six TurboChannel slots. (DEC)

Gecko: Motorola's PDA. (Motorola)

Guppy: Hub router. (Bay Networks)

Jaguar: Early PowerPC codename. (Apple)

Kangaroo: An early version of MASM (Microsoft Assembler). (Microsoft)

Kestrel: Paradox for DOS 3.5. (Borland)

Longhorn: Am386DX. (AMD)

Lynx: Electronic file distribution system for Notes. (Lotus)

Mako: Lotus Notes 4.0. (Lotus)

Next Big Fish: Query and access tool connecting VB to back-end databases. This is one of my favorite animal names. (Progress)

Pelican: DEC 3000 Model 300 AXP. (DEC)

Penguin: Set top box for interactive television. (Microsoft)

Salmon: IBM PC/AT. (IBM)

Sandpiper: DEC Alpha desktop workstation with three TurboChannel slots. (DEC)

Sparrow: Low-end video editing program. (DiVA)

Stallion: Set of computers from AST. (AST)

Tasmanian Devil: Voice recognition system. (Microsoft)

Tiger: Microsoft Media Server. (Microsoft)

Viper: Iomega Jaz line of removable internal drives, based upon their Zip drives. (Iomega)

Wildcat: Core logic controller for the SuperCore 590 chip set. (VLSI Technology, Inc.)

Wombat: Apple Quadra 25 and 40. (Apple)

Worm: Xerox 820. (Xerox)

Mythological Animals

I suppose one could argue that many of these are real and not mythological. Note that many programmers are big fans of Godzilla movies, so I'm sure that I've missed many Godzilla-based code names.

Argus: Enterprise development tool for NT. (Microsoft)

Big Foot: 32-bit DOS extender. This name originally came from the idea that a 32-bit application could use a big memory footprint. (See also *Godzilla*.) (Borland)

Big Foot: Avantra 44 image setter. (Avantra)

Dragon: Multiprocesser server. (Sun)

Godzilla: PowerPack for DOS. (Borland)

Gryphon: VIS CD-ROM player. (Tandy)

Mothra: Paradox for DOS 4.0. While Mothra is a foe of Godzilla, Mothra is also a giant bug, so some say this is a poor choice of a code name for a software product. (Borland)

Pegasus: PDA operating system. (Microsoft)

Pegasus: Data dictionary tool. (Gupta)

Pegasus: ESCALA PC line. (Bull HN)

Phoenix: A marketing distribution strategy. See also the discussion under "Ten All-Time Great Code Names," page 121. (NEC)

Mythological and Magical Gods and Figures

Ali Baba: A plan, which was shelved, for including an encrypted version of Microsoft Office applications with Windows 95. (Microsoft)

Aladdin: PCI motherboard for 100 and 135 MHz Pentiums. (Intel)

Amazon: First-generation interactive television OS. (Microsoft)

Amazon: Superbase. (SPC)

Apollo: SQL Links for connecting to Oracle. (Borland)

Aquarius: PC development project prior to Acorn (the IBM PC), that was shelved. (IBM)

Athena: The first code name for Paradox for DOS 4.0. This was a short-lived code name, because programmers used to say things such as "I just shoved my code into Athena." The sexual overtones (and the breadth of variation) didn't lead to a healthy work environment, so the name was changed to Mothra. (Borland)

Aurora: DRS 3000 computer. (ICL)

Crom: Quattro Pro 4.0 for DOS. Crom is the god that Conan prayed to. And thus, this was a retort to Lotus's Conan. (Borland)

Delphi: Windows help desk software. See also *Delphi,* in "Code Names That Stuck," page 139. (S&S)

Gemini: SQL Links for connecting to RDB. (Borland)

Genie: Early name for Tsunami project at Sun. (Sun)

Hermes: NT-based systems management product. An amusing code name, because Hermes is the god of good fortune and prudence, as well as fraud and theft. (Microsoft)

Hobbit: RISC PDA chip. (AT&T)

Jupiter: 5100 Automatic Tape Library. (Memorex Telex)

Mars: NetWare support for NT. (Microsoft)

Mercury: Distributed agents technology. (IBM and Legent)

Mercury: SQL Links for connecting to Sybase. (Borland)

Mercury: Nok Nok Pro. (Trik Incorporated)

Merlin: Mass storage system. (SunDisk)

Orion: Multimedia authoring system. (Quark, Inc.)

Orion: MIPS chip for desktop systems. (QED)

Pele: VAX 4000. (DEC)

Saturn: PCI local bus chipset. (Intel)

Snow White: A style guide for machine appearance used for machines prior to the PowerBook series. (Apple)

Thor: Quattro Pro for Windows. (See figure 8-3 — Borland)

Triton: Cray T90. (Cray)

Vulcan: 80860-based multiprocessor. (IBM)

Figure 8-3 Thor was the code name for Quattro Pro for Windows. Here you can see the team t-shirt that played off the code name.

Astronomical and Related Names

Note that many of the mythological names could easily be classified here as well.

Comet: Multimedia project. (IBM)

Eclipse: workgroup architecture for NetWare. (Novell)

Lunar: The first PC development project at IBM. Shelved. (IBM)

Pulsar: Two-way intelligent messaging product. (Microsoft)

Saturn V: RocketShare. An obvious pun on the *Rocket* part of the product name. (Radius Incorporated)

SkyLab: Macintosh-compatible server. (Radius Incorporated)

Voyager: dBASE for Windows 6.0. (Borland)

Cartoon and Comic Book Figures

College kids often love watching cartoons: it brings back memories of stress-free childhood. Developers often name products after cartoon and comic book figures, as well, in part to evoke memories of stress-free collegiate life. And in part because comics and comic books — particularly Dilbert, Calvin and Hobbes, Ren and Stimpy, and Batman — are regarded as cool.

Astro: DOS 6.0. The dog in the Jetsons. (Microsoft)

Bart: Visual Basic clone for OS/2. (IBM)

Calvin: Electronic forms designer for Microsoft Mail. (Microsoft)

Calvin: SparcStation II. (Sun)

Casper: Voice recognition system. (Apple)

Elroy: DOS 6.2. The boy in the Jetsons. (Microsoft)

Hobbes: Set of predefined forms to run with Calvin. (Microsoft)

Opus: Word for Windows 1.0. Named after the cartoon character, but also a pun on using the word processor to create great works. (Microsoft)

Phantom: netOctopus Agent. (MacVONK)

Popeye: Multimedia player. (Toshiba and Apple)

Roadrunner: 3.5" 135M removable media hard drive. (SyQuest Technology, Inc.)

Sweat Pea: Multimedia PDA, supposed to follow Newton. (Apple)

Programmers love comic books. This stems from a deep love of science fiction and fantasy, and perhaps the role programmers see themselves playing in the computer world. This shirt comes from Paradigm, makers of an embedded systems debugger.

Code Names That Stuck

Sometimes it is hard to get rid of a code name. If the product is under development for a long time, the name may have established itself with the press and the user community. Sometimes marketing departments get enamored with code names and decide to keep them for the product. And in some cases, by the time the product ships no one has enough energy left to come up with a new name. Here are some code names that stuck once the product shipped:

Alpha: The chip and RISC microcomputer from DEC. Note that the full name is Alpha AXP. Some say that AXP stands for Almost eXactly Prism, which was a code name for a predecessor. (See "And Yet, Still Other Code Names," page 142.) (DEC)

Delphi: A Pascal-based client/server development product from Borland. The code name was chosen for a variety of reasons, including "seeing the Oracle," as one of the key features of Delphi is its ability to connect to database servers such as those from Oracle. (Borland)

Lisa: The computer. Allegedly named after Steve Jobs' daughter, though officially standing for "large integrated software architecture." (Apple)

Macintosh: The computer. (Apple)

Newton: The PDA. (Apple)

NT: Windows NT. The NT stands for "new technology." Also, if you take the letters in VMS (the Vax OS) and add one, you get WNT, or Windows NT. This is similar to taking IBM and subtracting one letter to get HAL. (Microsoft)

Warp: OS/2 Warp 3.0. (IBM)

Code Names That Suck

Hardware companies, and especially chip manufacturers, are known for having really boring code names. Here are a couple:

Dru2: 486SX clock doubler. (Cyrix)

EV-4: First Alpha chip. (DEC)

H4C: 486SL. (Intel)

K5: Competitor to Pentium. Code-named Krytponite as well. (AMD)

M6: Cx486S2/50. (Cyrix)

M6N: 3.3-volt version of M6. (Cyrix)

M6NB: Low-power 486SL50. (Cyrix)

M7: 486 chip from Cyrix. (Cyrix)

P23T: OverDrive 486. (Intel)

P24T: Pentium overdrive chip. (Intel)

P5: Pentium. (Intel)

P54: 3.3V 100 MHz Pentium. (Intel)

P6: Chip after Pentium. Sometimes jokingly called the Sexium. (Intel)

Ultra-P: This was the code name for the first MIPS Technologies upgrade kit. The big question is, if this is the code name for upgrade #1, will they call upgrade #2 Ultra-Poo? (MIPS)

ZX: Update to 8051. (Intel and Philips)

Figure 8-4 Lego was the code name for the IDAPI engine at Borland. After the code name was leaked, it was changed to Ogel. Here you can see the team t-shirt.

And Yet, Still Other Code Names

Just in case you think all code names fall into neat categories, or I have been lax in my writing, here is a set of even more code names. As you can see, there are hundreds and hundreds of code names for products. And, of course, there are hundreds more products than those I have discussed here. In fact, listing all code names for all computer products could fill a phone book.

Acorn: First IBM PC. (IBM)

AJ: PowerBook Duo model with a larger hard drive and screen than the 280c. (Apple)

Alar: An add-on to Visual C++ that let programmers target the Macintosh. Alar is a pesticide put on apples that received much negative press in Washington State. (Microsoft)

Alarm Clock: Set of PDAs. (Motorola)

Alchemy: Upgrade to Power Mac 6300. (Apple)

Alchemy: Another name for Forms Cubed. (Microsoft)

Alex: Add-on for Telephone Access Server that connects it to GroupWise. (Novell)

Alive: Video compression and decompression software. (Media Vision)

Amber: Early name for OpenDoc. Amber is often regarded as a poor choice for a code name, because Amber is old pine sap filled with bugs. (Apple)

Amber: Paradox for Windows. (Borland)

Bento: Cross-platform document storage format. (Apple)

Blackbird: User interface design tool for Microsoft Network. (Microsoft)

Blackbird: Commucations program. (Traveling Software)

Blackjack: Indigo. (SGI)

Blaze: Local non-server database engine for Oracle Power Objects. (Oracle)

Blueprint: DataLens portion of Lotus 1-2-3 Release 3. (Lotus)

Bonsai: Apricot LS Pro. (Apricot Computers PLC)

Bullet: Mail server. (Microsoft)

Bushmaster: HP Series 700 workstation. (HP)

Carat: CA-RET/Xbase. (CA)

Carousel: Adobe Acrobat. (Adobe)

Catalina: Paradox for DOS 4.5. (Borland)

Catapult: Internet security firewall being developed for NT. (Microsoft)

Chronicle: Version Manager feature of Lotus 1-2-3. (Lotus)

CIA: InfoCentral. Apparently, WordPerfect was thinking of calling the product CIA, but marketing tests indicated customers would not react positively. (WordPerfect)

Cinnamon: PowerBook subnotebook. (Apple)

Columbus: Database library product. (Cascade)

Concorde: Symantec Enterprise Developer. (Symantec)

Cobra: Color LaserWriter 12/600 PS. (Apple)

Converse: PowerBook 180. (Apple)

Coral: Successor to TC2000. Cancelled. (Bolt Beranek and Newman, Inc.)

Crystal: Visual C++ 2.1. (Microsoft)

Darwin: Lotus 1-2-3 for Windows 2.0. (Lotus)

Destiny: Unixware System V, Release 4.2. (Novell)

Dossier: An email program. Turned into Eagle. (Borland)

Dr. Pepper: AppleTalk tunneling protocol. (Wellfleet Communications, Inc.; Shiva Corp.;

Novell, Inc. (Cisco Systems, Inc.; and Cayman Systems, Inc.)

Duplo: Paradox engine. (Borland)

Eagle: An email package. (Borland)

Egg: After Effects. (Company of Science and Art)

Emerald: HP 3000 992/400. (Hewlett-Packard)

ENCOMPASS: Distributed enterprise network management system. (SunConnect)

Eric: Alex for Windows 2.0. (VisionWare)

Espresso: A style guide for machine appearance used when designing the PowerBook 500. (Apple)

Exemplar: Early name for OpenDoc. (Apple)

Foghorn: Microsoft Sound Card. (Microsoft)

Forms Cubed: Forms layout tool. (Microsoft)

Fred Font Machine: Font design program. (Letraset)

Genesis: 386SL. (Intel)

Green: First name for Ada.

Haiku: Modular Windows. (Microsoft)

Harmony: IBM 4391. (IBM)

Iris: Object-oriented database. (Hewlett-Packard)

Ivy: Enterprise Network Services for NetWare. This is a product that communicates with NetWare and VINES servers, hence the joke. (Banyan)

Jah: Second code name for dBase for Windows. Later turned into Bladerunner. (Borland)

Jedi: Early name for OpenDoc. (Apple)

Jensen: Minitower Dec Alpha machine. (DEC)

JetSki: Middleware for IBM PowerPC-based PDA. (IBM)

Juice: Symphony. (Lotus)

Jumbo: Windows Printing System. (Microsoft)

Kagera: OLE-enabled version of ODBC. (Microsoft)

Karat: Series of System View applications. (IBM)

Kryptonite: K5 chip. (AMD)

Laser: Alpha system. (DEC)

Leaf: Lotus Add-In Toolkit for 1-2-3. (Lotus)

Lego: IDAPI. See also *Ogel*. (See figure 8-4 — Borland)

Little Guy: HP 1000. (Hewlett-Packard)

Lonestar: ObjectVision 1.0. This name was chosen for two reasons. First, many of the people on the ObjectVision team were from Texas. Secondly, instead of using a formal version control system (that is, a program to help coordinate programmers so that multiple people can work on the same code file), the team used a bottle of Lonestar beer. Whoever had the bottle of beer was allowed to check in their changes. No one else was allowed to apply their code changes. Thus, files didn't get changed by several people at once. Allegedly, the bottle of beer was drunk once the product shipped. (Borland)

Lookout: InfoPump. (Channel Computing, Inc.)

Malcolm: PowerPC daughter card for PowerBook 500. (Apple)

Marconi: System 7 upgrade for PCI-based computers. (Apple)

Medley: AV Office 2. (Data General)

Menagerie: 68040 network server. (Apple)

Monarch: Vines for UNIX. (Banyan Systems)

Morgan: Alpha-based computer. (DEC)

Mosaic: Sidekick for Windows 1.0. (Borland)

Mystery House: A spreadsheet Apple deisgned for the Apple II, which some said Apple built because the engineers didn't like the president of VisiCorp. It was written in part by Steve Wozniak, and never shipped. (Apple)

Neon: First version of Laser. (DEC)

Notebook: ViP (Visual Programmer). (Lotus)

Obex: Object Exchange, a technology shipped in Quattro Pro for Windows and Paradox for Windows. (Borland)

Odyssey: A technology that links PCs to mainframe applications. (Sterling)

Odyssey: Excel 1.0. (Microsoft)

Ogel: The second code name for IDAPI. Apparently a high-level executive leaked the Lego code name so they needed to find a new code name. They reversed the letters to come up with Ogel. (Borland)

Ojai: DocuBuild. (Xerox)

Omega: Microsoft's first database program, which never shipped. Later turned into Cirrus. And eventually, Access. (Microsoft)

Omega: 68LC040-based M2 computer. (Apple)

OpenROAD: Windows 4GL framework, code generator, and other tools. (ASK Group)

Opera: 3D0 player. (3D0)

Orbit: Multimedia project. (IBM)

Peanut: IBM PC/jr. (IBM)

PET: PDA from IBM. Note that this is also the name of an early computer, the Commodore Pet. (IBM)

Pike: Interactive appliances. (Hewlett-Packard)

Pink: Taligent OS. (Taligent)

Pinnacle: hyperSPARC. (Cypress)

Pippin: Power Player game and multimedia machine. (Apple and Bandai Corp.)

Primavera: QuickDraw color management system. (Primavera)

Primrose: Set of C -based parallel processing tools. (Tesseract Corporation)

Prism: Code name for Alpha's predecessor, headed by Dave Cutler, and cancelled in 1988. Some say that AXP — the name for Alpha— stands for Almost eXactly Prism. (DEC)

Project Chess: The code name for the mission of creating PCs at IBM. The first project that came into being was Acorn: the IBM PC. (IBM)

Project Commodore: EasyWriter for the IBM PC. IBM contracted with Captain Crunch to port this from the Apple to the IBM PC. But the NDA with IBM prevented them from mentioning anything relating to IBM, so they needed to choose a code name. (Information Unlimited Software)

Project X: Oracle Power Objects. (Oracle)

Project X: Image-editing application. (Wright Technologies)

Project X: User interface integration product. (Microsoft)

QuickSilver: Forms package. (WordPerfect)

Ratpack: Holographic storage project. (MCC)

Redwood: 20GB tape backup. (Storage Technology)

Reporter: Previous code name for Rosebud. (Apple)

RIP Plenty: Raster image processor. In this case, RIP stands for "raster image processor," but it is amusing because in the software world, RIP often stands for "rest in peace;" in other words, a fatal bug. (Hyphen, Inc., and Radius Corp.)

Rosebud: Text-filtering and retrieval program. (Apple)

Rosetta: Pen-based Macintosh software. (Apple)

Royal: TrueType. (Microsoft)

Ruby: Alpha version of Laser. (DEC)

Ruby: A precursor to Visual Basic. (Microsoft)

Sage: Device for controlling home appliances. (AT&T)

Salsa: Application development tool. (Wall Data)

Scribble: An interactive environment development tool for Microsoft Network. (Microsoft)

Sequoia: A precursor to Quick C for Windows. The name was chosen because almost everyone working on the product was over 6 feet tall. (Microsoft)

Shiner: PowerPC-based server from Apple. Some say it is an appropriate name because Apple has gotten a black eye every time it has tried to compete in the server marketplace. (Apple)

Small World: NetWare system management facility for NT. (Microsoft)

Snowball: Windows for Workgroups 3.11. (Microsoft)

Sonic: SOM. (IBM)

Spiral: Electronic notepad for PowerBooks, which is based on a spiral notebook metaphor. (TechWorks, Inc.)

Summit: PC chip set. (NCR)

Sundance: Open PIC architecture for interrupt controllers. (AMD and Cyrix)

Sweep: Designer Macintosh prototype. (Apple)

Synergy: OpenView 5.0. (Hewlett-Packard)

Tangerine: Macintosh tailored for China. (Apple)

Tangora. RS/6000 based voice recognition system. (IBM)

Tesla: PIM product. (Common Knowledge)

Tiger: OS/2 to NT upgrade tools. (Microsoft)

Tiger III: A series of 486 computers from DEC, including the DECpc 466d2 MT, DECpc 433dx MT, DECpc 450d2 MT, DECpc 433dx MTE, DECpc 450dx MTE, and DECpc 466d2 MTE. (DEC)

Tiny Tunes: At Ease. (Apple)

Titanium: Cross-network database engine. (MDBS)

Torque: Microsoft Exchange. (Microsoft)

Touchdown: Microsoft Exchange Server. (Microsoft)

Touchstone: Video Vision. (Radius)

Trailblazer: RS/6000 machine. (IBM)

Trailblazer: LC 5200 Macintosh. (Apple)

Triumph: Alpha PC specifically designed for NT. (DEC)

Utopia: Microsoft Bob. (Microsoft)

Vail: Performa 400. (Apple)

Velcro: NetPort. (Intel)

Viper: Norton Desktop for Windows 2.0. (Symantec)

Viper: SPARC-type RISC processor. (Cypress)

Viper: Early NT code name. (Microsoft)

Walden: Lotus 1-2-3 G. (Lotus)

Wasabi: The beta-tester code name for Borland Delphi, chosen because Wasabi is real hot stuff. (Borland)

Wedge: Early code name for Newton. (Apple)

Whiplash: A word processor. Turned into Picasso. (Borland)

Windsor: Storage management platform. (Epoch)

Wings: An early name for Alar. (Microsoft)

Wizard: AccessPC. (Insignia Solutions Incorporated)

Zone V: Mac IIfx. "Going Zone V" is a military term for pushing an aircraft to its design limits. (Apple)

"We're past the anger phase. Now we're in acceptance mode."

—Third-party vendor, regarding the impact of Windows 95 shipping date slips

Developing for a future operating system can be a frustrating experience. Not only do you need to work with inherently buggy software, but planning marketing and product campaigns is difficult because schedules often change. For example, Windows 95 slipped several times during its development, altering the plans of third-party developers waiting for its release.

Riding on the Vapor Trail

After you've chosen a code name and begun development, news about your product will invariably leak out to the world. While sometimes this is because the press has persuaded beta testers to talk or has gotten their hands on secret documents, most of the time, leaks are intentional. At this point, the marketing team jumps into action and extols the product's virtues. If the product doesn't ship shortly thereafter, it will invariably earn the vaporware tag.

The computer industry is filled with stories of "vaporware." A vaporous product is simply one that is talked about, but doesn't yet exist for customers. Originally, vaporware referred to products that were completely fake. They were talked about purely for some marketing advantage, but they weren't under development and, in fact, weren't even in the planning stages. The term was popularized in the 1980s by Ann Winblad. At the time, she was the president of a Minneapolis-based accounting firm called Open Systems Corporation — though now she is a partner in the prestigious venture capital firm Hummer Winblad Venture Partners and the one-time girlfriend of Bill Gates. In 1982, a Microsoft engineer told her that a piece of software promised by Microsoft was not going to be produced, and that it was "vaporware." She spread the term, and it has been widely used ever since.

Today, vaporware more often describes a product that is in the planning or development stages, and is widely publicized, but is not yet available for customers. Note that there is a subtle difference between a beta product and a vapor product. If a company is developing a product and isn't marketing it yet, it isn't vaporware. But as soon as the company announces that it is forthcoming, talks about how it will shortly be shipped, or uses it to stall sales of a competing product, it is vaporware. That's because it is talked about as if it existed, but no customers can get their hands on it.

There are several reasons why companies announce vaporous products, as discussed in the following sections.

Discussing Long-Term Strategic Directions

Companies often discuss their long-term plans with customers, so that customers understand and feel comfortable with a company's direction. This shows the customers that the company understands their needs and has a strong vision for the future. Companies do this with the underlying intent of keeping customers loyal.

For example, Microsoft talked about its 32-bit operating system strategy long before any products were available. Though in this case, the products talked about eventually switched from OS/2 to NT.

Preannouncing to Stall Competitive Sales

When a competitor announces a new product, companies often react by preannouncing their next releases. This is done to keep customers from

Nerd Humor:

NT Source Code Chain

Completing Microsoft Windows NT was a gargantuan undertaking. This message, which floated on the Net, described one theory as to how NT was created:

I have SOLID information that Windows NT will be distributed in chain letter form. Within 60 days you will receive a letter containing a list of names and addresses, along with instructions to write 10 lines of C code and send them to the address at the top of the list before you add your name at the bottom and mail copies to 84 of your friends. Having done that, you will simply sit back and wait a few weeks to receive 12.5 million lines of NT source code, which you will then compile and link to form your NT system.

switching to the other companies' products. Sometimes the product preannounced is very close to release; in other cases, the product hasn't even been planned prior to the competitor's announcement.

In a famous example, Microsoft preannounced the availability of one of their language products, QuickBasic, in November 1986. This was to stall sales of the competing Turbo Basic, an announced but also unavailable product from Borland. Rob Dickerson, the employee responsible, bragged about this effective technique on his self review. Unfortunately, when Rob left Microsoft to work for Borland, Microsoft sued him, and the self review became part of the evidence used in the lawsuit. Later on, when the Department of Justice investigated Microsoft for monopolistic practices, this document surfaced again. Judge Sporkin, in reviewing the government's finding, focused on this review, making much of a documented case of a vaporous announcement.

In other cases, the preannounced products are quite far from release. For example, Microsoft has received a large amount of media attention about Windows 95. In order to avoid being eclipsed, and to demonstrate their commitment to future Macintosh releases, Apple announced Copland and Gershwin, neither of which was slated to appear within two years of the announcement.

In still other cases, products are announced that aren't even planned. This is often done when a company is completely surprised by a competitive announcement or by the success of a competing strategy. For example, when Lotus announced 1-2-3 for the Macintosh, in part to compete with Excel for the Macintosh, some say they didn't even have plans for the products' features or how they would create it. Not surprisingly, Lotus 1-2-3/Mac stayed a vapor product for a very long time, with a two-and-a-half year gap between its announcement and its ship date.

In another example, Borland was caught by surprise with the success of Microsoft Office. Some of the key features of Microsoft Office were the common look and feel of the applications, the interoperability, and a common scripting language called Visual Basic for Applications. Borland's response was a joint effort with WordPerfect, in which WordPerfect for Windows, Paradox for Windows, and Quattro Pro for Windows were bundled. The two companies gave a very different look and feel to their applications, but worked hard to add options so that each application could change to have either the WordPerfect look or the Borland look. Most reviews, however, lauded the common scripting language Microsoft provided. In reaction to this, a Borland executive announced a product called Object Automator, which would provide a common scripting language across Borland products. Object Automator, however, was just an experiment at the time, mostly designed for creating scripts for interactive tutorials. It had huge technical obstacles to overcome in order to work the way the executive claimed it would and, not surprisingly, never shipped. (Though it was used for tutorial creation quite successfully.)

Nerd Humor:

Lightbulb Jokes

Q: How many programmers does it take to change a lightbulb?

A: That's a hardware problem.

Q: How many programmers does it take to change a lightbulb?

A: Two. One always quits in the middle of a project.

Q: How many Windows programmers does it take to change a lightbulb?

A: 472. One to write WinGetLightBulbHandle, one to write WinQueryStatusLightBulb, one to write WinGetLightSwitchHandle...

Q: How many OS/2 programmers does it take to change a lightbulb?

A: I think that's a device driver problem.

Q: How many program managers does it take to change a lightbulb?

A: Let's get the marketers involved. We can sell this as a feature.

Q: How many managers does it take to change a lightbulb?

A: Three. Two to hold the ladder and one to screw the lightbulb into a faucet.

Q: How many support people does it take to change a lightbulb?

A: We have an exact copy of that lightbulb here and it seems to be working fine. Can you tell me what kind of system you have? OK. Just exactly how dark is it? OK. There could be four or five things wrong. Have you tried the light switch? Well, try it now. OK. Look over by the door. Is there a little rectangular thing on the wall? It might be a beige color. Good. That's called a light switch.

Q: How many help writers does it take to change a lightbulb?

A: None. In the future, we can move all of our docs on line, which means people won't need books or lightbulbs.

Q: How many developers does it take to change a lightbulb?

A: The lightbulb works fine on the system in my office. Not reproducible.

Q: How many C++ programmers does it take to change a lightbulb?

A: You're still thinking procedurally. A properly designed lightbulb object would inherit a change method from a generic lightbulb class, so all you'd have to do is send it a bulb.change message.

Q: How many group assistants does it take to change a lightbulb?

A: One.

Award Deadlines

Many magazines give awards for products. For example, there is the *PC Computing* MVP award, the *PC Magazine* Technical Excellence award, and the *Byte* Readers' Choice award. Such awards often have strict deadlines. That is, the magazines must receive a finished version of the product by a specific time. And, because of the long lead time of publishing a magazine, sometimes they will accept the promise that a program will ship instead of an actual copy.

Both situations occasionally lead to vaporware. Because winning such an award is a huge publicity win (and losing is a huge loss), companies will sometimes promise that they will make a date when they know they can't. In such cases, they apologize after they win the award, and laugh all the way to the bank. This usually doesn't work more than once.

If, on the other hand, magazines require a golden release, companies sometimes resort to further trickery. In such cases, if a product is very close to release, companies will create what they claim is the final release, and send that along with documentation, saying that the product has gone to manufacturing. They then continue to finish the product, change what actually ships, but claim that the disks the magazine received really went out. If the magazine complains that the package they bought in the store is different, the vendors claim bugs were found and the store release was just a slightly later cut. It is pretty hard for magazines to catch this ploy, but it doesn't lead to good long-term relations with the press.

Related techniques are often used to avoid public embarrassment, as is discussed in "Some Tricks to Avoid the Vapor Claim," page 156.

Great Quotes:

I'm a Steamroller, Baby

In May 1991, Rob Dickerson, who was General Manager at Borland at the time, promised that a suite of products including Paradox for Windows, Quattro Pro for Windows, and dBASE for Windows, would be released shortly: "It will be like a steamroller hitting in a short amount of time with a wide range of products." A short amount of time turned out to be several years.

Why Vendors Miss Ship Dates

Determining when a software product will ship is tricky. In fact, there is a joke that says building software is like building a cathedral. It takes far longer than you think, costs far more than you think, and when you are finished, you pray.

There are lots of reasons why products don't ship when a company says they will. Many of these relate to the process by which a ship date is determined.

1. A rough design is created for the product.

2. The engineers get together, discuss the project, and create schedules for their pieces. Engineers naturally underestimate how long it will take them to create a piece. After all, they want to look like hotshots.

3. The marketing people look at the feature set and add some extra features.

4. The finance department determines how much revenue will be derived from the ship quarter based on the ship date. If the date is too late in the quarter, the sales team, which is often compensated on the number of sales in a quarter, pushes upper management to pull the date in.

5. The date is then announced. Steps 2–4 ensure that the date is optimistic by at least three months.

6. Development begins.

7. During testing, customers find more bugs than expected. The product begins to slip.

8. The competition announces a new product, so more features have to be put in. The product slips even more.

9. Beta testers don't like the user interface for the new features. The product slips even more.

By now, the product has unavoidably slipped. And the person who announced the product in step 5 now has a vapor problem. Before you know it, customers scream, the press hollers, and heads roll.

Several mugs change their pictures when hot. It is hard to see the cursor on many laptops; the mug on the left celebrates a solution with the cursor appearing clearly once the mug warms. With the mug on the right, a Quattro Pro spreadsheet appears through the letters WYSIWIG.

ABOVE BOARD 286 IS SO ADVANCED IT'S COMPATIBLE WITH VAPORWARE.

OS/2™ SOFTWARE

The Above™ Board 286.

It'll run every one of the terrific new OS/2 applications.

Just as soon as they're written. Which by all accounts looks to be mid-1988.

In the meantime, it's almost mandatory with the memory-intensive applications you're using today: spreadsheets, networks, Microsoft® Windows™ pop-up utilities, or whatever.

In all, Above Board 286 can give you up to 4 MB of expanded memory, based on the Lotus®/Intel/Microsoft standard.

And since it looks like you'll be working with DOS at least another year, those 4 MB should come in handy. Especially when your spreadsheets develop middle-age spread.

And your pop-up utilities are popping up all over the place.

Then, when OS/2 finally arrives, that same Above Board you've come to know and love will give you up to 4 MB of OS/2 memory. Ready to run.

What's more, our new Above Board 286 comes with switchless installation, a five-year warranty and the toll-free technical support you'd expect from Intel.

All of which makes this a very special sort of proposition.

Because we're promising you the moon in the future.

And giving it to you in the present.

To give you the full story, we've written a paper called "The Memory Implications of OS/2." Just call (800) 538-3373 and we'll send you a free copy.

Above is a trademark and Intel a registered trademark of Intel Corporation. Lotus is a registered trademark of Lotus Development Corp. Microsoft and Windows are registered trademarks of Microsoft Corp. OS/2 is a trademark of International Business Machines Corp. © 1987 Intel Corporation.

This Intel ad makes fun of OS/2's early vaporware status. As you can see from the copy, many at the time believed OS/2 would mark the end of DOS.

General Incompetence and Shifts of the Market

A lot of times, vaporous announcements are due to honest incompetence or unpredicted changes in the market. For example, consider the leader in the table on page 159: dBase for Windows. It was originally announced in May 1991 as a forthcoming product called Turbo xBase. A Borland executive exuberantly declared that it and numerous other Borland products, Borland would ship in 1992. Then Borland bought Ashton-Tate, and in the process, Borland scrapped their original dBase plans, instead deciding to use Ashton-Tate code. The product changed directions and management numerous times after that. And finally, Borland bought WordTech, makers of a dBase clone called Arago that happened to run on Windows. By the time they were finished with all the twists and turns, it was August 1994, but the market had long since migrated to Paradox and Access.

Some Tricks to Avoid the Vapor Claim

Once a product is announced, customers expect the company to make its date. After all, when dates are missed, customers get upset and move to the competition. The company may have staked its reputation and even key contracts on making dates. And finally, if the company runs on a quarterly basis, it may desperately need product revenues for a particular quarter.

Moreover, the industry press puts great pressure on making dates. The various weeklies watch what happens and pounce at any sign of a product slipping. There is even a newsletter called *PC Letter* that features a regular column on vaporous products.

Because of these factors, vendors sometimes go to great lengths to keep customers from thinking a product has slipped. In fact, there are a slew of tricks that have been used to make it look like a product is available.

One technique is to ship a product before it is fully tested. In this case, the company creates a small number of units, shrink-wraps them, sends them to friendly dealers, the press, and a few customers, and claims that the product has shipped. The programmers stay hard at work, though, finding and fixing bugs. When the product is finally ready, the company sends it out for mass duplication. This technique can buy a few weeks of time, but is risky. If customers read that a product is shipping and rush in droves to the stores, they may be upset that they can't get immediate gratification, and they might forget to order again. Of course, if they ordered by phone, the company has six weeks to send the goods after taking customers' money, before having to send a refund.

This technique is used sometimes even when a product is finished. It can take one to two weeks to get products back from manufacturing. But, if a company is willing to pay for it, it can get a dozen or so products built overnight. Some will do this, ship the products to key press members, and announce that the product is widely available. Just to make sure, they will also send a small number to key distributors and stores, so that they can truthfully tell the press and customers that the product is available in the market. Many large vendors have used this technique over and over.

Another trick is to send out boxes with blank disks. Lotus allegedly did this with Jazz. They apologized once customers received the product, claimed it was a manufacturing problem, and sent them new disks. This can buy a few weeks of time, but also costs several dollars per customer. It isn't a trick vendors want to use too often.

Another approach is to send out or charge for a very wide beta program. For example, Microsoft is said to have sold or given away 400,000 copies of Windows 95 prior to its official release. Borland gave out hundreds of Delphi betas at the Delphi launch. Novell gave out numerous beta releases of AppWare Foundation before shelving the product.

And still one more trick is to give out coupons. This works for products that have cleanly separable features or components. For example, when IBM first shipped DOS 6.1, it provided a coupon for customers to receive a data compression package. By doing so it could tout that as a feature, be competitive with Microsoft DOS 6.0, but not have to hold up the ship date until the software was ready.

During one Microsoft Office upgrade, Microsoft shipped a new version of Word along with coupons for Excel 5.0 and PowerPoint 4.0. Once those packages were ready, Microsoft did an inline revision that replaced the coupons with the real software. Borland did the same thing when they had an office product: they shipped Quattro Pro and provided a coupon for Paradox for Windows and WordPerfect 6.0 for Windows.

All-Time Vapor Greats

In case you (or Judge Sporkin) think Microsoft is the only company to have vaporous products, on the following page is a list of some of the all-time vapor trail leaders. You can see dBase for Windows leading with an over-three-year vapor period, closely followed by Lotus 1-2-3/G.

There are two parts to a vaporous announcement: the date that a product is announced and the date the company says the product will ship. The dates on this chart are based on when a company starts talking about a product publicly, not on the official announce dates. That's because companies will often "unofficially" announce products long before they are ready. Yet they claim the products were never vaporware because they shipped at the time of the "official" announcement.

You'll also note some products at the end of the table that have been announced, but haven't shipped as of the time of this writing.

One caveat with the following chart. Because I calculated the time between the announce and ship dates as if the product were announced at the beginning of a month and shipped at the end of a month, there can be as much as a two-month error. For example, if dBase for Windows were announced at the end of May 1991, and shipped at the beginning of August 1994, then the difference in months is really 38, instead of 40.

Product	Date Announced	Date Shipped	Difference (Months)
dBase for Windows	5/91	8/94	40
Lotus 1-2-3/G	4/87	3/90	36
ScriptX	6/92	12/94	31
Windows NT	4/91	7/93	28
Lotus 1-2-3/Mac	10/87	12/91	27
System 7.0	5/89	5/91	25
Windows 1.0	11/83	11/85	25
Lotus Notes	2/88	12/89	23
NextStep 3.0 DB Kit	12/90	9/92	22
Windows 95	12/93	8/95	21
Telescript	2/93	9/94	20
Windows 3.0	2/89	5/90	16
Ashton Tate SQL Server	1/88	4/89	16
Newton	5/92	7/93	15
NetWare 4.0	2/92	4/93	15
Lotus Notes 3.0	4/92	5/93	14
Novell DOS 7.0	3/93	3/94	13
Word 6.0 for Macintosh	10/93	9/94	12
cc:Mail wireless client	10/92	9/93	12
Quattro Pro for Windows	10/91	9/92	12
Envoy PDA	3/94	1/95	11
Power Macintosh	5/93	3/94	11
InForms	10/92	8/93	11
Microsoft Network	11/94	8/95	10
3DO	1/93	10/93	10
Zoomer	1/93	10/93	10
WordPerfect Office 4.0	10/92	6/93	9
Borland Delphi	8/94	3/95	8
SCO Win-tif	10/93	5/94	8
Adobe Acrobat	11/92	6/93	8
UnixWare	6/92	1/93	8
Apple Duo Dock/Express Modem	10/92	2/93	5
OpenDoc	6/93	Fall 95	27
Copland	3/94	1996	
Gershwin	3/94	1996	
Microsoft Exchange	6/94	1995	
Open Messaging Environment	8/94	1996	

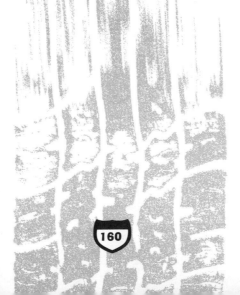

"We made Amiga, they f***ed it up."

A classic frustration easter egg appears in version 1.2 of the Amiga 1000 computer operating system. Apparently this message was put in shortly after Commodore purchased Amiga, and it reflects the developers' opinion of new management. After holding down the Left-Shift, Left-Alt, Right-Alt, Right-Shift, and a function key all at once, and placing and ejecting a disk, you get the message above. Not surprisingly, this message got replaced in later versions with "The Amiga—Born a Champion, Still a Champion."

Hiding and Finding Easter Eggs

You've learned about choosing a code name and the unfortunate slip into vaporware status. Between this and getting a product ready, there are thousands and thousands of hours of sleepless nights, stress-filled days, and general nervousness as the team readies the product. The engineers design hardware or create software. The testers test it. The product goes through numerous beta cycles and revisions. Marketers get customer feedback. The PR team stokes the press. And sales pounds the pavement getting the stores and corporate customers ready.

But before a product ships, there is one final step programmers undertake. Is this final sign-off from management? An assessment of whether the product met the goals? No. This final step is often done without management knowledge. This is the hiding of the "easter egg."

Easter eggs, sometimes called "credit screens," are hidden screens that list the developers that worked on the program. Often corporations don't like this. They want an anonymous, professional look to their applications. They don't want to admit that their products are the work of a bunch of eccentric programmers. (Some corporations don't have this fear. For example, the splash screen for Adobe Photoshop lists all of the developers.) To get even, the programmers hide their names in the applications. When a special set of undocumented keystrokes or actions occurs, lo and behold, up come their names. It is then a challenge for customers to find these lists.

Sometimes easter eggs simply contain a list of developers' names. Other times, they contain elaborate animations showing the application destroying its competition. And on occasion, easter eggs contain messages about the frustration developers sometimes feel with having to ship a product before all the bugs are out, or before their favorite features have made it in.

A classic frustration easter egg appears in version 1.2 of the Amiga 1000 computer operating system. Apparently this message was put in shortly after Commodore purchased Amiga, and it reflects the developers' opinion of new management. After holding down the Left-Shift, Left-Alt, Right-Alt, Right-Shift, and a function key all at once, and placing and ejecting a disk, you get the message "We made Amiga, they f***ed it up." Not surprisingly, this message got replaced in later versions with "The Amiga—Born a Champion, Still a Champion."

Other easter eggs pay tribute to the significant others of the developers. Perhaps this is in the hope that such attention will make up for the many long nights spent in front of computers. For example, in the Amiga (the same one with the nasty message), you can find a picture of the programmer's girlfriend by pressing and clicking a special combination in the mouse settings control. In the Coleco Adam, if you held a special set of keys down while booting CP/M 2.2, you'd get a picture of a woman with the title "Pam's Face." In SmartBASIC 1.0 on the Adam, you can find the message "Hi Cathy," while in version 2.0 you can find the message "Hi Jan."

In the remainder of this section, I'll take you on a tour of easter eggs in some popular applications. There are many more than I've listed here.

Windows Easter Eggs

The following easter eggs all show up in Windows applications. If you follow the steps listed, you too can see these hidden visual treats.

Microsoft Windows 3.1

There are two parts to the easter egg in Windows 3.1. To find the easter egg, do the following:

1. Run the Program Manager.
2. Select Help | About Program Manager.
3. Hold down the Ctrl and Shift keys and double click on the left side of the Windows flag.
4. Click on OK.
5. Select Help | About Program Manager once more.
6. Hold down Ctrl and Shift and double-click on the flag.

The first easter egg screen will appear, as shown in Figure 10-1. This display is relatively tame. But don't give up — the second one is much more fun. To find the second one, follow the steps on the next page.

Figure 10-1: The first of the Windows 3.1 easter egg screens shows a waving flag.

1. Click on OK to close the About box.

2. Select Help | About Program Manager.

3. Hold down Ctrl and Shift and double-click on one of the four panes in the flag.

You'll see a list of the developers who worked on Windows. Depending upon the pane you click on, you will get a different picture. Figure 10-2 shows Steve Ballmer, Executive Vice President and long-time Vice President of Systems, giving the roster. Figure 10-3 shows the bear, a generic term for a manager who gives one grief for having bugs in code. In addition, you can find Brad Silverberg, Vice President of Systems, and Bill Gates himself.

Note that if you want to go back to see the other variations once you have watched one version, you will have to go through the full set of steps.

Figure 10-2: Steve Ballmer shows the list of developers in one version of the Windows 3.1 easter egg.

Figure 10-3: The bear shows the list of developers in another version of the Windows 3.1 easter egg.

Microsoft Windows NT

The NT easter egg provides an elaborate display of every developer on the product. The names fade in and out in a cascading and rotating set of dots (figure 10-4). A large number of folks worked on NT, so if you want to watch this easter egg to completion, you'd better arm yourself with a good snack.

1. From the control panel, click on the desktop icon.
2. Select the Bezier screen saver.
3. Hit the Test button.
4. While the Bezier is drawing, type the following, with no spaces: **ilovent**. (In case you are wondering, this says I Love NT).
5. Hit Return.
6. Now hit the Test button once more.

Figure 10-4: The NT easter egg lists all the developer names through a series of expanding and contracting balls.

Microsoft Office Manager

This is a simple easter egg, saying "Hi Mom" and listing developers. By the way, if you don't get the joke, Microsoft Office Manager is sometimes called MOM, because of the initials of each letter. Not to be outdone, Borland added a similar feature to its office suite called DAD.

1. Click on the Microsoft Office icon in the Microsoft Office Manager toolbar. (It is typically on the far right, showing a pencil and a notebook.)
2. Select About Microsoft Office.
3. Hold Ctrl and Shift and double-click on the icon.

The screen shown in Figure 10-5 will appear.

Microsoft Word 1.0 for Windows

Word for Windows 1.0 displays fireworks with the team names. To see this list, do the following. Note that the final characters to type, **O**, **P**, **U**, and **S**,

Figure 10-5: The Microsoft Office Manager easter egg says, "Hi Mom."

spell the code name for the product. Many products use the code name to trigger the easter egg. It makes it all the more special to be in the know:

1. Choose Format | Define Styles.

2. Press the Options button.

3. Type **Normal** in the Based on box.

4. Click on OK when you get the error message.

5. Click on Cancel to close the Define Style dialog.

6. Select Help | About.

7. Turn on CapsLock and press **O**, **P**, **U**, and **S** at once.

Microsoft Word 2.0 for Windows

This is one of the great competitive easter eggs. It also is a very complicated one. Here's what to do:

1. With a document open (such as the default blank document), select Tools | Macro.

2. Type **spiff** as the macro name and hit enter.

3. Select the lines Sub MAIN through End Sub.

4. Delete these lines.

5. Close the macro and save the changes.

6. Select Help | About.

7. Click once on the icon.

Now the easter egg will appear. It is a complex, animated sequence that starts with a bunch of figures (presumably Microsoft programmers) amassing. A dragon appears which, judging from the control characters within it, clearly represents WordPerfect. (In case you never used WordPerfect, the control characters in the easter egg are some of those used for formatting WordPerfect documents.) The Microsoft programmers then run over and jump on top of the evil dragon. You can see a still from this animation in Figure 10-6.

Figure 10-6: The rival WordPerfect is in trouble in the Microsoft Word for Windows 2.0 easter egg.

When you exit Word for Windows, it will ask whether or not to save global changes to the glossary. Say no.

Microsoft Word 6.0 for Windows

Once again, the Word team has created a fairly complex easter egg to find, though in this case it is far less interesting than the egg in Word 2.0 for Windows.

1. In a document, type **T3!**
2. Select these characters.
3. Hit the Bold button.
4. Hit the AutoFormat button.
5. Select Help | About Microsoft Word.
6. Click on the icon.

The easter egg shown in Figure 10-7 will appear. The names of the various developers scroll up the screen.

Figure 10-7: The Word for Windows 6.0 easter egg is much calmer than the previous version.

Microsoft Access 1.0

Access 1.0 has two easter eggs built into it: one from the help team, and one from the developers.

The help easter egg is pretty simple — just a list of names inside of a help file. To find this screen, shown in Figure 10-8, do the following:

1. Open Help.

2. Search for Error messages:Reference.

3. Click on the T section.

4. Press Page Up.

5. Click on Syntax error in LEVEL clause.

6. Click on the period after the sentence "Punctuation is incorrect." (It will be underlined.)

Figure 10-8: The names of Access help team members are hidden in the help file.

The development team easter egg is far more complex and much more amusing. It starts with a pair of ducks calmly sitting in a pond. (Gee, could that stand for Paradox, Access's competitor?) A cloud appears, lightning strikes and blows up the two ducks (though with pretty low-tech animation), and then the credits roll, as shown in Figure 10-9.

Figure 10-9: Like Word 2.0, Access sports a competitive easter egg. If you look closely, you will see two ducks get hit by lightning, followed by the cloud and credits shown here.

Note that the steps to find the easter egg use the product code name.

1. Open any Access database.
2. Create a new table.
3. Create one field of any type, with no primary key.
4. Save the table as "cirrus." (Be sure to use lowercase letters.)
5. Highlight "cirrus" in the table container.
6. Select Help | About Microsoft Access.
7. Hold down Ctrl+Shift and double-click the right mouse button on the Access logo.

Microsoft Excel 5.0

The steps for finding this easter egg are a little complex. To find it, do the following with a blank worksheet.

1. Right-click on the toolbar.
2. Select Customize.

3. Select Custom.

4. Drag the Solitaire icon onto the worksheet.

5. Click on Cancel to close the Assign Macro dialog box.

6. Click on Close to close the Customize dialog box.

7. Press Ctrl+Shift and click on the Solitaire icon.

Figure 10-10 shows the first screen that appears, listing the developers. This is followed by a list of testers. Then, the various names appear one at a time, with whirling dots transforming one name into the other.

Figure 10-10: The Excel 5.0 cast list.

Paradox for Windows 1.0

Paradox for Windows contains a fairly amusing easter egg. It starts with a set of ducks (again, a takeoff on the name Paradox) sitting in a pond. One duck asks a number of questions, such as, "Who tested this product?" and another duck responds with the names of those involved. At the end, it asks who played saxophone, blasts a short tune on the speaker, and the other duck responds, "Oh, that was Philippe Kahn."

To see it (figure 10-11), do the following:

1. Select Help | About.
2. Press Alt+Shift+C.

Figure 10-11: In Paradox for Windows, you'll find a lake filled with talkative ducks.

You can also hit Alt+I to see the internal version number.

Quattro Pro for Windows 1.0

Quattro Pro displays the names of the team members in a restaurant menu, along with a few jokes (figure 10-12). For example, the product manager, Song Huang, is listed as "Song 'and Dance' Huang." The screen also refers to a quote from Philippe Kahn regarding Lotus, in which he said he would eat their livers with fava beans and chianti. One word of caution: this easter egg doesn't like to go away. You might need to Alt+Esc back to Quattro Pro, then cancel all the dialogs and shut down Quattro Pro to get it to disappear.

1. Type text in a cell, for example, type **Hello**.
2. Press Enter.
3. Select Data | Parse.
4. Click on the Create button.

Figure 10-12: Here you can see the names of the Quattro Pro developers.

5. Click on the Edit button.

6. Hold the Shift key and press the **?** key three times.

dBase for Windows 5.0

This application contains four different easter eggs. Two are fairly tame, one is downright boring, and one is great fun. All of the easter eggs stem off the About box.

To see the names of the dBase for Windows team (figure 10-13), do the following:

1. Select Help | About.

2. Hit Alt+I.

To see a picture of the Borland campus (figure 10-14), do the following:

1. Select Help | About.

2. While holding the Alt key, type **CAMPUS**.

Figure 10-13: Here you can see the names of the dBase for Windows developers.

Figure 10-14: This is a low-resolution scan of Borland's headquarters.

To see the number 28 go across the About box, do the following:

1. Select Help | About.

2. While holding the Alt key, type **28**.

You might think that the programmer spent his 28th birthday working on dBASE, and thus embedded this message. Actually, it is the number of NASCAR racer Davey Allison. Allison was the hero of the developer who snuck in the easter eggs. After Allison died in a 1993 helicopter crash, the programmer resolved to pay tribute by embedding this animation.

And finally, for the best easter egg in dBase for Windows by far, do the following:

1. Select Help | About.
2. While holding down the Alt key, type **FOX**.

The OK button will rise to the top of the About box, revealing a fox underneath. Once the OK button reaches the top of the screen, it turns into a guillotine and comes crashing down on the fox's head, as shown in Figure 10-15. (FoxPro is the name of a competing database, now owned by Microsoft.)

Figure 10-15: This is a still from a great animated sequence of dBase's competition getting its head chopped off.

Borland C++ 4.0

This same set of keystrokes works in most versions of Borland C++. The easter egg lists the names of the extended Borland development team. Note that "B" and "I" stand for Borland International.

1. Select Help | About.
2. Hit Alt+B+I.

You'll get the screen shown in Figure 10-16.

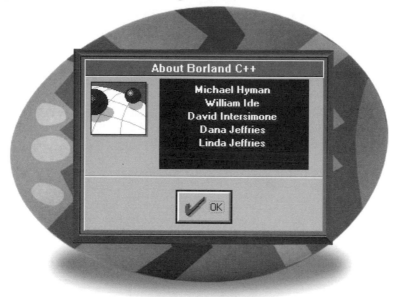

Figure 10-16: Borland C++ lists the various members of the development team.

Resource Workshop

To see a picture of the developer's hat, do the following:

1.   Select Help | About.

2.   Hit Alt+B+I.

You can see a picture of the result, as well as learn more Resource Workshop stories, in "The Resource Workshop Splash Screen" section later in this chapter.

Borland Delphi

The lead architect for Delphi is Anders Hejlsberg. He has been with Borland since its inception, and in fact he programmed the first version of Turbo Pascal. Anders got married during the middle of the development of Delphi. (Originally, he was going to get married after Delphi shipped. But the schedule slipped, and Anders made the wise decision not to slip his wedding along with the product.) During an all-hands meeting held on Borland's outdoor dining area, the Delphi team organized a bit of a wedding send-off. They dressed him in the first Borland t-shirt, made him put on a duck-shaped inner tube, and forced him to swim in the pond. The team slipped a photo of this grand event into the product, and only showed it to Anders after the product went to manufacturing.

To see it for yourself (figure 10-17), do the following:

1. Select Help | About.
2. Hit Alt+**A**+**N**+**D**.

Figure 10-17: See the architect for Delphi looking foolish and very wet.

Borland C++ for OS/2 Debugger

This is the only easter egg I know of that requires a bit of coordination and rhythm to expose. Turn down your radio, start humming, and do the following to see the list of developers:

1. Bring up the About box in the stand-alone GUI debugger for Borland C++ for OS/2.

2. Click anywhere on the About box bitmap, tapping out the rhythm to "shave and a hair cut, two bits."

Quicken for Windows 4.0

This works with Quicken for Windows 3.0, too. You'll see a screen with a windsurfer and the names of the developers (figure 10-18). Pressing **r** will cause a dragon to run across the screen. Pressing **v** will show you the version number.

1. Select Help | About.

2. Hit **s**.

3. Hit **r** to see the dragon.

4. Hit **v** to see the version number.

Figure 10-18: Here you can see a windsurfing board with the developers of Quicken for Windows.

Norton Desktop for Windows

In Norton Desktop for Windows, you can see pictures of the various developers. In addition, you'll see quotes such as, "A foolish consistency is the hobgoblin of little minds," and congratulations to some team members who had a baby. Here's how to find the egg.

1. Select Help | About.
2. Hold down the **N**, **D**, and **W** keys. (This stands for Norton Desktop for Windows, of course.)
3. Click three times on the icon.
4. Release the **N**, **D**, and **W** keys.

Ami Pro 2.0

The Ami developers have an obsession with Elvis, as you will see in this and the following easter egg. The Ami Pro 2.0 easter egg is very elaborate. It fills the screen with rapidly bouncing heads, each representing team members, as shown in Figure 10-19. One of the heads, which you can see towards the top in the middle of the screen, is named T. King. This stands for, obviously, The King, or Elvis. You can click on the heads to cause them to disappear.

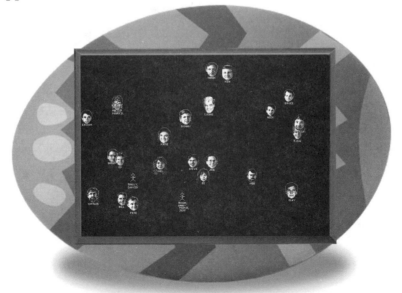

Figure 10-19: An easter egg that ain't nothing like a hound dog.

Here's how to find the easter egg.

1. Select Help | About Ami Pro.
2. While pressing Shift+Ctrl+Alt, press F7 and type **SPAM**.
3. Note the amount of available memory listed in the lower left corner.
4. Type the last number and the third-to-last number.
5. Release the Shift, Ctrl, and Alt keys.

Ami Pro 3.01

This easter egg is very similar to that in Ami Pro 2.0. Only, Elvis now chases a jelly donut (figure 10-20).

Figure 10-20: This time Elvis is hungry.

1. Select Tools | User Setup.
2. Change the user initials to GPB.
3. Select Help | About.
4. Holding Ctrl+Shift+Alt, press the function key that corresponds to the day of the week (where F1 = Sunday, F2 = Monday, F3 = Tuesday, and so on).

5. Type **SHANK**.

6. Release the Ctrl, Shift, and Alt keys.

CorelDraw 4.0

Speaking of Elvis, CorelDraw 4.0 has a great easter egg. It starts with a hot air balloon that you can control by pressing on the left and right mouse buttons or the up and down arrows. If you click on the right mouse button several times, Elvis will parachute from the sky, as shown in Figure 10-21. To see it, do the following:

1. Select Help | About CorelDraw.

2. Double-click on the hot air balloon icon.

3. Raise or lower the balloon by clicking the left and right mouse buttons.

4. Right-click several times.

Figure 10-21: CorelDraw 4.0 lets you control a hot air balloon and see Elvis.

HSC Digital Morph 1.1

The easter egg in this product shows a scanned picture of the developer (figure 10-22).

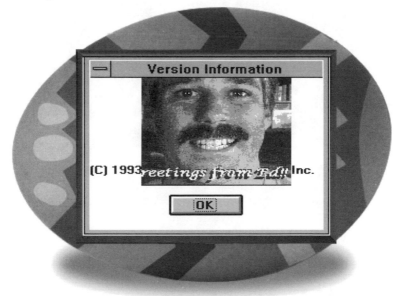

Figure 10-22: A picture of the developer of HSC Digital Morph appears in the About box.

1. Select Help | About.
2. Double-click in the About box.

SimEarth

In this easter egg, the earth appears with the names of the developers scrolling underneath (figure 10-23). The names are given a humorous twist, however. To find the easter egg, do the following:

1. Hold the Shift key.
2. Type **joke**.

Figure 10-23: The easter egg for SimEarth.

Macintosh Easter Eggs

Almost every operating system and every software product ever shipped has an easter egg somewhere. The Macintosh is no exception. In fact, Macintosh programmers seem particularly prone to including easter eggs in their products. Perhaps it is part of MacReligion.

Macintosh System 7 Finder

To see the easter egg in the Finder or Multifinder (figure 10-24) do the following:

1. Hold the Option and Command keys down.
2. Bring up the About box.

You'll see a mountain landscape with the names of developers below. Note that if you set the creation date of the Desktop Folder (an invisible folder) to any date after May 13, 1991, then you'll see the names of all Finder developers through Macintosh history.

Lisa Desktop Manager 1981-1983 by Dan Smith, Frank Ludolph a

Figure 10-24: The development staff for the Finder.

Caches 7.0.1

You can see the name of the Caches developer by doing the following:

1. Hold down the Option key.
2. Click on the version number in the upper right corner.

Color Control Panel 7.0

Dean Yu and Vincent Lo wrote this program. Here's how to see their names (figure 10-25).

1. Hold down the Option key.
2. Click on the sample text a few times.

Memory Control Panel 7.0

In this application the easter egg appears as a series of pop-up menus. Instead of selecting a swap file, you'll see a list of the developers. The names are shown in a cascading menu, with amusing quotes for each developer. Some of the quotes are quite strange. To see them (figure 10-26), do the following:

1. Turn on virtual memory.

2. Hold down the Option key.

3. Click on the pop-up menu used for choosing the swap file hard drive.

Figure 10-25: The color control panel easter egg says that Dean and Vincent wrote the program.

Figure 10-26: Here you can see a comment from one of the programmers.

Monitors Control Panel 7.0

This easter egg begins by listing the programmers. If you hit the Option key after the easter egg appears, the face will stick out its tongue. If you hit the Option key more times, the names rearrange and some of the first names get replaced with "Blue" or "Meanies" (figure 10-27).

1. Click the version number.
2. Hold down the mouse button and hit the Option key a few times.

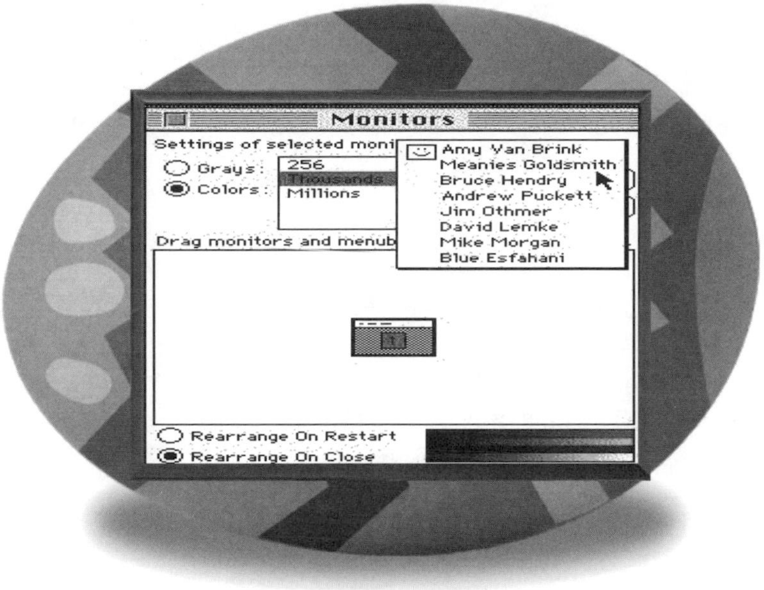

Figure 10-27: If you click the Option key enough times, the Blue Meanies come forth.

Microsoft Excel 3.0 for the Macintosh

Here's how you see the credit screen for Excel.

1. Open a new worksheet.
2. Select a cell.
3. Select Format | Style.
4. Make the style **EXCEL**.
5. Open the About box.
6. Click on the Excel symbol.

The Resource Workshop Splash Screen

Easter eggs aren't the only source of fun in applications. Many splash screens contain interesting images as well. Resource Workshop is a prime example of this.

Resource Workshop is a program for editing the user interface of Windows programs. It ships with a variety of Borland development tools, including Borland C++. Resource Workshop has gone through several splash screens. The version of Resource Workshop that shipped with Borland C++ 3.0 contained two different splash screens. Both were based on the Jeff Beck *Guitar Workshop* album cover, appropriately changed to show modifying computer programs rather than musical instruments. (Why is the splash screen based on the *Guitar Workshop* cover? Not only is it a pun on Resource Workshop, but the graphic designer and product manager were hard-core, long-haired guitar players.)

The VGA screen depicted a woman (Figure 10-28), while the EGA screen showed a man (Figure 10-29). I once overheard two people arguing over whether the splash screen showed a man or a woman. The person who had the VGA system told the other guy that he really needed to get away from the computer more often if he didn't know what a woman looked like. Neither knew that they were looking at different images, and both were convinced the other was crazy.

Notice the hat hung on the wall in both figures. The programmer who wrote Resource Workshop always wore a hat that looked like this. In fact, for Borland C++ 3.1, the splash screen was changed because some customers found the picture of the woman offensive. The new splash screen was a ray-traced green planet. But you can still find a hat in the background constellations.

In Borland C++ 4.0, the humorous splash screen was removed completely, leaving a tame corporate screen with the Resource Workshop icon.

Figure 10-28: The Resource Workshop VGA splash screen.

Figure 10-29: The Resource Workshop EGA splash screen. (Figure caption. Place under figure.)

Nonetheless, the hat remains, this time in an easter egg. If you bring up the About box and hit Alt+B+I, you will once again see the hat, as shown in Figure 10-30.

Suitably enough, when Peter Eden, who wrote Resource Workshop, left Borland, he bought several of his trademark hats and gave them out to his friends.

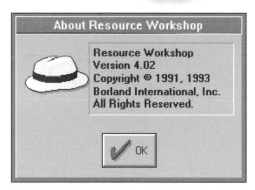

Figure 10-30: The hat returns in the Resource Workshop easter egg.

Microsoft Word 4.0

The easter egg for Word lists the testers.

1. Select About Microsoft Word.

2. Hold the Command key.

3. Click on the icon.

Simple Player for QuickTime 1.0

In this easter egg, you'll see a picture of two cats (figure 10-31).

1. Hold down the Option key.

2. Select About Simple Player.

Figure 10-31: This easter egg shows two cats.

QuicKeys 2

If you wait long enough, this easter egg will show an Energizer-type bunny walking across the screen beating a drum.

1. Open the macro definition window.

2. Click on the logo.

Wolfenstein 3-D

When you install Wolfenstein 3-D, there is a help file that shows swastikas to the left and right of the Wolfenstein 3-D logo. If you run a special program called !Help when you move the mouse over one of the swastikas, you will see this message:

"The reversed swastika, the symbol of menace and oppression."

If you repeat this five times, the message changes to this:

"The reversed swastika, still the symbol of menace and oppression."

And by the seventh time, you'll see the following:

"Is it:

      a) Quite a nice, flowery sort of symbol,

      b) Not a very nice symbol at all, really,

      c) The symbol of menace and oppression or

      d) Geoff Hurst in the 1966 World Cup?"

After the eighth time you see the final message:

"(You can tell I used to write adventure games)"

MacPaint 2.0

The very first run of MacPaint contained a painting of a nude, zebra-striped woman. It was quickly removed. If you have one of the early copies, try the following:

1. Hold the Tab and Space keys.
2. Select About MacPaint.

Newton Easter Eggs

Here are some things you can try out on your Newton. Note that once again, Elvis lives on through computers.

Displaying a Newt instead of a Lightbulb

1. Go to the Extras drawer.
2. Tap Preferences.
3. Tap Personal.
4. Type **Graceland** as the country option.
5. Restart.

Finding Elvis

1. Go to the Notes section.
2. Type **find Elvis**.
3. Highlight "find Elvis" by holding the pen down a second and drawing across.
4. Tap the Assist option.

And Yet More Easter Eggs

Just in case you think Windows, OS/2, and Mac users are the only ones who can see easter eggs, here are some other easter eggs you can run into on other systems.

Lotus Improv 1.0 for NeXT

To see a man with big bug eyes, do the following:

1. Go to the Info Panel.
2. Hold down Shift, Alt, and Command and then click the mouse in the space to the left of the Improv title.

3B1 PC

On the AT&T 7300/3B1 machines, type the following at the command prompt to see a list of the author's names:

.!.

Did You Know?

High Rollers

A number of people on Microsoft's OS/2 team (and thus, later on, the NT team) were avid gamblers. Their ringleader, Chuck Whitmer, created an extremely complex set of equations for modeling the way six-deck black-jack worked. From that, he and his group created a very sophisticated counting scheme. They would practice gambling late into the night, and make jaunts to casinos where they often played under false names.

They became extremely talented at the skill, and often received free airline tickets, fancy hotel rooms, and meals.

PCs for Guns

The Boston Computer Exchange started a program where it donated computers to schools in return for students' weapons. The type of computer donated depended on the type of weapon received. Several police stations have taken a similar approach.

Meanwhile, an ad in the Microsoft company classifieds offered to exchange a bulletproof vest for computer equipment.

Shoplifting

A ring of shoplifters stole $1.6 million in merchandise from Egghead between 1991 and 1993.

A Pregnant Pause

Before Bill Gates started Microsoft, he worked for a number of companies debugging their systems by trying to crash them. He was famous for cracking a Control Data Corporation computer. When he was caught and sternly reprimanded, he stopped using computers for nine months.

Activision Smurfs Game

Allegedly the Smurfs game has a bit of a naughty easter egg in it. Here, if you have successfully made it through the game to where Smurfette waits for you at the top of the screen, wait a long time instead of jumping to her platform. She supposedly will throw off her clothes to "convince" you to jump to her platform.

Activision Pitfall: The Mayan Adventure

Here again naughtiness strikes. If you leave the game on pause for over 20 minutes, the hero of the game will turn his back to the screen and pee into the bushes.

HP 150

If you do the following, the HP 150 will print "My mind is going..." Type the following:

<esc>&a?

This will also work on HP 2625 and HP 2628 terminals.

"If this product comes out with severe flaws, we're dead."

— Marc Sokol, Computer Associates
In suggesting that CA Visual Objects had better be bug free.

That's Not a Bug, That's a Feature

What happens after the Easter eggs have been added, the final touches are made, and thousands of units are shrink-wrapped and sent out the door? The product enters its most important phase: consumer testing. This is different from the beta test cycle. This is when testers (uh, I really mean *customers*) go to the local computer store, buy a product, and try it out for real. Now, no one will ever officially call this a test stage. But it is impossible to find all of the bugs in a product, so it is not until it hits the street that the strange bugs start to appear. This is also the time that people find and complain about the bugs the company didn't get around to fixing.

Vendors do a number of things to minimize the impact of bugs. Some approaches, such as releasing work-arounds, extensive technical support notes, and bug lists directly address the problems consumers face. Other techniques focus on market perception. For example, it's a well-known fact that it often takes three revisions for a product to stabilize. To get around this, vendors number products starting with 3.0 or greater. Windows NT started as Version 3.0, and dBASE for Windows started as version 5.0. While the official reason is that this puts the numbering in line with products on other platforms (e.g., Windows 3.0 or dBASE for DOS), there is certainly a lot of psychology behind the number selection.

This is also a favorite trick of startup companies. Just as serial numbers and check numbers usually begin with numbers greater than 1000, startups will begin their products with versions such as 2.7. That way, customers feel as if there have been several releases and they aren't guinea pigs. It also suggests that the startup has been around a lot longer than it really has.

Until a product has gone through several release cycles and the various kinks, shortcomings, and bugs are worked out, users are left finding a lot of glitches. At a software development trade show in Australia, a Microsoft speaker once plugged the Microsoft Test product, indicating that it allowed vendors to try out a product, fix bugs, try it again, fix bugs, and finally send it out when it was ready. The audience burst out in laughter when another panelist quickly retorted, "Just like Windows 1.0, Windows 2.0, and Windows 3.0."

The word *bug* was used to describe a mechanical defect by well-known inventors such as Thomas Edison as far back as the late 1800s. Popular computer legend has it, though, that the term really took off in September 1945, when Grace Hopper found that a problem in the Harvard University Mark I computer was caused by a moth. The moth, which had shorted the circuit, remains today in Admiral Hopper's logbook.

Since then, there have been a huge number of bugs in software products. In fact, legend also has it that there is a three-line mainframe assembly language program produced by IBM that went through several bug-fix releases. If it is hard to get three lines correct, imagine what it is like trying to get two million lines correct. Especially when those millions of lines need to work on thousands of different computer configurations.

It is no surprise, then, that there are a lot of gotchas. Bugs have run the gamut from the infamous Pentium division error, to bugs that only show up on obsolete hardware under obscure conditions, to bugs that are more a result of programming shortcomings.

For an example of the latter, many mainframe programs are written assuming that the first two numbers of the year are "19." They don't know how to print year numbers greater than 1999. When the year 2000 comes, there will be many programs, whose authors have long since retired or been forgotten, that suddenly fail.

Nerd Humor: Pentium Jokes

After Intel faced severe embarrassment over the math flaws in the Pentium chip, numerous jokes popped up. Following are some of them:

Q: What is the successor to the RU-486 birth control drug?
A: The RU-Pentium; it prevents cells from dividing properly.

Q: How many Pentium designers does it take to screw in a lightbulb?
A: 1.99904274017, but that's close enough for nontechnical people.

Q: What's another name for the "Intel Inside" sticker they put on Pentiums?
A: Warning label.

Q: Why didn't Intel call the Pentium the 586?
A: Because they added 486 and 100 on the first Pentium and got 585.999983605.

Q: What do you get when you calculate your Intuit tax return on a Pentium computer?
A. Audited.

Q: What do you get when you cross a Pentium PC with a research grant?
A: A mad scientist.

Q: What do you call a series of FDIV instructions on a Pentium?
A: Successive approximations.

How Many Bugs Are There?

Every product has bugs. No matter how carefully it is tested, there is bound to be something that is forgotten or overlooked. It is simply a matter of statistics. To begin, computer programs contain branches. In other words, there may be several different paths through a particular program. For example, take the program Leather Goddesses of Phobos. The user starts by walking into either a men's or women's bathroom. Depending upon which bathroom the user walks into, the user is assumed to be male or female. A different set of code executes in each case. This is called "branching" or "executing a conditional."

Once a user starts executing down one path of a program, there could be several other branches. It is similar to driving, in that there are many turns one can take. Each turn can lead to more turns. Sometimes the roads are clear. And other times, users run into traffic and potholes.

Suppose a company has a program with 10,000 lines of code. It could very easily have 100 conditional statements in that code. In the worst case, that could lead to 2^{100} or over a quadrillion quadrillion different possible paths. And that is just the tip of the iceberg.

Borland Bug Zappers

Beta testers are very important for finding bugs in products. This t-shirt was created for the extended QA team—the beta testers and others who helped find and track down bugs in Borland's C++ product. It features a lineup of hideous-looking bugs with Latin names. Going left to right, top to bottom, they are

Latin name	Actual error
Vagus Use Error	Unrecognizable Application Error
Faulticus	G.P. Fault
Stacus Flauae	Stack Overflow
Screenus Endae	Hanging Screen Shutdown: end
Floatus Pontus	Floating-Point Error: Domain
Non Systema	Cannot Run Command Com System Halted
Exitus Bugae	E. X. Bug
Assertae Fallia	Assertion Failure
Crasius Bukius	Crash Bug

200

Trying to test that many combinations is impossible. So testers break it into smaller pieces. If instead of testing the 100 conditions as a whole, they test each condition by itself, all of a sudden there are only 200 tests to run. That is a much easier task. But, knowing that the individual parts work doesn't mean that they function when put together. After all, connecting a perfectly working television set to a perfectly functional set of wheels doesn't create a perfectly working car.

Most software programs, however, are far more than 10,000 lines of code. For example, WordPerfect 6.1 for Windows is over 1,000,000 lines of code. So there tend to be thousands of branches in computer programs.

Testers use many techniques to find bugs. Baseline analysis determines a set of tests that should exercise the code within each branch, though not under each unique condition. Coverage analysis shows whether tests have, in fact, at least executed every piece of code. Complexity metrics help determine the complexity of the code. Normal-condition testing checks the typical paths. Edge-condition testing tests for strange usage. And so on. But no matter what, there is no way to test how the software will behave under every circumstance.

The problem is even more complex. With sophisticated, complex operating systems such as Windows and OS/2, several programs may be running at once. So a program might work fine by itself, but bomb abysmally when used with other programs. Or a program might work well unless you are low on memory or disk space. So testers try system-wide testing, in which applications are used with other applications running; and stress testing, in which applications are run under extreme situations.

Furthermore, there are many different types of hardware available. Each unique combination of hard drives, CD-ROMs, disk drives, memory sizes, CPUs, graphics cards, network cards, machine BIOS, keyboard types, and device drivers generates a particular environment. A program that works perfectly well on a 50 MHz Pentium with a Matrox Marvel II card with a BIOS dated May 1995, might not run at all on the same machine with a differently dated graphics card. Or it may not run on a 486 with a VGA card.

That's why beta testing is critical, because it exposes a program to all types of usage behaviors, hardware sets, and application combinations.

Between beta testers and in-house testing, vendors end up running hundreds of thousands of tests on products. But that still is not enough to find all of the bugs. The problem is complicated by the trouble of finding good beta testers. It can cost vendors several hundred dollars per beta tester. After all, they need to have a top-notch support person handle the incoming messages, they need to devote QA resources, they need to provide many beta copies of a product (which are very expensive to produce in low quantities), and then they often throw in a free product at the end. Yet, for that price, only 10 percent of the beta testers end up consistently reporting bugs. So if you send a product out to 200 people, maybe 20 provide really good feedback. And typically, the feedback comes late in the cycle. For example, people who provide add-on products often participate in the beta cycles of every release of every product for which they've created an add-on. They realize that early releases will have lots of bugs. And since they are short on time, they don't devote any cycles to testing the products until the late betas (sometimes called *gammas)*. Of course, once they start testing, they immediately complain loudly about conspiracies to break their products. To get around this, vendors sometimes call the second beta the *final beta*, hoping to pressure testers into giving more feedback.

Even though completely testing a product is a Herculean task, vendors (and beta testers) find huge numbers of bugs. A Lotus Development Corporation product manager said that Lotus typically found 5,000 bugs per product. Over 30,000 bugs were logged against NT during its development phase. This isn't quite as scary as it sounds, since large products go through hundreds of internal revisions before they are released, each of which fixes some bugs and often adds a few more.

Great Quotes:

Ignore These Bugs

Bugs that "only happen in the middle of the night when Venus is aligned with Mars" were ignored, commented a Lotus executive regarding its quality control for products. Statements such as these are often *doublespeak*, meaning that a lot of bugs were kept in.

Clocks and watches are another favorite giveaway in the computer industry. Shown here is a Microsoft NT watch, a wind-up alarm clock from Borland's office in Spain, and a dBASE stopwatch. The best thing about computer watches is that they rarely keep good time. The dBASE clock, of course, required constant maintenance (winding) to keep it working. The NT watch (shown here) and OS/2 watch both ran slow, leading to many jokes about the operating systems they promoted.

Of course, finding bugs is one thing, and fixing them is another. Corporations can't fix every bug. After all, if they tried to, they would never be able to ship. So vendors go through the difficult process of trying to figure out what to ship and what to fix.

What Do We Fix?

This is what it is typically like during the tail end of a product cycle — the time when a team determines which bugs get fixed and which don't. Picture the following scene. It is 8:00 at night. Programmers, development managers, testers, technical support members, and a few product managers fill a cramped room. A third of the people in the room have been up the whole night before fixing bugs. People are tired and not everyone has had a shower. A few boxes of half-eaten pizza litter the table. Everyone gathers around the bug database to discuss the bugs.

Unless the bug came from an outside program, the bug is probably described by someone who knows the innards of the system. How that effects the outside world might not be clear. Even if the bug is reported from the outside, it might be isolated to a very specific piece of code. Once again, it can be hard to tell how a specific bug would effect an application.

Let's see what it is like to participate in the meeting:

Tester: The automatic scaling of an embedded graphic is incorrectly adjusted for the previous paragraph spacing if the spacing changes between the paragraph before the graphic and after the graphic through a predefined style, instead of through an actual character-specific override of the default style.

Programmer: Oh, yeah, I remember that. It's this funny condition where you make your own styles instead of using the built-in buttons, and then you drop in a graphic, but only if the graphic is in a certain format, and you are pasting it with OLE instead of as a bitmap, and I think you might only see it if there isn't any text behind it.

Tester: Yeah, it is a pretty obscure one, but I think it is important to get it right.

Product Manager: But will the customer ever see it? I mean, is it easy to find? Will we be embarrassed?

Tester: Hmm, says here a user found it when using our product and our spreadsheet together. Let's try it out here. (Shows the bug.)

Product Manager: Sh**. How much work is it to fix?

Programmer: A couple of hours, probably. It won't destabilize anything.

Development Manager: Great, let's fix it.

Of course, such conversations sometimes conclude in a slightly different way. Let's look at another hypothetical discussion:

Tester: Hey, here is a bizarre one. Using full floating-point mathematics, creating the following in your spreadsheet: =A1-(A1/B1)*B1. It works just fine when you put the value 4100 in cell A1 and 5400 in cell B1. In fact, it works for every number we tried, except if you set the cell A1 to 4195835 and the cell B1 to 3145727, you get 256.

Product Manager: Who would ever type in numbers like that? That seems pretty questionable.

Development Manager: It's even stupider. Why would you use such a formula? That just evaluates to A1–A1.

Product Manager: Yeah, you're right. So you have to type some very strange numbers into a brain-dead formula.

Developer: I don't know. Maybe I should look at it.

Product Manager: Come on. We are three weeks late with the product as it is. We have a million-dollar ad campaign that kicked off last week, and people are screaming for the product. I know we should have a great product, but who would ever do this? We have to get the product out. We have 30 more bugs to go through tonight. How many more all-nighters do we need to pull?

Developer: OK. Let's defer it.

Sound strange? Would you have made the same calls? The first scenario is pretty similar to what happened with a bug in Word for Windows 6.0 that was reported by a customer and subsequently fixed in a point release. The latter scenario describes the infamous Pentium bug. Of course, these discussions never really took place, but similar ones do.

So Then What Happens?

It is impossible to fix every bug. So development teams decide which ones to leave in. And of course, they leave in those that they haven't yet found — because after all, they don't know what they are. Once the product is in the hands of the customers, the customers find lots of bugs, call up their friendly technical support department, and report them. And if there are enough bugs, or there are enough people who find bugs, or the bugs are sensational, news spreads.

At that point, vendors do a number of things: belittle the bugs (no one will ever run across it), ignore the bugs (they are small cosmetic defects, nothing out of the ordinary), promise to fix them (they'll be taken care of in the next release, thanks for letting us know), fix them (a fix is now available on our BBS), or, in extreme cases, send out a free update or issue a recall.

Sending out free updates can cost hundreds of thousands of dollars, or in some cases, even several million dollars. And it is almost impossible to fix single bugs and quickly send out a patch, because vendors want to make sure that the bugs they fix don't cause other bugs to appear.

Because of this huge expense, most vendors simply collect bug reports, maintain them in a bug database, and try to fix them in a later release. Some vendors make their bug releases public, figuring it is better for a customer to see what is wrong and be able to adjust for it than to be befuddled. Others keep the bug lists private, so the competition doesn't know where to poke and customers don't become aware of bugs they otherwise wouldn't find, and also because it takes a large amount of time and people to produce a bug list that anyone except the product developers can understand.

NuMega is famous for their debuggers and funny t-shirts. This shirt is no exception, making light of NuMega's penguin mascot. It is available on boxer shorts as well.

Some of the Classic Bugs

Although there are thousands and thousands of bugs shipping today, there are some bug stories that stand out as more sensational than the rest. The following sections detail some of these high-profile bug stories and how the vendors dealt with the bugs.

Great Quotes: All Apologies

"I am truly sorry for the anxiety created among you by our floating-point issue." —Andy Grove, President of Intel

Intel's Failed Strategy of Divide and Conquer

Bugs in chips are not a new phenomenon. Just as with software, it is safe to assume all chips have bugs in them. For example, the 386 had a multiplication bug that forced a slight redesign, and the 486 had a division bug that was silently fixed. Motorola has recalled chips. Cyrix encountered a nasty floating-point bug with one of its runs of its 486DX and 486DX2 chips.

The chip bug that gained the most notoriety was that of Intel's Pentium. Roughly two million Pentium chips shipped with a bug where division of certain numbers would return incorrect results. The bug was discovered by a mathematics professor who reported it on the Internet. While the bug itself was relatively minor, the PR disaster that surrounded it was not.

The bug resulted from five missing values in a 1,066-entry lookup table used to speed division. For these entries, where the table should have contained a 2, it contained a 0 instead. It would have been easy to check, but the engineers had mathematically proven that they only needed to check half of the values in the table. Unfortunately, their mathematical proof had a mistake in it, and they really needed to check more of the table. While they also ran several billion random equations through the chip to check the results, that wasn't enough. In fact, it would have taken roughly nine billion tests to have a chance of finding the bug.

Intel began by denying that it was an important bug, and claimed it would only be encountered once in 27,000 years by the average user. IBM, perhaps anxious to push the PowerPC chip, claimed it would occur every 24 days and halted building Pentium-based machines, expecting other vendors to follow. None did, and the Pentium continued to sell well, but publicity about the bug mounted.

Regardless of the probability of actually encountering the bug, the issue was that it was a real bug with great potential for making users feel uncomfortable with the results of calculations. To fix the problem, Intel initially said it would replace chips for free for anyone who could prove that they were impacted by the bug. Proving this could be somewhat difficult. It would require showing Intel proprietary code, or otherwise jumping through hoops. This angered users and added fuel to the flames.

Vendors such as Microsoft rushed to provide work-around fixes in operating systems and compilers. The work-arounds, though, causes applications to ignore the floating-point processor, which can dramatically reduce application performance.

Eventually, Intel ended up making a large public apology, and volunteered to replace all Pentium chips for free. It then budgeted a $475,000,000 write-off to cover the cost. Despite all the furor, few customers returned chips. Financial institutions exchanged roughly 25 percent of their chips, while only 1–3 percent of the average consumers exchanged chips.

More Pentium Jokes

Top Ten New Intel Slogans for the Pentium

9.9999973251	It's a FLAW, Dammit, Not a Bug
8.9999163362	It's Close Enough; We Say So
7.9999414610	Nearly 300 Correct Opcodes
6.9999831538	You Don't Need to Know What's Inside
5.9999835137	Redefining the PC—and Mathematics As Well
4.9999999021	We Fixed It, Really
3.9998245917	Division Considered Harmful
2.9991523619	Why Do You Think They Call It *Floating* Point?
1.9999103517	We're Looking for a Few Good Flaws
0.9999999998	The Errata Inside

Here Comes the Tax Man

Intuit is the dominant vendor of personal finance software. At the beginning of the 1995 tax return season, users found a nasty bug in Intuit's MacInTax Personal 1040 software. When numbers were imported into MacInTax from Quicken, which Intuit also makes, the thirtieth entry would sometimes be lost. As a result, tax returns contained errors. A number of users, in fact, got hit by the IRS for penalties resulting from bugs in the tax return software, or from bugs that also impacted Quicken's other tax products, TurboTax and TurboTax for Windows.

Revelation of the bug shortly followed the Pentium fireworks, so Intuit adopted a very aggressive program of public apology. The President of the company immediately offered a free upgrade and volunteered to pay any IRS penalties, including interest, that resulted from the error. To cover this, Intuit took a one-time, 1.3-million-dollar write-off.

Great Quotes: MacInTax

MacInTax, a tax program from Intuit, caused much grief after several bugs came to light that would cause incorrect tax returns. This forced a major write-off for Intuit. Asked how the errors could have occurred, Intuit responded, "It's programming."

Leave Lots of Room for WordStar

WordStar had a number of bugs, but perhaps the most famous one occurred when a user tried to save files to a floppy disk. Remember, of course, that hard disks were rare and hideously expensive during WordStar's heyday, so almost everyone saved their files on floppies. That worked great, unless the floppy didn't have enough free space on it. In this case, WordStar would crash. The user would be left at a DOS prompt, and the precious document would be gone.

This created a bit of an after-market. For example, there was a product called Failsafe that sprung up, which, among other things, would search through memory for a WordStar document. It could then save the memory block to a file. That way, you could restart WordStar, load in the file, and get most, if not all, of the information back.

No More UAEs

Windows 3.0 was a dramatic improvement over Windows 2.0. With so many changes, however, came a lot of instability. Windows 3.0 was famous for UAEs (*unrecoverable application errors*). These would sporadically appear, forcing users to exit Windows and in many cases lose what they were working on.

Microsoft fixed many of the UAEs in Windows 3.1, in part by providing stricter parameter checking to prevent bad system calls. And, in part, it got rid of UAEs by renaming them to GP faults (or *general protection faults*). It could then safely claim that users would no longer encounter annoying UAEs.

Nerd Humor:

Kosher Commands

If your program attempted to access memory that it wasn't allowed to or otherwise did something illegal, Windows 3.0 displayed an error message that said, "Unauthorized Application Error." During the beta process, this message said, "This command is traif" instead. *Traif* is a Yiddish word meaning that something isn't kosher; hence, that the command that was encountered was not legal.

Did You Know?

Nuts

On August 1, 1994, the NASDAQ exchange was shut down when a squirrel chewed through a power line and the backup power system didn't kick in. A squirrel took down NASDAQ in 1987 as well.

Thank Heavens for Reviewers

This is a classic story of vendor mishap. Symantec was in the middle of manufacturing Symantec Team Enterprise Developer 2.0, and had already sent numerous copies out to reviewers in the press. A reviewer from *InfoWorld* found a curious thing when he tried to install the product: it wouldn't run because a DLL was missing. (A *DLL* is a special file that contains code. Windows programs are broken into a main program — the one that you run — and a set of DLLs that are called by the main program. Each DLL contains code that the main program needs. Breaking a program into DLLs saves memory and space. If a program can't find the DLLs that it needs, it won't run.)

It turned out that if you had run an earlier beta or an earlier version of Team Enterprise Developer, the DLL in question would already be on your system. But if you installed onto a machine that had never seen Team Enterprise Developer before, you wouldn't have the DLL. And the program would fail. Symantec apparently didn't do enough testing of its installation procedure, so none of the duplicated disks would work on customer machines unless the customer also happened to be a beta tester or user of an earlier version.

After being notified, Symantec had to halt production, add the file to the disk set, and reduplicate the disks. Fortunately for Symantec, the bug was found before the product went out the door. Symantec was embarrassed in the press, but not nearly as much as if it had shipped thousands of units, only to have to send out free disks to everyone who bought the product.

Nerd Humor: Viruses

A *computer virus* is a rogue program that infects your computer and then causes some sort of malfunction. Virus activity ranges from benignly posting messages to erasing everything on hard drives. The following mail circulated on the Net for a bit, speculating what some mythical viruses would do.

AT&T VIRUS: Every three minutes, it tells you what great service you are getting.

MCI VIRUS: Every three minutes, it reminds you that you're paying too much for the AT&T virus.

PAUL REVERE VIRUS: This revolutionary virus does not horse around. It warns you of impending hard disk attack—once if by LAN, twice if by C:>.

POLITICALLY CORRECT VIRUS: Never calls itself a "virus," but instead refers to itself as an "electronic microorganism."

RIGHT-TO-LIFE VIRUS: Won't allow you to delete a file, regardless of how old it is. If you attempt to erase a file, it requires you to first see a counselor about possible alternatives.

TED TURNER VIRUS: Colorizes your monochrome monitor.

ARNOLD SCHWARZENEGGER VIRUS: Terminates and stays resident. It'll be back.

DAN QUAYLE VIRUS: Their is sumthing rong wit your komputer, ewe jsut cant figyour out watt!

GOVERNMENT ECONOMIST VIRUS: Nothing works, but all your diagnostic software says everything is fine.

FEDERAL BUREAUCRAT VIRUS: Divides your hard disk into hundreds of little units, each of which does practically nothing, but all of which claim to be the most important part of your computer.

GALLUP VIRUS: 60% of the PCs infected will lose 38% of their data 14% of the time (plus or minus a 3.5% margin of error).

TEXAS VIRUS: Makes sure that it's bigger than any other file.

ADAM AND EVE VIRUS: Takes a couple of bytes out of your Apple.

AIRLINE VIRUS: You're in Dallas, but your data is in Singapore.

ELVIS VIRUS: Your computer gets fat, slow, and lazy, then self-destructs, only to resurface at shopping malls and service stations across rural America.

A Vice-Presidential Pardon

Microsoft is the dominant vendor of application software for the Macintosh, selling roughly $400 million dollars of Macintosh software a year. The release of Word 6.0 for the Macintosh, however, was not one of Microsoft's highlights. It caused enormous flames, as it was dramatically slower in performance than the previous version and very buggy. For example, one magazine benchmark determined that counting the number of words in a document was almost 11 times slower than in the previous version, Word 5.1. Even starting up the program could take several minutes on certain Macintoshes.

Coming at the wane of the Apple-Microsoft look-and-feel lawsuit, many Macintosh customers claimed it was a conspiracy to hurt the Macintosh. Reviews were negative, with headlines such as, "Pass the Cranberry Sauce, This One's a Turkey."

Microsoft provided public apologies from a Vice President and blamed the performance degradation on its technique of using common code across Windows and Macintosh versions. To keep customers happy, it extended the money-back-guarantee period and provided a free update to all registered customers.

How Much Is that Bug in the Peachtree for Windows?

Peachtree Software has been plagued with problems in its recent accounting software. For example, one user tracked his inventory using Peachtree software, only to find that a camera he purchased for $325 was listed as costing him $4,567,896. Numerous users found similar calculation errors.

Peachtree shipped at least four maintenance releases to try to fix bugs. Unfortunately, many of these releases caused more problems than they fixed. For example, one maintenance release, instead of fixing the aforementioned bug, simply warned customers not to do certain things that would cause the bug to appear. Another fix, which Peachtree sent for free to 100,000 customers, caused many problems with saving data.

It Works Fine If You Don't Have a Hard Disk

During one of the version 3.x upgrades of IBM DOS, there was a bug that prevented DOS from properly understanding the boot partition information. As a result, if you upgraded to it on a machine with a hard drive, you could wipe out all information on the hard drive. This bug was found at the last minute, forcing IBM to pull 300,000 copies of DOS from manufacturing. Fortunately, the bug never made it to the customers' hands.

Just Don't Try to Install It

IBM experienced numerous problems with OS/2 Warp 3.0. Most notably, users had trouble installing the system. For example, it wouldn't install on some models of IBM's own ThinkPad computers. It wouldn't install on certain machines using IBM's 486SLC chip. And it had trouble on Gateway 2000 systems with Phoenix, AMI, and Micronics BIOSs, certain IBM PS/2 systems with a variety of CD-ROM drives, systems with Sound Blaster cards, and systems with Media Vision ProAudio Spectrum 16s.

Not only did the shipping version have installation woes, but the product was held from release for several days when a number of testers and reviewers found an installation bug that prevented it from installing on almost every computer. With great embarrassment, IBM acknowledged and fixed the problem before too many customers ran into it.

Follow These Instructions Carefully

When Windows NT or OS/2 crash, they tend to crash with a fury, bringing up a screen full of hex numbers describing the state of the machine when it died. The background of such windows is blue, leading to the name "blue screen" or "blue screen of death." You can use this as a verb, as in, "I blue-screened NT this morning." While blue screens are rare, they are alarming when they occur. Usually they contain a message suggesting how to resolve the problem. One NT blue screen apparently says: "Reboot your machine. Do not reboot your machine."

Did You Know?

Unsportsmanlike Conduct

At a trade show, IBM's Lee Reiswig deliberately crashed Microsoft Windows to show that it was unstable, suggesting that anyone who needed a crash-proof system should switch to OS/2. Not to be outdone, in a press tour that followed Reiswig's speech, Microsoft's Steve Ballmer demonstrated several ways to crash the allegedly crash-proof OS/2 2.0.

And You Thought the Postal Service Had Problems

Prodigy upgraded its email software in March 1995, so as to increase performance of sending mail to and from the Internet. Unfortunately, the upgrade had a slight bug in it, and during the few hours the new software was active, over 5,000 messages were lost or sent to the wrong recipient. Prodigy quickly found and fixed the bug, and posted numerous apologies to its two million subscribers.

Buggy Databases

Early versions of Microsoft Access were notoriously buggy. In fact, Access even crashed twice when it was launched at Comdex. Microsoft wasn't the only company plagued with database woes. Ashton-Tate's dBASE IV (the last version before being acquired by Borland) was so buggy that it took several years for dBASE to lose its reputation of being plagued by problems.

Some Altqweront with System 7.5

Apple's System 7.5 has a number of interesting quirks. One famous problem is that if a user accidentally pushes Command+Option+Spacebar in an application, the keyboard layout can switch from a U.S. layout to an international layout, resulting in very unexpected results when typing.

Shocking, Simply Shocking

IBM recalled 32,000 power adapters for ThinkPads after discovering they could cause an electrical shock.

More Shocking News

HP has had a number of problems with printers, and has withdrawn RuggedWriters, LaserJets, and InkJets. It sent 1.5 million repair kits to inkjet owners, to keep older inkjet rubber rollers from failing to grab paper in the DeskJet 550C, 560C, 520, 510, and DeskWriter 520 and 510 printers.

HP also recalled 10,000 OfficeJet printer-fax-copiers to prevent an electrical shock that could occur. During a particular manufacturing run, some metal shavings got into some of the power supplies. If the printer were not in a grounded outlet, someone touching a metal part of the printer could get shocked.

Toshiba T3400

A keyboard controller chip problem in some Toshiba T3400 chips caused characters to be dropped at random when a person typed very quickly.

Of course, it could have just been a prank.

Go Out for a Long Bomb

Federal Express introduced software to help customers ship and track packages. It advertised the software during the 1995 SuperBowl. Unfortunately, the program had a bug that would delete all of a customer's data on February 1. Federal Express sent fixes to the 13,000 people who had the software. The question is, did it FedEx the fix disk?

Technology to the Rescue

The Envoy PDA, from Motorola and General Magic, had a nasty bug in which, after periods of heavy use, the system slowed down so much as to be unusable. The vendors were very proactive about announcing that they found this bug, and, via the wireless modem in the PDA and the built-in Telescript scripting language, they created a patch and automatically sent it to all the PDAs.

Nerd Humor: What If Operating Systems Were Airlines?

This is an operating system discussion that circulated on the Internet.

DOS Air: Passengers walk out onto the runway, grab hold of the plane, push it until it gets in the air, hop on, then jump off when it hits the ground. They grab the plane again, push it back into the air, hop on, jump off . . .

Mac Airways: The cashiers, flight attendants, and pilots all look the same, talk the same, and act the same. When you ask them questions about the flight, they reply that you don't want to know, don't need to know, and would you please return to your seat and watch the movie?

Windows Airlines: The terminal is neat and clean, the attendants courteous, the pilots capable. The fleet of Lear jets the carrier operates is immense. Your jet takes off without a hitch, pushes above the clouds and, at 20,000 feet, explodes without warning.

OS/2 Skyways: The terminal is almost empty—only a few prospective passengers mill about. The announcer says that a flight has just departed, although no planes appear to be on the runway. Airline personnel apologize profusely to customers in hushed voices, pointing from time to time to the sleek, powerful jets outside. They tell each passenger how great the flight will be on these new jets and how much safer it will be than Windows Airlines, but they have to wait a little longer for the technicians to finish the flight systems. Maybe until mid-1995. Maybe longer.

Fly Windows NT: Passengers carry their seats out onto the tarmac and place them in the outline of a plane. They sit down, flap their arms, and make jet swooshing sounds as if they are flying.

Unix Express: Passengers bring a piece of the airplane and a box of tools with them to the airport. They gather on the tarmac and argue about what kind of plane they want to build. The passengers split into groups and build several different aircraft, but give them all the same name. Only some passengers reach their destinations, but all of them believe they arrived.

Slight Delays in Shipping

Computer Memories, Inc., supplied the hard drives used by the first IBM PC/ATs. The drives were notorious for crashing and occasionally losing data. IBM held shipment of some machines by as much as nine months as it searched for different hard drives to use.

But Wait, There's More

There are thousands of other bugs with software products that gained less notoriety than those just discussed. Here are a few of the more amusing ones:

- The Microsoft Windows calculator caused certain round-off errors. For example, 2.11–2.10 resulted in 0.00. The error got attention when people used the calculator to check for the Pentium bug, and in face of the publicity, Microsoft fixed it.

- Norton Utilities for Macintosh 3.0 had a bug in Speed Disk that could corrupt data and often required system reinstalls. Norton halted shipments and sent a free upgrade to users.

- Windows for Workgroups 3.11 had incompatibilities with certain disk-compression packages and network drivers.

- Using the PowerBook 150 with an internal modem could crash the computer.

- The MacPro Plus keyboard from KeyTronic didn't always work with a trackball. Likewise, the KeyTronic SynerG didn't always work if a system had a mouse.

- KeyCAD from SoftKey crashed when trying to load any of the sample images shipped with the product.

- When a PowerBook 540c was left idle, it sporadically crashed.

- The Windows UNDELETE program from DOS 6.0 lets users rename files so that they contain lowercase letters in the name. Because DOS 6.0 doesn't recognize lowercase letters, once users have so renamed a file, they can't rename, delete, or open the file.

- Norton Desktop 3.0 for Windows caused occasional hangs when expanded memory was enabled.

- When the Rocfish character in Learning Company's Reader Rabbit Interactive Reading Journey went to sleep, the program sometimes hung the computer.

- Walt Disney shipped a huge number of its Lion King CDs during the 1994 holiday season, only to receive thousands of complaints about the product not installing or sound not playing.

- When DoubleSpace came out with DOS 6.0, there were numerous complaints that it corrupted disk files.

- Novell halted shipments of its SoftSolutions 4.0a document management system. It reportedly caused numerous GP faults and other such errors, stemming from two modules.

- Compaq halted production of the Contura 400 to fix a PCMCIA controller bug, and stopped production of the LTE Elite to fix a bug that prevented it from recognizing more than 16MB of RAM in some cases.

- Novell NFS 1.2 was incompatible with Novell NetWare 4.1 until an update came out.

- A bug in the Windows driver for the Diamond Stealth 64 VRAM card caused the animated characters in Arthur's Teacher Trouble to move across the screen with their heads to the side of the screen.

- Photoshop for Windows 3.0 wouldn't install on a system that had LaserMaster printer drivers. The warning from Adobe about the bug, however, only appeared after users installed the product. But they couldn't install the product because of the bug.

- Lotus put a free version of Lotus Organizer 2.0 on ZiffNet. Customers flooded Lotus with reports of crashes, forcing Lotus to delay plans for wider release.

- The AT&T 6300 PC had a bug that wouldn't let its internal clock update beyond December 31, 1991.

Did You Know?

If Kicking It Doesn't Work

In 1994, Inacom held a PC-Pitching contest to see how far people could throw a PC across a parking lot. The winner chucked a machine 137.4 feet.

Tales from the Front Line

Once a product ships, the bulk of the interaction between a company and its customers is through the technical support department. The stated mission of tech support is to help customers better understand how to use a product. Tech support also hand-holds customers who have little computer experience, provides work-arounds for product bugs, and listens to complaints about products that don't work as well as advertised.

The quality of tech support varies from company to company, but it can be a critical factor for customers' use of a product, as well as a product 's success in the market. With small companies, the engineers tend to take technical support calls. This is great for customers, because they talk with the experts, but the practice takes away valuable R&D time. And engineers aren't always the most sociable people. If they think you are an idiot, they will often let you know. ("So, you aren't quite sure how to use Eigen values to solve your antenna theory equations? Then why the hell are you using our product?") By contrast, technical support people are trained (or learn quickly) how to be relatively polite to customers from all types of backgrounds.

Larger companies have elaborate technical support setups, often complete with multitiered support (so if you pay more, you get better support) and hold jockeys, who play music and entertain customers who are waiting for technical help. This can be particularly useful in calming down customers who are put on hold for sometimes as much as three and one-half hours to get help.

Technical support folks tend to form their own circles within a company. Even though they play a vital role in a company's survival, they aren't too respected by the engineers. (Engineers ask, "If they are good, why aren't they engineers?") They aren't respected by senior management, because an average technical support call costs a company $12, so they are a financial burden. And they aren't respected by customers, simply because customers are upset about a problem when they call. As a result, support engineers tend to bond together pretty tightly to help each other out after dealing with lots of angry customers.

Tip of the Day

💡 **Did you know...**

You can hurt yourself if you run with scissors.

OK

<u>N</u>ext Tip

More Tips...

<u>H</u>elp

☒ Show Tips at Startup

Word for Windows, like many Microsoft applications, can print helpful tips every time you start it. The idea is that by learning one small trick every day, you will soon master the application. This tip provides a helpful safety hint.

Nerd Humor: ✓

Engineering Solutions

A software engineer, a hardware engineer, and a departmental manager were on their way to a meeting in Switzerland. They were driving down a steep mountain road when suddenly the brakes on their car failed. The car careened almost out of control down the road, bouncing off the crash barriers, until it miraculously ground to a halt, scraping along the mountainside. The car's occupants, shaken but unhurt, now had a problem: they were stuck halfway down a mountain in a car with no brakes. What were they to do?

"I know," said the departmental manager. "Let's have a meeting, propose a Vision, formulate a Mission Statement, define some Goals, and by a process of Continuous Improvement, find a solution to the Critical Problems, and we can be on our way."

"No," said the hardware engineer. "That will take far too long, and besides, that method has never worked before. I've got my Swiss Army knife with me, and in no time at all, I can strip down the car's braking system, isolate the fault, fix it, and we can be on our way."

"Well," said the software engineer, "before we do anything, I think we should push the car back up the road and see if it happens again."

Who are these people? Tech support folks tend to be smart and fresh out of college with a computer background. They are looking for a start into a company. Usually they have very little experience with the product they are supporting, so they learn through on-the-job training. They will start by supporting installation or other relatively easy aspects of a product, and take classes and listen to senior support engineers to learn all the product's various ins and outs. Since much of support really involves knowing what the bugs are in a product and how to work around them, it takes months for an engineer to get really hot. The learning process can be frustrating, both for engineers and for customers. Most companies create elaborate computer systems to help engineers figure out whether odd behavior is the customer's ill behavior or the product's. They also create escalation paths, so that a new tech support engineer can defer to a more experienced engineer when he or she gets stuck.

When customers find a bug, the tech engineer often needs to fill in a bug report so that R&D can fix the problem. While many bugs are legitimate, there are three common terms for ones that are questionable.

- **DDT** — Don't Do That. If opening a particular file always crashes the program, don't open that file. Also used to describe bugs caused by the user doing something dangerous, such as deleting a bunch of files the program needs and then wondering why it doesn't work. And used to describe bugs that won't occur very often and therefore probably won't be fixed.

- **SUE** — Stupid User Error. Also known as Ignorant User Error or Operator Error. This is when the problem is caused by the user not understanding how to use the program. For example, "Whenever I click on the I button, my letters become italicized. It doesn't insert the letter 'I' in my text." If the I button is supposed to italicize text (as is the case with Word for Windows), then clicking on the I button will never insert the letter 'I' into the text.

- **RTFM** — Read The F***ing Manual. The problem is caused because the user hasn't read the manual. For example, the customer might say, "It is impossible to figure out how to italicize text." And the manual might say exactly how to do so on page 3.

Customers also have plenty of terms for what happens when a product doesn't work. Often, customers send extremely nasty messages, called "flames," to the support department. Eventually, support engineers become immune to such treatment, having developed "asbestos underwear."

There are many stories of strange and puzzling tech support calls. Here are a few I've gathered from tech support engineers at various companies. As you read through them, imagine that you are the support engineer. You are in a small cubicle, surrounded by computers and databases to help you with problems. The lights are dimmed. (Lights? We're support. We don't need no stinkin' lights.) The Clash wafts over the cubicle divide. You are wearing a telephone headset, and are connected to a million-dollar phone system that monitors the time you spend on every call as well as how long customers have been waiting. You have a six-pack of Jolt at the ready, the latest Gibson novel for when things get boring, and a lava lamp for decoration. The phone rings, and a customer's voice comes from the other end...

Any Key Won't Do

A customer called up very upset because he couldn't install the product. "Your installation screen keeps telling me to put in the next disk and then hit any key to continue. My keyboard doesn't have an 'any' key. I want my money back."

Almost every tech support department has gotten this call at one time or another. One company had an innovative answer. Some of the Gateway 2000 computer keyboards have a blank key between the arrow key cluster. The support engineers told people that was the 'any' key. It was easier than explaining what "Hit any key" really meant.

Saving on Postage

A customer called up saying that he had lots of trouble with some files on a particular disk. We asked him to send us a copy of the disk so we could investigate further. He did. About three days later, we got a photocopy of a disk in the mail. It certainly didn't help us any, and making the photocopy probably fried the disk.

Nerd Humor:

Taking Care of Your Keyboard
This advice comes from the Gateway 2000 user manual:

If you use the system in a dirty environment, open it periodically and vacuum the boards and components with a small vacuum designed for this kind of work. Don't loosen anything in the process — sucking all the chips off the system board with an industrial strength wet/dry vac is not covered by your warranty!

Cooked Disks

A frantic customer was escalated from customer support through to product management. "Please, I desperately need your help. My husband is evaluating a beta of one of your products — I'm not sure which. He's out golfing right now, and while cooking dinner I accidentally baked the disks. Is there anyway you can get me a copy before he gets back?"

Help with Homework

I was supporting the C++ compiler. Every now and then, we'd get calls and we'd just know it was for homework problems. Especially towards the beginning of semesters — things like linked lists, word wrap, and so forth. Once I got a call from someone asking for help on a particular problem — and it happened to be the same as the homework assignment I'd gotten that week. It turned out the person who called was taking the same class I was. That was one of the funny things about supporting a programming language.

Cut Disks

When Borland first shipped products on 5.25-inch disks, the installation instructions told the user to take the disk out of the sleeve and insert it in the computer. Instead of taking the disk out of the Tyvek sleeve, many customers cut open the disk jacket itself, removed the actual media — which is very thin and flimsy — and stuck that in the drive. Needless to say, Borland changed the instructions pretty quickly.

Nerd Humor:

And Now for Something Completely Different

Borland is famous for having extraneous items show up in the indices of their user manuals. (Which is not to be confused with references to missing sections, which sometimes happens too.) In the Turbo Vision manual from Borland C++ and Application Frameworks 3.1, you can find the following listing:

Dead parrots, see 'Parrots, dead.'

Jamming Them In

We had a product that shipped on several 5.25-inch disks. We'd get calls from customers who said, "Your installation instructions don't work. I've gotten disks 1 and 2 in the computer, but disk 3 just won't fit." Instead of inserting the disks one at a time, they just kept jamming more and more into the drive.

Magnetic Encounters

We once had a customer call because the installation diskette was unreadable. We sent him a new set. That didn't work either. By the third set he was really irate, and we were concerned about our quality control. So we had him walk through the exact steps he had gone through. "First, I got the disks in the mail. I opened the envelope. To make sure I didn't lose them, I stuck them on the refrigerator with a magnet. That night I put them in the machine." It's amazing that people don't realize that magnets destroy disks.

Well-Filed Backups

I consulted for the MIS department of one company and had a chance to watch how they backed up their critical company data. First, they ran archiving software to save all information to floppies. A clerk then carefully labeled a piece of paper with the date and contents, stapled the disk to the page, and put it in a folder. I'm sure glad I never had to read any of those floppies.

It's Magic

A woman called very upset that she wasn't able to print a database report. I walked her through the steps of selecting and printing the file, and she was doing everything perfectly. I then asked if the printer was on. "Yes." Was the cable connected? "It doesn't need a cable. It's a laser printer — it sends the information by laser beam." Once she got a parallel printer cable and actually hooked the printer up to the computer, things worked much better than with the magic beams.

In a similar story, a woman asked her relative who worked at Microsoft to check out her computer at home. When he arrived, he asked if she made backups. "Of course," she said. "What do you use?" he asked. She told him she had a very nice tape backup system. Which she did, only it was in the closet. She had thought the mere presence of the tape backup, sitting in the closet, meant that the machine occasionally backed itself up.

Several of the many Microsoft mugs, including two from the technical support group.

My Clothes Don't Match

In Borland Australia we did a good business selling Borland clothing — t-shirts, sweatshirts, running shorts, and so on. We got a call from a customer demanding his money back, because after he washed the clothes the colors changed and his black Borland shorts no longer matched his black Borland shirt.

Quick, Shut the Door

A customer called, unable to get the software to install. He kept getting a message saying, "Not ready reading drive A." Did you put the disk in the drive? "Yes." Did you close the door? "Wait one moment." In the background, we heard him walk across the room and shut his office door.

It's the Little Men That Make the Computers Work

I was supporting Quattro Pro for DOS. A customer called saying, "All I have on my screen is little men holding hands." At first, I thought it was a crank call. After a while I figured out he was using it in WYSIWIG mode, but the columns weren't wide enough for his numbers, so they showed up as a row of asterisks. He thought the ***** on the screen were really pictures of people holding hands. I didn't get into why he knew they were men and not women.

Cut Down to Size

I worked the help desk at a law firm in downtown Chicago. One time, a lawyer called me and asked why his 3.5 inch floppy drive didn't work. I went to his office and saw there was a disk in the drive, so I tried to access it. It didn't work at all. I took the disk out and found it was a 5.25 inch floppy cut down to the size of a 3.5 inch diskette. He thought that if he just cut the disk down, that would allow him to access it.

Did You Know?

Digital Art

There is a large piece of art in the lobby of one of DEC's New Hampshire buildings. A set of vertical metal tubes extend across the lobby. Each represents a bit in 7-bit ASCII code, where white tubes mean 1 and black tubes mean 0.

The art was supposed to say "Digital Software Engineering" — which was the group that worked in that office complex. Unfortunately, there was a slight mistake, and the sign instead said "Digital Softwa Reengineering."

Technicians' Revenge

Of course, sometimes the support engineers get to play tricks on the customers. At a DEC users' group convention, after hearing numerous complaints about DEC hardware and incompetent support engineers, one field technician told this story.

"I got a call from the client about a hard drive that no longer worked. When I showed up at the site, no one was in the MIS department. Since I had been there several times, I went in, examined their system, fixed it, and shut it down again. I then went back to my car where I had a rubber chicken in the back seat. I put the chicken in my toolbox and waited. Soon I saw the MIS staff coming back from lunch. I then went into the building, met with them, and marched up to the machine. I took out the chicken, waved it over the hard drive several times, and chanted. Then I hit the power button and the machine came up perfectly."

This illustration comes from a 1984 Memorex diskette ad. The ad states that Memorex provides the best protection from disk disasters because its Solid-Seam Bonding technology makes seams that are harder to rip open. As you can tell from this chapter, such seams were definitely needed.

More Abused Disks

Support departments often get hit with questions about disks that have been abused. Here are some more stories about strange things done to floppy disks.

- Someone accidentally put a 3.5 inch disk in the washing machine. It survived the whole washing, detergent, and exposure to the magnetic fields from the motor with only one bad sector.

- People occasionally mail disks. One person took this to an extreme. He took a 3.5 inch disk, wrote a mailing address on a disk label, put a stamp on it, and sent it through the mail. It arrived fine.

- Often, 5.25 inch disks get folded because they don't fit in a post box. They usually survive.

- In another story, a technician repaired a 3.5 inch drive that had broken when a user folded a 5.25 inch disk to get it to fit into the slot.

- And for the ultimate disk abuse, during a thunderstorm, a computer dealer's window broke and soaked a computer and a very important floppy that was in the drive. The owner cut open the floppy, put the magnetic media out in the sun to dry, and then very carefully put it into a new 5.25 inch sleeve. Amazingly, the disk still worked.

PART 3

Marketing

Developers have many theories about marketing:

- It's easy (false)
- All marketers are slime (false, only half are)
- All marketers wear ties (false, sales and accounting wear ties)
- Marketers can't program (false, many high tech marketers are ex-programmers and ex-engineers)
- Marketers like to take free trips to exotic locations (true)

Marketing high tech products is a difficult task. Customers vary in technical understanding, so marketing needs to address needs ranging from purchasers new to the market to seasoned rocket scientists. Marketing needs to create demand for very complex products whose benefits can't always be summarized in a few pithy statements. And, marketing needs to react quickly to changes in the competitive landscape.

In this section, you'll take a look at some of the key activities of the marketing team, ranging from choosing a product name to creating the product t-shirts. You'll also learn about some of the more amusing marketing screw ups.

Did You Know?

Product Name Conflicts

In Kuala Lumpur, Compaq is the name of a smokeless charcoal briquette.

The Name Game

One of the first and foremost activities for a
marketing team is picking a product name. Names are extremely important. A catchy name, such as Apple, will stick in people's minds, leading to
good brand recognition. A bad name, such as Professional Object
Elucidation Management Analysis Collector (which is too long to remember) or Flaky (which suggests instability) can lead to product death.
Therefore, companies spend much time and effort choosing product
names, sometimes spending hundreds of thousands of dollars on name
impact studies and consultants who specialize in name selection.

The marketing team needs to choose the product name early in the development cycle. After all, it will be used throughout marketing materials —
the box, ads, fact sheets, and press releases — as well as throughout the
documentation, so changing the name late in the cycle costs a lot of
money. Unfortunately, though, coming up with a product name can be
pretty hard.

Nerd Humor:

More Merger Names

When IBM bought Lotus, a rumor floated around that Lotus Notes would be renamed Blue Notes.

Let's see what it is like for a hypothetical marketing group to find a name for a new spreadsheet. First, the marketing group brainstorms names. This is a critical part of the naming process, requiring much concentration, so the group usually tries to do it at an off-site. Preferably somewhere where they can avoid day-to-day fires and phone calls, like Hawaii or Nice.

Product NAME Ideas: Maui 95

SuperSlickSpreadsheet
Not Your Fathers Excel
Instacalc
Between the Sheets
Good Sheet
This is some good
Sheet MAN!
Bread Maker
Bread Winner
Financial Vision
QuickCalc
NumberCruncher
Calc it

The group returns from the off-site and presents the list to the broader development team. Typically this turns into a big debate, separating the "we are a serious corporation" developers from the "we are the wild pirates" developers. Development usually kicks in a few name suggestions too, with a very high honesty quota. (For example, "Let's call this version .5, because I don't think we will fix as many bugs as we should.) The list narrows:

InstaCalc

Between The Sheets

Good Sheet

Bread Maker

FinancialVision

QuickCalc

NumberCruncher

CalcIt!

Then, the legal department joins in. Lawyers like names that are trademarkable and don't infringe on other names. They thus narrow the list further, and then head off on a trademark search. This is an expensive process whereby they look for products in the same industry with similar names. For our hypothetical company, they might decide that QuickCalc was too close to Microsoft's Quick C, and that Good Sheet was not trademarkable.

With a smaller list in hand, the marketing team sets out to make a difficult decision, narrowing down the names. They survey the team once more, consult the executives, and pick the final name. In this case, we'll say they go for FinancialVision.

Products with a Sense of Humor

Even though our mythical company picked the conservative FinancialVision name, not all companies feel so restricted. In fact, there are some very strange and clever product names in the industry. The following lists some of my favorites. The jokes and quirks in the names should be pretty evident.

**Bear Bone$** — An inexpensive communications package that works with an IBM utility called IND$FILE.

Being There — Video conferencing software with a takeoff on the Peter Sellers movie with the same name.

CanOpener — A program for opening files on the Macintosh even if the application that created it isn't present. Without software such as this, you can't always open every file.

ComponentGlue — Software from Novell that connects OLE and OpenDoc.

DiskTop — A program for finding files on the Macintosh.

EasyBall — Microsoft's mouse for kids, not to be confused with the Happy Fun Ball. Somehow there are too many sexual connotations with this name.

Echo Lake — A multimedia diary and story-maker program.

Forest & Trees — Information management software.

GatorLink — Network management software.

GraceLAN — AppleTalk remote access server software, with a clever joke mixing Elvis and local area networks.

Grapevine — Add-on administration software for Lotus Notes.

HotJava — A Web browser from Sun that uses the Java scripting language.

LanRover — Remote access network software with another good local area network joke in its name.

Macro Spitbol — A programming language that for some reason reminds me of straws and high school.

MPEGthere and MPEGanywhere — Two MPEG transmission solutions.

NetOctopus — Network management software.

NewtWare — Network software for Newton that connects to Novell NetWare.

NNTP Sucker — A Net newsgroup reader.

Nok Nok Pro — Network software.

Same<>Same 2.2 — Software for transferring files between computers.

SlipKnot — Many Internet browsers require that you have a SLIP connection. This software doesn't, and thus the name alludes to "SLIP, Not!" as well as the famous way to tie a knot.

SniffMaster — Network analyzer software.

Son of a Batch — A batch file compiler.

StrongARM — A set of RISC chips designed for PDAs, where ARM stands for Advanced RISC Machines Ltd.

StuffIt — A popular file-compression program.

SubBrick — A portable computer from Ergo, makers of another computer called the Brick.

Sunscreen — A network security system from Sun. This is, of course, a joke on the ability to screen out undesired users, as well as on the goop that keeps you from getting sunburned.

ToadNews — A Net newsgroup reader.

Total Recall — A set of data-retrieval APIs.

TribeLink8 — Remote-access server software.

WHATSIT — A 1978 database manager with a name that stood for Wow! How'd All That Stuff get In There?

Win, What, Where — Software for tracking user activity in Windows.

Did You Know?

Does It Come with a Condom?
Acer Computer was very excited about the laptop computer it was about to unveil in the United States. It planned to indicate that it was an easily carried business computer by calling it Hand Job. Fortunately for Acer, the name was changed before it hit the market. Of course, now that Microsoft has its EasyBall mouse, there are plenty of good product combinations.

Amusing Company Names

Not only are product names sometimes amusing, computer company names don't always convey conservatism. Here are a few clever and bizarre company names.

Barn Owl Software

Baudville

Berkeley Voo Doo

Buzzwords International

Canopus Research — While this company, run by Will Zachmann, is named after a star, it always sounds like Cannabis Research, which would be something completely different.

Chili Pepper Software

Chips&Dale

FYI, Inc.

Gandalf Technologies

Grumpfish, Inc.

HockWare, Inc.

Hummingbird Communications LTD.

Lose Your Mind Development

No Hands Software

Pickles & Trout

Rabbit Software

Radish Software

Tadpole Technology, Inc.

The Bit Bucket System

Thought I Could

Twinhead Corp.

Very Early Amusing Company Names

While the names just listed are fun, the truly great company names stem from the early days. The personal computer industry started during the mid-seventies, and was heavily influenced by the counter-cultural movement of the sixties and the continuing age of rock 'n roll. This influence is evident in the list that follows. If you close your eyes, you can easily visualize the company founders standing next to their headquarters' entrances, wearing tie-dyed shirts and grooving to the sounds of Jefferson Airplane.

Loving Grace Cybernetics

Golemics Incorporated

Itty Bitty Machine Company — A takeoff on IBM.

Chicken Delight Computer Consultants

Kentucky Fried Computers — Run by the same people that ran North Star and Applied Computer Technology, it was shut down after Kentucky Fried Chicken complained about the name. The owners concentrated on North Star instead.

Thinkertoys

Computer Headware

Parasitic Engineering

Confusing Names

Despite the effort to come up with exciting, unique, trademarkable names, companies don't always succeed. After all, with hundreds of computer companies and thousands of products, the chances are high that a few names will seem surprisingly close. When this happens, one of four things occurs: the two companies ignore the similarity and tough it out; one company decides to change its name; the bigger company buys the name from the smaller company; or one company sues the other.

The following lists a few examples of company or product names that seem pretty darn similar. In a few cases, some of the similarities led to legal threats and actions. For example, NCC acquired Novell's LANalyzer hardware, but Novell retained the rights for the name LANalyzer.

After a brief legal skirmish, NCC changed their product name to LAN Network Probe.

Company or product name	Similar name, different company
Access (Microsoft Corp.)	**Access for Windows 3270** (Eicon Technology Corp.)
Act! (Symantec Corp.)	**Actfast** (Daprex)
Alaris, Inc.	**Claris Corp.**
Delphi Internet Services, Inc.	**Borland Delphi** (Borland)
Director 4.0 (Macromedia, Inc.)	**Backup Director 4.0** (Palindrome Corp.)
Generation 5	**Fifth Generation Systems, Inc.**
Logic Arts	**Electronic Arts**
NCC LANalyzer (NCC; now called LAN Network Probe)	**LANalyzer for Windows** (Novell, Inc.)
Newer Technology (Spectrum Technology, Inc.)	**Windows NT** (Microsoft Corp.)
P.Ink 2.1 (P.Ink America Corp.)	**Pink** (Taligent, Inc.)
Rational Systems	**Rational**
Sterling Software, Inc.	**Stirling Group**
Teknosys	**Techgnosis, Inc.**
Uninstaller (MicroHelp, Inc.)	**IYM Uninstall** (It's Your Money, Inc.; IYM)
Veritas Software Co.	**Qualitas, Inc.**

Thirty Products That Jumped On the Visual Bandwagon

Sometimes, names are similar on purpose. This happens when a particular word becomes a fad. "Visual," "Object," "Open," "Pro," and "Cyber" all were hot words at various times. When a product, such as Visual Basic, takes off in the market, companies jump on the bandwagon hoping to emulate the success.

For example, Microsoft released Visual Basic in 1991. After a slow start, it took the world by storm. By 1993, when Microsoft released Visual C++, the word *visual* had become an in word for describing products. Everyone wanted to use it when describing their products, as you can see in the following list of 30 products, all using the word *Visual*:

CA-Visual Objects	Visual FoxPro
Turbo C++ Visual Edition for Windows	Visual Help Builder
Visual Access for Windows	Visual MATRIX
Visual Ada for Windows	Visual MuSQLe
Visual Age	Visual Planner
Visual Appbuilder	Visual Programmer
Visual Baler	Visual Prototyper
Visual Basic	Visual SlickEdit
Visual BBS	Visual SQL
Visual Builder	Visual WorkFlo
Visual C++	Visual XL
Visual COBOL/XO	Visual-DCE
Visual Cyberquery	Visual/db
Visual Debugger	Visual/Recital
Visual Designer for Windows	VisuaLab

Keeping Track of Openings

Like *visual*, *open* is another buzz word frequently used in product and committee names. Amusingly enough, when *open* is used with committees, it usually indicates that the committee is closed. For example, it might be an "open" committee for determining a proprietary standard.

Here is a list of some committees or agreements with the word *open* in them:

1. **Open Software Foundation (OSF)** — a purveyor of open systems technology like the Distributed Computing Environment (DCE) and the Distributed Management Environment (DME). It includes companies like DEC, IBM, and other system heavyweights.

2. **Open Tools Agreement** — a Microsoft program for licensing operating systems files to competing tools vendors.

3. **Open Collaboration Environment** (OCE, also known as the Apple Open Collaboration Environment) — an organization centered around Apple's attempt to provide a universal email gateway. It's been less than an overwhelming success.

4. **Open Applications Group (OAG)** — founding members include Oracle Corp., Dun & Bradstreet Software, and PeopleSoft, Inc., along with a bunch of other database vendors.

5. **Open Set Top Standards Committee** — a subgroup of the Video Electronics Standards Association (VESA), members include hardware manufacturers, multimedia companies, and participants from the TV broadcast industry.

6. **PowerOpen Association (POA)** — a PowerPC-oriented industry association that includes IBM, Apple Computer, and Motorola, along with a host of other hardware and software developers.

7. **X/Open Committee** — an association of Unix hardware and software system developers that includes most of the major UNIX players, including Novell, IBM, DEC, HP, and AT&T.

8. **Open User-Recommended Solutions (OURS)** — a 60-member consumer organization that aims to streamline software licensing and purchasing procedures.

And here are some products with *open* in their names:

Apple Open Transport	OpenUptime
Open Integr8	Open Interface
Open/DB	Open ODMS
Open Office	Open Shutter
Open /TP1	Open RS/36
Open Cooperative Test System	OpenConnect/APPC
Open Networking Environment	OpenUI Development Environment
Open Media Framework	OpenPost
Openfile	OpenSNA
Open Software/TP	Open Mail System
Open Sesame!	OpenServer 400
OpenWin	OpenInsight
OpenVMS AXP	Open Link Extender
Open Channel Flow	Open Access IV
Open Draw	OpenForms
OpenODB	OpenWindows
OpenView NetLS	Open Genera
Open!Capture	Open Advantage
Open TransPort	Open System
OpenCase/Encapsulator	OpenUser Interface
OpenRead Plus	OpenFAX
Open M/SQL	OPEN/office
Open-PL/I	Open Plan
Open Ada	Open Architecture Development System
OpenSelect CASE Starter	

Did You Know?

Intel Inside

Next time you fly into San Francisco or San Jose, take a close look out the window when you fly over the Intel buildings in Santa Clara. One of the buildings has a big Intel Inside logo on top, because, after all, Intel is inside.

Slogans: The Best Chapter Ever

In addition to picking product
names, the marketing group creates product and company slogans. Slogans
are those inspired lines of copy that typically show up under a company's
name in an advertisement. Terse and catchy, they epitomize a company's
spirit in a few brief words. They communicate a mission. And more often
than not, they include an element of braggadocio. After all, a small company run out of a basement can declare that it is the "Best Software
Creator in the World" in an ad. If enough people read the slogan without
pausing to think about it too much, maybe it will sink into their subcon-
scious minds. For example, our hypothetical software company from "The
Name Game" chapter (Chapter 13) might choose "The Leader in
Spreadsheets" as their slogan, hoping that a customer will say, "Hmm, I
could buy Microsoft Excel, or I could buy this product called
FinancialVision. I've never heard of FinancialVision, but the company is
the leader in spreadsheets, so it must be a good product."

Slogans are used everywhere, from Nike's "Just Do It" to Burger King's "Have It Your Way." The personal computer industry has used slogans from its inception, perhaps starting with Microsoft's slogan from the mid-seventies, "What's a microprocessor without it?"

Some companies keep slogans for a long time, while others shed them every month, taking on new personas or missions. Of course, slogans as well as products are prone to competitors' bashing. Slogans also seem to circulate through the industry, starting at one company, only to appear a few years later in a slightly different form at another company.

Let's take a look at some of the slogans.

Microsoft

Microsoft, one of the oldest software companies, has gone through numerous slogans. Here are a few.

What's a Microprocessor Without It?
This was the first Microsoft slogan.

Better Tools for Microcomputers

The Higher Performance Software

We Set the Standard

Making it Easier
Amusingly, Eagle, the maker of the Eagle PC, had a similar slogan, "Eagle makes it easier."

Information at Your Fingertips
This successful slogan was frequently used by the press and in general descriptions of the power of computers. Years earlier, NEC had a comparable slogan, "Productivity at your fingertips," and a few years before that, a hard disk manufacturer named Konan ran ads with the lead, "New power at your fingertips."

Making It All Make Sense
This slogan was unveiled with much internal fanfare at Microsoft. There was a contest in Microsoft's employee newspaper where the slogan was

listed in hangman style, with blanks for each letter. Each week, more letters were filled in, and the first employee to guess the new slogan would win a prize. During one week a clue was "Ma _ i _ _ i _ _ _ _ _ a _ _ _ _ _ _ . "An employee ran a dictionary program against it and came up with "Maniac in the Fast Track."

Where Do You Want to Go Today?
This was Microsoft's most recent slogan, accompanied by a very aggressive print and TV advertising campaign. Lotus immediately ran a counter ad, showing a frustrated worker saying, "Where do I want to go today? Home."

Borland

Borland ran through numerous slogans, especially as it hit turbulent times. Changing a slogan often meant changing strategy, which sometimes indicated that the previous strategy didn't work, or its proponent had left or fallen out of favor. Here are a few of Borland's slogans.

Power Made Easy
The idea of power is a very popular one. Claris presented "Simply powerful software." Corona, a maker of IBM PC clones in the early 80s suggested "Feel the power." Likewise, another early PC vendor, Northstar, offered "Simply powerful solutions."

The Leader in Object-Oriented Programming

Software Craftsmanship
The idea of software production as a craft is a popular way to express the idea that some people just crank out software, while others do a superior

job. In fact, this was a concept used by a numbers of companies other than Borland. Almost a decade before Borland used it, Okidata had the slogan, "Technological Craftsmanship," and Oryx Systems had "Craftsmen of the new technology." Preceding both of them, Whitesmiths, Ltd., a maker of compilers and other tools, had "Software Craftsmen."

The Database Company

The Power of Things to Come
Gupta, one of Borland's competitors, seemed to like this slogan enough to adopt a similar one, "The Power To Get Client/Server Done."

Software with the Future Built In

Software for the Way You Work

The Upsizing Company
This slogan received a mixed response in the general media. At first, no one could figure out what *upsizing* meant. Because Borland was going through troubled times, many people referred to it as "The Capsizing Company" instead.

Computer Associates

Computer Associates, one of the largest software companies, has long pushed its slogan, "Software superior by design." CompuAdd had a similar slogan, "Customer Driven, By Design." "Superior In Every Detail" was Nanao's slogan. Ten years prior, Olivetti had "The intelligent choice. By design."

Lotus

Lotus has gone through numerous slogans, including "The hardest working software in the world" and the most recent, "Working Together." This slogan, of course, should not be confused with Datapoint's "Systems That Work Together Now" or Digital Research's much earlier motto, "We make computers work."

Did You Know?

No "3" for IBM

IBM will never use the name OS/3 for a future version of OS/2, since that is trademarked by Unisys.

IBM

IBM has gone through numerous slogans as well, including

Operate at a Higher Level

Software for Application Productivity

We're Putting the Personal in Personal Computing

A recent slogan, "There is a difference" has been widely criticized by columnists who ask, "Different from what?" Others wonder what about IBM's sometimes miserable performance is different.

Then, of course, there is one of my all-time favorite slogans, which was the rallying cry for OS/2 2.0, "A better DOS than DOS, a better Windows than Windows, a better OS/2 than OS/2." Sometimes it even makes sense.

The introduction of Windows led to this die-hard DOS sentiment.

Nerd Humor:

What It Really Means

PCMCIA — This abbreviation stands for Personal Computer Memory Card International Association. Many people say it really means People Can't Memorize Computer Industry Acronyms.

LISP — LISP is a somewhat strange programming language popular among artificial intelligence researchers and MIT students. It is famous for containing lots of parentheses in the code. While officially its name stands for list processing, many say it really stands for LISP Is Stupid Parentheses, which is a self referential acronym, and thus cool. Another theory is that it stands for Lots of Irritating Single Parentheses.

JOVIAL — is a programming language. Its name is an acronym for Jule's Own Version of the International Algorithmic Language.

TWAIN — the Aldus image acquisition format, is said to stand for Technology without an Interesting Name.

YAHOO — is an extremely popular site on the web (www.yahoo.com), because it provides categorized lists of thousands of web sites, thus serving as a kind of electronic phone book. YAHOO stands for Yet Another Hierarchical Officious Oracle. Many computer abbreviations start with Yet Another. For example, YACC is Yet Another Compiler Compiler.

Early Hardware Vendors

Slogans from the early computer vendor's give a glimpse into the mindset of the time. Many of these slogans show a strong sense of revolutionary mission. While Heath would not turn out to be the strongest partner, and Radio Shack is by no means the largest company in microcomputers, these companies all played a role in changing and advancing the industry.

Computers for the Advancement of Society (Vector Graphics)

Creating Useful Products and Services for You (Texas Instruments)

Follow the Star (NorthStar)

Packed with Fresh Ideas (Altos)

The Biggest Name in Little Computers (Radio Shack)

The Most Computer you Can Carry (Compaq)

The Personal Portable (Kaypro)

We Build Computers As If Your Business Depended on Them (IMS)

Your Strong Partner (Heath/Zenith)

We Brag the Most

While some slogans convey a mission, others sound more like excerpts from teenage boasting contests. The following slogans win a trophy in the "most pompous" category.

A Better Way (Microfocus)

First in Software Technology (SuperSoft)

Nobody Gives You Better Performance (Fuji)

One Great Idea After Another... (Quasar)

Outperform the Very Best (QMS)

Somebody Has to be Better Than Everybody Else (Dysan)

The Best of Everything in Software (Digital Research)

The Difference Between Toys and Tools in Microcomputers (NNC)

The Future in Software (UVEON Computer Systems)

The Past, Present, and Future of Network Computing (Novell)

The Picture of Success (Micrografx)

We Change the Way the World Thinks (DEC)

We Make Modern Times Better (Maynard Electronics)

You'll Never Look at Computers the Same Way Again (Hyperion)

Plenty of other companies promoted their leadership position in future technology. In most of these cases, the companies didn't bring about the change they anticipated. For example, Exxon is no longer a powerhouse in the personal computer market.

A New Kind of Power for a New Kind of Computing (PowerSoft)

Extending Your Reach with Innovation, which was shortened to **Extending Your Reach** (Texas Instruments)

In Touch with Tomorrow (Toshiba)

Micros for Bigger Ideas (Intersystems)

Start with Us. Stay with Us. (Exxon Office Systems)

The Future...Without the Shock (Exxon Office Systems)

The Languages of the Future. The Tools of Today. (insoft)

The Burger Awards

Many slogans have little to do with the companies' technology and sound more like general merchandise slogans. Here are some slogans that could just as easily promote fast food, running shoes, or designer underwear.

Building on the Power of People (PowerSoft)

Connecting People (Nokia)

Make the Connection (Zenith Data Systems)

Now You Can (Canon)

Quality Runs in the Family (Epson)

See, Hear, and Feel the Difference (NEC)

Setting You Free (Hewlett-Packard)

Software for a Small Planet (IBM)

The Freedom to Communicate (DCA)

The People's Choice (PC Brand)

There's a Lot More to it (Microfocus)

Uncomplicating Your Life (Compuware)

You've Got a Friend in the Business (Gateway 2000)

And Some Funny Ones

Of course, no list of slogans would be complete without some of the more amusing ones, such as the following:

Because Slow is Dead (Speedware)

Don't Plug in Without Us (EPD)

Financial, Workflow/Image, and Cold Solutions (Computron)

Have You Kissed Your Computer Lately? (Components Express, Inc.)

Naturally Bug Free (Organic Software)

Software for People Who Aren't Easy to Please (Datasoft, Inc.)

And Now for a Few More

Just in case you missed your favorite slogan, here are a few more, illustrating the breadth and popularity of slogans.

Backup so simple it's advanced (Colorado Memory Systems)

Connectivity for a Changing World (Reflection)

How the World Says Project Management (Primavera)

I/O. Now More Important than Ever. (Adaptec)

Increasing the Speed of Business (Hayes)

Making PC Connections Count (Reflection)

Making Small Printers for People Who Think Big (Okidata)

Managing the Enterprise (Symantec)

Opening Windows to Multimedia (Sigma Design)

PCs designed and Built in America (Hyundai)

People Bet Their Business on Us (Sybase)

Software for the Real World (Telos)

Solutions for Workgroups (Northgate)

The Document Company (Xerox)

The First Name in Small Business Accounting Software (Peachtree)

The Senseware Company (Logitech)

The Storage Answer (Conner)

Tools that Build Business (Cognos)

We're Keeping Pace with your Business (Okidata)

Hello, information.

Or, how the IBM Personal Computer can bring you the world.

In 1983 IBM launched its memorable Charlie Chaplin campaign, one of the most expensive and elaborate advertising campaigns in the personal computer industry at the time. Slick print and TV ads bombarded customers, marking one of the first uses of celebrity endorsements for PC products. It was a time in which IBM was widely perceived as an industry leader. Apple, not to be out done, would retort with its famous 1984-like TV spot at the 1984 Super Bowl.

Oh Please, Mr. Ad Man

Creating ads is an integral part of a marketer's life. Ads are the most leveraged form of marketing. A small team can create an ad that will be viewed by millions of potential customers. Advertising is also the least targeted type of marketing — of the millions of people who look at an ad, only a small number might really need the product. Writing ads is a lot of fun, but at the same time very stressful. Ads take a long time to produce, and magazines need to get copies of ads as much as three months before they run. Therefore, marketing needs to plan its first ad campaigns very carefully. If the product changes or slips in the three months between when an ad is submitted and when it runs, marketing can look very stupid. During these few months prior to a product launch, marketing teams pull very long hours, readying all the materials they need for a successful campaign.

When opening any computer magazine today, readers will be confronted with the best Madison Avenue has to offer. Microsoft uses the same advertising firm as Nike. Apple kicked off the Macintosh with a surreal television ad during the 1984 Super Bowl. IBM has sponsored bowl games and plastered the world with TV and radio spots on Warp.

But the early days of computers were far humbler. Instead of flashy ads, most were black and white and got to the facts in a hurry. In many of the early magazines, only Texas Instruments stood out, using Bill Cosby as a spokesperson for its calculators. Later, IBM would use Charlie Chaplin and the crew of "M.A.S.H." to endorse its PCs.

Nonetheless, with the hunger in the market, these simple early ads were incredibly successful. Borland's first ad, for example, launched the company, generating instant demand and a revenue stream.

Let's take a look at some of the early ads from some of today's giants.

Microsoft

This was Microsoft's first ad (Figure 15-1), from when it was still based in Albuquerque, near the MITS headquarters. The fine print under the cartoon says, "Microsoft is the company that will efficiently produce and implement quality software for any microprocessor, in any amount, at any level of complexity. Why not contact them about your micro-software needs?"

Flight Simulator

For many years, the Microsoft Flight Simulator was the coolest thing around. It was used to check PC compatibility and also to show the hottest and fastest computer graphics available. It became a best-seller and continues to sell extremely well, fifteen years after the ad in figure 15-2 ran.

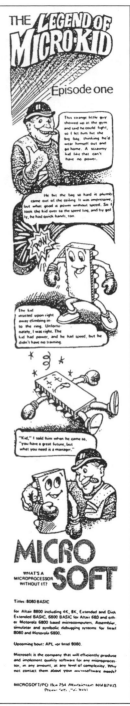

Figure 15-1

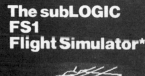

Figure 15-2

Microsoft licensed the Flight Simulator from subLogic. The ad shown here predates that arrangement. Because the IBM PC wasn't invented yet when this ad ran in early 1980, subLogic didn't have any software for that platform. Instead, the ad gives instructions on receiving the program on paper tape, cassette, or various floppy formats.

Figure 15-3 This mug advertises Microsoft's Flight Simulator, which was used to test compatibility of early IBM PC clones.

CompuServe

While this wasn't the first CompuServe ad (see figure 15-4), it was a very early one. It ran in late 1981 to announce a Halloween adventure gaming contest where the grand prize was two hours of connect time. At the time, CompuServe had 10,000 members.

Get yourself a **real** chill on

HALLOWEEN

in the nationwide
CompuServe Adventure Tournament.

Prizes: Grand Masters win two hours of free time on CompuServe.

Runners-up win a CompuServe Adventure T-shirt (Grand Masters win this too.)

Everyone who enters can, on request, receive a large poster of the Gray Morrow art on the opposite page in full color. We'll charge your account $2.00 for postage and handling.

When? Starting at 6 PM local time on Friday, October 30, running through 5 AM on Monday, November 2.

How? Since this will be our first nationally-advertised tournament, we may have to make some last minute changes following our "in-house" tournament on Labor Day. So check the "What's New" section of the CompuServe Information Service for details preceding the contest. So enter. Collect treasures. Slay dwarves. And practice, practice, practice. How else will we be able to afford the T-shirts?

CompuServe

5000 Arlington Centre Blvd.
Columbus, Oh 43220
Information Service Division
(800) 848-8990

If you're not already a member of the country's largest personal computer network, get on-line now!

How does it work?
Your computer talks to our computers. You need a modem and some special software. Software for the TRS-80® and Apple II® computers are available at many Radio Shack® outlets and all Radio Shack® Computer Centers. Atari® users can access the system via Telelink™ software. Persons owning other brands of computers or terminals can also purchase the CompuServe Information Service through Radio Shack®. In more than 260 U.S. cities you can reach the CompuServe Information Service via a local phone call. The cost is $5 per hour, billed in minutes, to your charge card, for service between 6 PM and 5 AM local time on weekdays and all day on Saturday, Sunday and most holidays. Limited daytime access is available at a higher rate.

What do I get?
There are more than 175 topics listed in the on-line index. Most first-time users are interested in:

1. News, weather, sports. We offer the electronic editions of many of the major daily newspapers and the AP news and sports wires.
2. CB simulation. "Talk" to other computer users anywhere in the country. We also offer electronic mail.
3. Games. Many, including the multi-player Space War, Star-Trek, four Adventure games.
4. Finance. Again, a wide variety for both historical and current data on stocks, bonds and commodities.
5. Computer user groups (including national bulletin boards) and computer manufacturers' newsletters.
6. Home information. Family Service. Government publications. Aviation news. Energy-saving tips. And more.

When you are ready, CompuServe Information Service can provide you with a lot of big mainframe computer power. But see a demonstration at Radio Shack® right away so you can get on-line before the tournament.

Radio Shack and TRS-80 are trademarks of Tandy Corporation. ATARI and Telelink are trademarks of ATARI, Inc. Apple is a trademark of Apple Computer, Inc.

Figure 15-4 An early Compuserve ad.

IBM PC

IBM released the IBM PC in August 1981 and, by doing so, irrevocably changed and consolidated the market. The ad shown in figure 15-5 was the

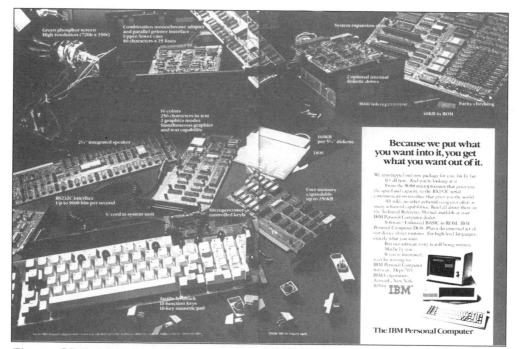

Figure 15-5 This IBM ad focuses on the "nuts and bolts" of the PC.

first IBM PC ad to run in a monthly computer magazine. Compared to the first Apple ad, and to the Apple ads of the time, it was a very stark, technically focused advertisement.

Microsoft Mouse

In the beginning, mice were a curiosity. It wasn't until the Macintosh came out, half a year after this first ad for the Microsoft Mouse appeared in the June 1983 issue of *Byte* (figure 15-6), that mice became popular and were no longer viewed as strange and awkward devices. In one of the first reviews of the very same Microsoft Mouse, the reviewer stated that the Microsoft Mouse "opens up the possibility of a whole new generation of software." The reviewer, Chris Peters, was then a software engineer working on the mouse at Microsoft and is now a Microsoft vice president.

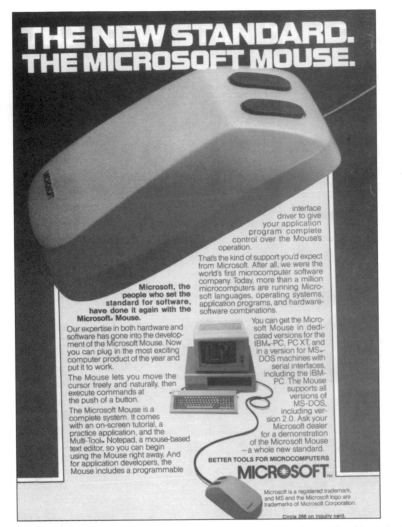

Figure 15-6 This ad for the Microsoft Mouse predates the Macintosh.

Columbus Used It

Microsoft ran an ad for a package called the Visual Basic Power Tools Bundle. To make customers jump on the special $149 price, Microsoft added a time limit, saying, "this offer expires January 31, 1492."

MicroPro

MicroPro was one of the first software companies. Its founder, Seymour Rubenstein, started in the military defense contracting world. He became a marketing manager at IMSAI, and gained fame as one of the few people ever to out negotiate Bill Gates. He left IMSAI to form MicroPro. In this October, 1978 ad (Figure 15-7), MicroPro hawked its first two products, SuperSort and WordMaster. Within a year, MicroPro released WordStar, which became one of the most popular word processors of the time.

Figure 15-7

Figure 15-8

dBASE

dBASE was originally called Vulcan. Response to this March, 1980 ad (Figure 15-8) was so strong that George Tate decided to form a small company called Ashton-Tate to sell the product. In the process, it renamed Vulcan as dBASE, and turned it into the best selling database product ever. Eventually Ashton-Tate hit financial problems, and was bought by Borland for $440 million.

Lotus

Lotus didn't invent the spreadsheet, but it did make it a household word and a staple of the business community. Promising to put raw power at your fingertips, Lotus kicked off 1-2-3 with this 1983 ad (figure 15-9), and built an empire. In 1995, IBM bought Lotus for over three billion dollars. That's quite a change from this simple, black and white ad.

INTRODUCING 1-2-3™. IT'LL HAVE YOUR IBM/PC JUMPING THROUGH HOOPS.

Meet 1-2-3 – the remarkable new software package that puts more raw power at your finger tips than anything yet created for the IBM PC. 1-2-3 actually combines information management, spreadsheet, and graphing in one program that can perform all three functions interchangeably and instantly at the touch of a key. That's power.

To explain: since 1-2-3's information management, spreadsheet and graphing functions reside in memory simultaneously, you can go from retrieval to spreadsheet calculation to graphing instantly, just by pressing a few keys. So now you can experiment and recalculate and look at data in an endless variety of ways. As fast as your mind can think up new possibilities. There's no lag between you and the computer. And that's a new kind of power – power that's greater than the sum of its programs.

The spreadsheet function.

If 1-2-3 were just a spreadsheet, you'd want it because it has the largest workspace on the market (2048 rows by 256 columns). To give you a quick idea of 1-2-3's spreadsheet capabilities: VisiCalc's spreadsheet for the IBM PC offers 15 arithmetic, logical and relational operators, 28 functions and 32 spreadsheet-related commands. 1-2-3 has 15 operators,

41 functions and 66 commands. And if you include data base and graphing commands, it actually has 110!

In addition, 1-2-3 is up to 50 times as fast as established spreadsheets. With all the features you've ever seen on spreadsheets. 1-2-3 also gives you the capability to develop customized applications (with 26 macro keys) and lets you perform repetitive tasks automatically with one keystroke. If 1-2-3 were just a spreadsheet, it would be a very powerful tool. But it's much, much more.

The information management function.

Add to 1-2-3's spreadsheet a selective information management function, and the power curve rises at an awesome rate. Particularly since 1-2-3's information management capability reads files from other programs such as WordStar, VisiCalc and dBase II. So you can accumulate information on a limitless variety of topics and extract all or pieces of it for instant spreadsheet analysis. Unheard of before. Specific 1-2-3 information management features include sorting with primary and secondary keys. Retrieval using up to 32 criteria. 1-2-3 performs statistical functions such as mean, count, standard deviation and variance. It can produce histograms on part or all of the data base. 1-2-3 also

allows for the maintenance of multiple data bases and multiple criteria.

The graphing function.

1-2-3 enables you to create graphs of up to six variables using information already on the spreadsheet. And have it on screen in less than two seconds! Once you've made a graph, three keystrokes will display it in a different form. If data on the spreadsheet changes, you can display a revised graph with one keystroke. This instant relationship of one format to another opens up a whole new application area. For the first time graphics can be used as a "what if" thinking tool!

For a full demonstration of 1-2-3's remarkable power, visit your nearby 1-2-3 dealer. For his name and address, call 1-800-343-5414 (in Mass. call 617-492-7171)

Lotus Development Corporation, 55 Wheeler Street, Cambridge, MA 02138.

Spreadsheet, graphing, information management all-in-one.

1-2-3 and Lotus are trademarks of Lotus Development Corporation. All rights reserved. WordStar is a registered trademark of MicroPro Inc. VisiCalc is a registered trademark of VisiCorp. dBase II is a registered trademark of Ashton-Tate.

Figure 15-9 Lotus introduces 1-2-3.

Compaq

At the same time Lotus was popularizing the spreadsheet, Compaq was kicking off its empire. It redefined what it meant to make an IBM PC clone, and took over Kaypro and Osborne's role as the dominant supplier of portable PCs. The Compaq Portable, debuted in this June, 1983 ad, was lovingly called a "luggable" It looked and weighed like a medium sized suitcase filled with books (Figure 15-10). It wasn't the lightest or most convenient PC, but it helped Compaq establish a foothold that it would later use to overtake even IBM's sales.

Figure 15-10

Well Excuse Me

Sometimes ads get a lot of attention, but for the wrong reason. Companies withdraw ads on a regular basis due to complaints from readers or threats from other companies. For example, Borland received complaints from customers for an a direct mail campaign that used the term "visually impaired" to criticize Microsoft's Visual C++.

In one of the more interesting cases, Intel created a brochure promoting the 80387 chip. The front page stated, "Our entire Math CoProcessor public relations department promises to keep quiet until you've had a chance to evaluate Intel's new, improved 387 Math CoProcessors." Which seemed pretty normal until you flipped open the brochure to find an attractive blonde woman sitting on a wooden stool, her mouth taped shut, and her hands bound with a phone cord. The inner caption read, "Be quick. She's dying to talk to you about it."

After a flood of protests, Intel quickly changed campaigns.

Borland

When Borland started, it had no money, no customers, and it was based out of a room on top of a garage. Borland convinced *Byte* to let it run an ad on credit for its product, Turbo Pascal. It placed this ad (figure 15-10) in the December 1983 issue of *Byte* magazine, announcing the first cheap, easy-to-use Pascal compiler. It instantly received thousands of orders and catapulted into incredible growth, at one point becoming the largest database and language vendor in the world.

Figure 15-10 This ad for Borland's Turbo Pascal stimulated great demand.

Sidekick

This mid-1984 ad (figure 15-11) is the first ad for Sidekick, which cemented Borland's position as an up-and-coming software company. Sidekick was a pop-up utility that let users keep a calendar, take notes, and do many other things. It was written in tight assembly language and was part of the first wave of TSRs.

This ad features a miner named Frank Borland. A popular rumor ensued that Frank was the founder and namesake of Borland, having come down from the hills of Santa Cruz to write Sidekick. This rumor persisted even ten years later, with letters written to Frank instead of Philippe Kahn, the company president. Borland furthered this by putting Frank's name in credit screens as a tester. Without fail, at Comdex every year at least one customer would approach a Borland employee, complain about some problem, and threaten that since they knew Frank Borland personally, they damn well better get good service.

Figure 15-11 Fictional miner Frank Borland explains the virtues of Sidekick.

"I can't do that. Steve Jobs wears Armani suits."

— Bill Gates, Microsoft

After someone suggested that he wear Armani suits.

Take the T-Shirt Right Off My Back

Walk into any department store or thrift store and you will find t-shirts. These are simply clothing. Go to a bowling alley and you will also see t-shirts. These show who is on what team. T-shirts in the computer industry are different. Like Proust's madeleines, they evoke strong memories. They remind one of lost summers, late nights, stale pizza, and team camaraderie. But more so, they are trophies. They are proof that one was *there* when a product was created. They create a bond between customers and vendors. They are a pledge of allegiance. And they are one of the most important parts of high-tech marketing. After all, great ads may come and go, but a good t-shirt lasts forever. (Or at least a few hundred washings.)

Computer companies crank out thousands of t-shirts. Some commemorate trade shows. Many are for product launches. Some motivate employees. And others are statements.

Giving out t-shirts evokes fervor like no other giveaway, with the possible exception of vast quantities of cash. I've gotten hundreds of suit-clad businessmen to yell out "Cool" in unison, all for the chance of catching a t-shirt. At team events, developers flock around anyone disbursing t-shirts. During last minute crunches, teams will work extra long hours, jazzed by the cool t-shirt design created by marketing. Weary trade show attendees will even sit through lengthy technical lectures to get one.

Yet at the same time, t-shirts are extremely serious. They present a lasting outward image of a company. They are advertising that gets worn for a very long time. They can generate business, or turn it away. This has lead to many interesting shirts and interesting shirt-related battles. For example, an unhappy, longtime Microsoft employee discussed creating a "FYIFV" shirt. This stood for "F*** You, I'm Fully Vested" — a statement made by employees whose stock options were worth millions. No longer needing to work, they could begin to speak their minds, head off to race Ferraris, chase romance across Turkey, or buy sports teams. It's not an attitude that leads to hard, focused work, and Bill Gates apparently sent a lengthy flame mail to the developer considering such shirts — even though the shirts were just an idea and were never created.

Every good t-shirt has a story or a joke behind it. This chapter shows but a few of the many great t-shirts made in the computer industry.

Microsoft OS/2 Team Shirts

These two shirts, and the sweatshirt shown in chapter 8, "Shhh, It's a Secret Codename," are a rarity. Microsoft and IBM jointly developed OS/2 for many years. During the middle of OS/2 2.0 development, Microsoft and IBM's relationship disintegrated. IBM continued OS/2 development, while Microsoft pursued Windows 3.0 and Windows NT. The two shirts shown here are Microsoft OS/2 2.0 shirts — shirts for a jointly developed version of OS/2 that never shipped. The "Back to the Features" slogan on one of these shirts — a takeoff on the popular *Back to the Future* movie — is particularly amusing.

Microsoft Tiger

Tiger was the code name for Microsoft Media Server, a product that reliably stores and plays digital video off of an NT server. The polo shirt on the left is the official Tiger team shirt.

Microsoft announced Tiger at a trade show in Louisiana. By coincidence, one of the marketing managers for Microsoft was a big fan of a hot sauce called Tiger Sauce. He contacted the makers of Tiger Sauce and arranged for hundreds of bottles of Tiger Sauce to be used during the launch dinner. Furthermore, he even managed to get boxes of Tiger Sauce t-shirts, shown on the right, as unofficial launch giveaways.

Go Us!

This is a classic motivational t-shirt, with a caricature of Steve Ballmer, Vice President of Microsoft's systems group at the time, and oft regarded as the number 2 man at Microsoft. Steve is a very charismatic, energetic leader, known for pounding his fists on tables and walls and inspiring employees to super-human performance. Steve is also a runner, and at one point ran the New York

City marathon. After finishing the race, he apparently headed straight back to work, stretching out on the floor of the airplane to avoid leg cramps on the seven-hour flight back to Seattle. Here he bursts through a ribbon that says "Building the future one byte at a time."

Engineers Can't Spell

This is the back of the QuickBasic 4.5 team t-shirt. If you look closely, you can see the rallying slogan "There is no competiton." Fortunately, this isn't the team shirt for spell-checking software. Amusingly enough, a later Visual Basic t-shirt also has a spelling mistake on it.

The First NT T-Shirt

This is the first Windows NT t-shirt. The NT team was very proud that networking capabilities were tightly integrated into NT, as illustrated in this shirt.

I Want a Double Dipper

This shirt is from Qualitas, Inc., makers of numerous products, including 386Max. 386Max provides DOS memory management capabilities — giving more room for applications to run. One of the features it supplies is DPMI support. This stands for DOS Protect Mode Interface, and is a way of giving access to memory above the 640K barrier. DPMI is sometimes pronounced "Dip Me," as shown on the shirt.

RTFM

RTFM stands for Read the F***ing Manual. It is used as a reply to particularly stupid questions from users, especially when the questions are clearly documented in the manuals. This shirt, made by *Windows Tech Journal,* makes fun of the saying, with the caption "Read the Fine Magazine" below the bold letters. You can buy these shirts directly from *Windows Tech Journal* should you need to add one to your collection. I have heard that they are particularly popular for dress-down Fridays at corporate MIS departments.

McCarthyism

This is a classic competitive t-shirt from Microsoft, created by the Lan Man team. NetWare is a networking product from Novell that competes with Lan Man. Novell's corporate colors are red, and they use these colors on all of their logos and advertising. This shirt's competitive message comes from a clever use of the famous "Better Dead Than Red" political statement. It is similar to the use of the code name "Visine" for getting the red out of one's eyes.

Formal Wear

Finally, a t-shirt that program-mers can wear for black-tie affairs. This t-shirt shows a tuxedo on a penguin. It comes from NuMega, makers of power-ful debugging tools. They use a penguin on all of their market-ing materials and are known for amusing shirts, several others of which are shown in this book.

Life on the Loma Prieta Fault

A major earthquake struck the Bay Area in 1989, causing damage from its center south of Santa Cruz to as far away as San Francisco. It devas-tated numerous buildings, wiped out downtown Santa Cruz, destroyed highways, and shut down several high-tech companies. Borland, located a dozen miles away from the epicenter, received much damage. Whereas some Santa Cruz t-shirt vendors capitalized on the event with "Shift Happens" t-shirts, Borland brought out this unique computer-oriented shirt. One side says "The Epicenter of Software Design," while the other

says "Quake-proof software tested to 7.0." This is a reference to the strength of the earthquake. At first it was measured as 7.0 on the Richter scale, but it was actually 7.1.

A Protest Shirt

This is a very rare shirt created by a group of Microsoft employees. IBM and Microsoft had just signed an agreement, called the Joint Development Agreement, to make OS/2. A number of Microsoft programmers were not pleased by this agreement, fearing IBM's bureaucracy would drag them into an unpleasant series of never-ending meetings. Some even predicted it would doom OS/2 to failure, and created this shirt to protest the arrangement. In it you can see a takeoff of the *Saturday Night Live* "Oh No Mr. Bill" routine. At the time, the shirt seemed like unwarranted pessimism, but it proved to be prophetic.

You Decide

Company product lines can sometimes become confusing. For example, Borland produces dBASE and Paradox, two different databases that serve the same market. Likewise, for a period of time Microsoft developed both OS/2 and NT. Companies rarely produce conflicting product lines on purpose; usually they arise from historical or political circumstance. The marketing team devises messaging, rarely successful, to explain to customers who should use which product when. The t-shirt on the preceding page points out the awkward situation Microsoft was in at the time. On the front, there is a pair of dice that says "NT" and "OS/2." The back says "Hopefully, we'll come up with a rationalization which will make it easier to understand."

Tire Tracks All Across Your Back

This is another aggressive t-shirt, coming from the Microsoft languages group. Unlike the other BASIC team shirt shown in this chapter (page 272), the group managed to spell *competition* correctly this time. This shirt was created in celebration of shipping a number of languages products. The back features tire tracks driving all over the name "Borland."

Ugly Shirt Award

Vendors aren't the only creators of t-shirts. This shirt is made by Programmer's Paradise, one of the larger mail order houses catering to programmers. Programmer's Paradise creates shirts every year in conjunction with the launch of Microsoft language products. This particular shirt is for the launch of Microsoft C/C++ 7.0, the predecessor to Visual C++ 1.0. While most of the Programmer's Paradise shirts are both ugly and phallic, this one takes the cake.

Running Naked

This is one of the several shirts for the Microsoft Exchange team. The front says "Sacrificing Our Today for Your Tomorrow." On the back, a bunch of bare-bunned figures "run naked down the information superhighway."

Linux

Linux is a shareware version of Unix that's popular with hackers and with small companies establishing Web sites. If you are a Linux fan you will appreciate this hard to find t-shirt. Just as small companies and groups of users can create operating systems, they can also create t-shirts.

Pigs on the Wing

This is an early shirt from Borland's German office, featuring a pig flying around the globe. Several of Borland's European advertising campaigns featured flying pigs. It is strange and cute at the same time.

Nerd Humor

This shirt, created for the launch of Borland C++ 4.0, is a classic example of nerd humor. Borland C++ 4.0 was loaded with new features, one of the most important of which was exception handling. Exception handling is a C++ feature that makes error handling easier and safer. The syntax for exception handling uses the keywords *try*, *catch*, and *throw*. The tag line on the shirt says "try {throw} and catch the wave." Here, the "try {throw} and

279

catch" part is a takeoff on the popular saying "catch the wave" as well as on the C++ syntax, complete with the necessary { and }. The joke is continued in the design, which features a wave (in the sea — i.e., C) forming C++.

This shirt was extremely popular with programmers. When I gave them out at product launches (by making people yell "Cool," of course) I also revealed one of the better features of the shirt. Since the joke was obscure, non-programmers would surely approach the wearer and ask them to explain the meaning. This would turn into a great way for nerds to meet members of the opposite sex.

Splat!

This is another great competitive shirt. On it, a heavy dBASE box falls on and flattens a fox. Naturally this is a reference to FoxPro, dBASE's major competitor at the time. You may like to compare this shirt with dBASE for Windows' guillotining easter egg, as discussed in Chapter 10, "Hiding and Finding Easter Eggs."

All Types of Fun for The Family

Working at a high-tech company can be all-encompassing. Employees passionately embrace the corporate ethos, often involving their whole families. Many companies create shirts for babies saying things such as "Future Borland Programmer." This is one of the first shirts for the extended Microsoft family — a tribute to the Microsoft mom. They were popular Mother's Day gifts. Note that this shirt is unrelated to and precedes Microsoft Office Manager by many years.

IBM Attacks

IBM is known for its staid corporate image. This shirt is unique in that it is from IBM — traditionally a button-down-cotton-dress-shirt type of a company — and that it is extremely competitive. Most IBM shirts prior to this were corporate-looking polo shirts. This shirt is part of the OS/2 versus Windows NT wars. In it, IBM suggests that NT stands for "Nice Try." It was tied into a campaign with the slogan "Not just up and coming. Up and running." — reminding customers that OS/2 came out before NT, and already provided 32-bit multitasking.

Inside Out

Numega makes debuggers. The t-shirt shown here (front and back) has the slogan, "We're turning the debugging world inside out." And this is printed on an inside-out t-shirt. So the seam and label, as well as the printing, are all on the outside.

Cats and Mice

Computers have changed from being a strange device only used by strange nerds to an integral part of society. Computer jokes and shirts have similarly spread into pop culture. This is the sole non-industry shirt shown in the book. On it, a cat plays with a computer mouse.

Did You Know?

Overnight Steak

An early computer mail order firm, First Software, would send a free steak if a customer ordered software to be shipped overnight.

Shrink-Wrapping Blues

Creating a product involves much more than writing the software code and building the hardware. After all, for a product to be successful it must make it into the customers' hands. Creative product packaging can get it there.

Successful packaging can make a product succeed, where lousy packaging can often make it fail. There are typically two distinct types of packages: those sent directly to a customer, and those that will end up in a store. Packages that are sent directly usually come in plain brown boxes. There is no need for marketing material to make the products stand out, because customers have already bought them. On the other hand, packaging that will end up in a store is much more elaborate. After all, it must attract consumers' attention and convince them to buy the products.

There are all types of tricks that vendors use when designing packages. Some commission elaborate studies to determine the best colors. For example, orange and yellow, which are used in fast food restaurants to stimulate hunger, are often used for consumer software packages. You can find them on many Lotus and Borland packages, as well as Duraflame logs. Some choose a look to show corporate stability, to emphasize commonality across product lines, or to position the company on the cutting edge. Other products go for a unique look. For example, Fractal Design's FractalPaint ships in a paint can. A company called The Neon Software Co., Inc. sold software on clothes hangers.

Packaging has changed dramatically since the early software days. The early IBM PC manuals shipped in sturdy cardboard boxes, with metal three-ring binders. The size of these first manuals set a standard for computer book manuals and boxes that quickly replaced the competing 8.5 x 11 format. Slowly manuals became glue bound, boxes became thinner, and more and more manuals shipped on CD-ROM.

The reason for the evolution is simple: the market has grown. When shipping a small number of units, the unit cost isn't so important. Once a company ships several thousand, or more importantly several hundred thousand, the cost of each unit becomes extremely important.

For example, a typical computer manual costs around $3 to print, and a reproduced floppy disk around $.80. If a company has a product that has one manual and three disks, that's about $5.40. By contrast, a CD-ROM costs around $1.20. So if the company puts the manuals and programs on CD and doesn't ship disks, it can save roughly $3.20 per package. That might not seem like much, but if a company ships 100,000 units, it saves $320,000. That's why vendors spend so much time looking at compression software (to reduce the number of floppy disks), on-line documentation software (to put all documentation on CD-ROM), and box cost. Even shaving a few cents on a box can save a company tens of thousands of dollars.

Designing a product package takes several months and involves input from the marketing department, manufacturing department, artists, and the documentation group. The number of disks and the size of the manuals need to be estimated long in advance so that the proper box size and die vinyls can be created. The marketing art and carton copy are fit to this specific box size and shape. In fact, the reason why boxes often ship with *dunnage* (styrofoam and starch noodles, styrofoam sheets, or paper) is that the product actually required less room than estimated by the team. Dunnage fills the empty space to avoid damage during shipping. If, on the other hand, the product is too big to fit in the box, the marketing department may have to redesign the packaging at the last moment, thus wasting valuable time and money.

Once the package design is finished, an elaborate sign-off process ensures that the package has the correct text, the license agreement is put in properly, the box has the correct colors and illustrations, and everything else is in place and according to plan.

Despite such processes, however, manufacturers often make embarrassing mistakes and need to scrap inventory or otherwise put up with some humiliating customer complaints. The following are some stories about things that have gone wrong with product packaging.

What Should We Call It, Anyway?

One of the most important things to get right is the product's name. After all, the goal of all advertising and marketing activities is for a customer to remember the product name long enough to make it to a store or a telephone to buy the product.

Names, however, aren't the easiest thing to choose. Sometimes names are already in use. Before picking a name, vendors typically hire a trademark attorney to do a product name search. And often it is hard to decide on the best name for a product.

When the name changes early in the development cycle, the effects are minimal. Perhaps a few members of the press need to be informed of the switch, and a few manuals may need some reworking. But if the change occurs late in the game, the cost can be prohibitive. Manuals need to be scrapped, new box artwork and printing plates need to be created, and extra charges are paid to rush reprinting of the packages. Despite the cost, last-minute name changes occur suprisingly often.

For example, IBM printed 100,000 boxes with the name OS/2 Version 3.0. But a debate broke out. Some of the team wanted to call it Warp, after the product code name. Others wanted to call it Version 3.0, because it was the successor to version 2.1. To compromise, IBM called it OS/2 Warp Version 3.0, and as a result, scrapped all of the original boxes.

Great Quotes:

IBM on OS/2

"OS/2 will propel the industry forward into the '90s ... like racing through the doors instead of crawling through windows" — Joe Gugilemi, who later left IBM to head Kaleida.

IBM Amway

One of the campaigns IBM started to sell OS/2 involved getting IBM employees to sell OS/2 to their friends and neighbors. While the intention may have been to get broad awareness and excitement behind the product, the prospect of hundreds of thousands of IBM employees canvassing door to door to sell OS/2 was simply insane. Lee Levitt, an industry analyst for IDC, commented, "IBM created its own Amway program, having its 344,000 employees sell to neighbors, friends, family. If they announced it on April Fools' Day, I would have only half believed it."

Borland also changed names at the last minute. In a story similar to IBM's, Borland printed boxes for a product called Quattro Professional before deciding to shorten the name to Quattro Pro. In still another case, Borland created a product called the Borland Visual Control Pack. It printed boxes, placed pictures with the product name in reseller catalogs, and was ready to launch when Microsoft threatened to sue, because Microsoft had a product named the Visual Control Pack. Borland changed the product name to Borland Visual Solutions Pack, and scrapped the original boxes.

If You Are Having Problems, Just Smoke the Manual

The first run of the Borland Database Engine went out with "Reeference Manuals" instead of "Reference Manuals." Jokes circulated about what the proofreading team was smoking, and what advice the technical support team could give to customers who encountered problems.

And Speaking of Spelling Mistakes

The NetWare for SAA 2.0 manuals also had a misspelling in its reference manual. In this case, it spelled the product name wrong in the title, "Reference Guide for NetVeiw Operators."

Great Quotes:

I Hate dBASE

This is a public relations person's worst nightmare. In an article about dBASE 5.0 for Windows, Nicholas Petreley wrote, "I don't like dBase. I have never liked dBase. I didn't like it when it was dBase II and ran on 8080s with CP/M. I didn't like it when it was dBase II and it ran on 8088s under DOS."

It Won't Fit on the Shelves

For a product to succeed, it ought to appear on shelves at stores. The more store area a product occupies, the more chance someone will buy it. So vendors go through all types of schemes to get increased shelf space. Because store shelves are specific sizes, vendors also need to make sure the boxes will fit on shelves without trouble. When Borland released Borland Pascal 7.0, it tried a new style of packaging. Since the product contained much more software than the corresponding Turbo Pascal, the company wanted customers to sense immediately that it was a far more elaborate package. The idea was that hard-core programmers desiring the latest and greatest would find the product appealing. Unfortunately the design Borland chose, a cube, didn't fit well on store shelves, and thus many stores placed most of the copies in the warehouse.

Did You Know?

Turbo Wipes

When someone is running a successful computer company, all types of people flock around with business proposals, hoping the proposals will help catapult them to fame, and more importantly, to fortune. One of the stranger such proposals sent to Borland was for a product called Turbo Wipes. These were for a moist set of paper towelettes used to wipe, well, you know what. The only thing in common with Borland is that Borland was the maker of a series of software products with the name Turbo in them. (For example, Turbo Pascal.) Needless to say, Borland didn't take up the offer, despite the fully detailed business plan.

Crossed Wires

Borland printed the wrong phone number in a press release for ObjectVision 2.0. Instead of listing Borland's PR department, it listed the number of a local real estate office. It made a similar mistake with other releases, which inadvertently contained the unlisted number of a local priest.

Time Bombs

When vendors put software into beta test, they sometimes incorporate time bombs. Time bombs are pieces of code that prevent a piece of software from running after a certain date. Vendors add time bombs for a variety of reasons. Sometimes they are added to force beta testers to upgrade to the full version of the product. The free beta test version stops working when the time bomb dictates. Other times they are added to try to reduce piracy.

Unfortunately, vendors sometimes forget to remove the time bombs before they ship the shrink-wrapped versions of their software. Novell did this with PerfectOffice 3.0. The first 100,000 copies contained a time bomb. After December 31, 1994, anyone who installed it would get an error message. Work-arounds included resetting the system date before installing the software. A message, nonetheless, would still occur in many cases once the software loaded, saying, "Debug Message — Old THETA being updated." Several other errors, all stemming from the time bomb, would later occur.

Novell moved quickly to update the product and provided stickers, with a hotline phone number for customers to call, on boxes that had the out-of-date software.

Adobe ran into the same problem with Photoshop 3.0. It, too, had a time bomb in the beta program that would cause it to expire on January 1, 1995. And it, too, forgot to take it out of the shipping program. Unlike Novell, Adobe got part of it out. Instead of checking the month and date, it just checked that the year was 1994. Of course, that didn't do much good for any users during 1995. Adobe recalled the product and shipped version 3.0.1 to fix the problem.

Did You Know?

Lifeboat Associates was one of the very early distributors of microcomputer software. It sold a broad variety of products, and in 1980, it was the largest such distributor. Yet, in the Manhattan Yellow Pages it was listed under "Marine Supplies and Emergency Equipment."

Lifeboat was later bought by Programmer's Paradise, a popular mail order shop.

The World of Sex Objects

A rampant rumor (with variations for most computer manufacturers who make training video tapes) is that for the first run of Borland's World of Objects, the tape duplicator accidentally filled the remaining blank tape on the video with a pornographic movie trailer.

And Speaking of Sex

A tester at Borland wrote a sample Quattro Pro for Windows spreadsheet to test some aspect of the system. Because it was intended as an internal file only, and for some momentary amusement, he decided to name it "f***me." He renamed the file to "SECOND.BAR" before making it part of the official test suite.

Once others looked at the test program, they decided it provided interesting functionality. So they decided to expand the test program into a full-blown example program and ship it with the product. Thus, it ended up on the product disks.

Little did anyone realize, however, that Quattro Pro for Windows saves the original filename inside its files. So, the original "f***me" name remained embedded in the document.

Later, a user looking at the raw binary text in the Quattro Pro directory ran across the original filename. He immediately reported it to Spencer the Katt, and Borland quickly removed the naughty words from the sample program.

Did You Know?

Borland Office Chocolate Bars

Borland and WordPerfect collaborated to create a product to compete with Microsoft Office. Borland Office contained Paradox for Windows, Quattro Pro for Windows, and WordPerfect for Windows. In celebration, Borland created huge, custom chocolate bars that looked like the Office product. Many employees of WordPerfect, however, were Mormon. Since many Mormons don't eat chocolate, the gift didn't go over as well as it was intended.

So Who's Counting, Anyway?

And while we are on the sex theme, in an early version of Turbo Basic, the help team misspelled the word "Count." Programmers looking up this function found an entry for "C*nt" instead. This passed the spelling checker, but not the discerning eyes of several customers who found the function curious, if not offensive.

Getting Political

The French version of Lotus Ami Pro 3.1 contained the text "Impeach Clinton" inside of a DLL called AMIPROUI.DLL.

Did You Know?

How'd That Happen?

Lotus Jazz was a major flop. There is a rumor that not only was it a flop, but it was widely pirated, and Lotus received more returned units of Jazz than it shipped out.

And You Were Wondering About Nerd Breath

The Pennsylvania College of Technology once quarantined $400,000 worth of computers that were donated by IBM. When the machines arrived at the school, they smelled terrible. The school worried that they might be contaminated by toxic chemicals. In reality, the truck that brought the computers had also carried a leaky shipment of garlic oil.

Control Codes

The first 5,000 manuals of Paradox for DOS 3.5 had a typesetter control character at the beginning of a chapter instead of an illustration. This was corrected in subsequent runs.

Viruses

Viruses can strike anyone. Software development companies, trading disks and software back and forth on a regular basis, are particularly prone to viruses, and thus often have elaborate corporate procedures for virus checks. Prior to shipping a product, most companies check every single disk with the latest and greatest in anti-virus software. Sometimes, however, viruses slip through the cracks.

For example, Zinc Software accidentally shipped the Forms 18 virus with its C++ class library. Virtual Reality Laboratories inadvertently shipped the Michelangelo virus with some of its packages. In both cases, the companies worked quickly to clean the disks and rescue users.

WinDOS

Borland brought forth its much delayed Quattro Pro for Windows with great fanfare. It decided to take a bold step to differentiate itself from the competing Excel and Lotus, so it bundled the Windows and DOS versions of Quattro Pro in a single box, calling it WinDOS. Unfortunately for Borland, this turned into a nightmare. Customers couldn't figure out what WinDOS meant. Some thought it was a new operating system. Most customers, however, wanting to buy only a DOS or a Windows spreadsheet, figured they were paying twice what they should, and avoided the package. In an even more amusing twist, Microsoft had gotten wind of the name WinDOS through a trademark search, and thought Borland was about to release a competitor to Windows.

Borland withdrew the product from the market at great expense, and relaunched Quattro Pro for Windows as a stand-alone product. It later sold Quattro Pro to Novell.

This shirt commemorates the Quattro Pro for Windows release, complete with WinDOS.

I Don't Care What Your Name Is

When you install Microsoft Office (or any of the Microsoft Office products), the installation program asks for your name and company name. But when Microsoft shipped one version of Microsoft Office, the product support manager for Microsoft Office inadvertently entered his name on the disks before they went to the manufacturer. When a customer installed the product, the usual dialog box would pop up asking for the customer's name and company; however, "David Ferguson" and "Microsoft" were already entered. To make matters worse, there was no way to change the entries. Microsoft quickly corrected the problem.

PART 4

A Brief History of Time

The personal computer industry

has undergone enormous change since its inception in 1975. Slick Plug and Play Pentiums and PowerMacs have replaced the wood-paneled kit computers. Sophisticated spreadsheets chart data, whereas in the early days output consisted of blinking LED lights. And where one used to drive for miles to hear the latest computer news, one can hardly avoid hearing about computers no matter where one tries to escape.

This section takes a look at some of the history of the personal computer industry. It traces the evolution of computers from mechanical devices to today's desktop machines. It reveals the humble origins of today's corporate giants. And it traces the lawsuits that shaped the industry. Along the way, you'll walk down memory lane, looking at some of the editor keystrokes, dirty tricks, and activities from the past.

So, put on your bell-bottom jeans, dust off Osborne's 8080 programming guide, and jump right in.

"We were too tired, too arrogant, too stupid, I don't know what.."

— Gary Kawasaki, Apple
Regarding why Apple didn't fix some of the Macintosh's early speed and memory problems.

Gone but Not Forgotten

We'll begin our journey by taking a look at the evolution of the personal computer. Computers have been around long before the PCs we know and love today. In the early days, whole buildings were devoted to housing computers. With the introduction of the transistor, computers became dramatically smaller, but still required special, air-conditioned rooms. Such rooms, which often had their own power supplies, fire prevention devices, and air conditioning, were usually on raised floors. The cables connecting the computer to peripherals ran underneath. Glass windows allowed users to look in. The computer room was affectionately called the "glass house."

Integrated circuits enabled personal computers. Instead of needing a huge room, air conditioning, and industrial power, the same functionality (or much more) could fit in an awkward lunch box fed commands by flipping switches. With increasingly denser chips and more specialization, such computers have evolved to those we use and slave over today. What used to take a whole building now fits on a watch.

This chapter is a tour of some of the early computers, as well as some microcomputers that have long since fallen off the edge.

Early Iron

Inventors have designed mechanical computing devices for centuries. In the 1600s, Schickhard created a machine for performing six-digit addition and subtraction. During that same period, Blaise Pascal, the namesake for the computer language Pascal, created a series of weight-driven calculators that would eventually support eight-digit operations.

Charles Babbage, who lived from 1792–1871, is credited with designing the first computer, called the *difference engine*. He built a prototype, but the full project was canceled due to cost overruns. Meanwhile, he designed a more advanced machine called the Analytical Engine, as well as several other difference engines. These later machines were never funded and thus were not built. His plans, however, were not forgotten, and over a hundred years later a team at the London Science Musuem convened to create one of the advanced difference engines. They completed a working version in 1991.

Many inventors followed. Hollerith created a punched card machine tabulator used in the 1890 census. In 1892, William S. Burroughs created a machine that would kick off the calculator industry. In 1935, IBM created the IBM 601, a punch card–based computing machine, and sold roughly 1,500 of them.

Konrad Zuse created the V1, often viewed as the first computer built, in 1936. It was a mechanical machine that used binary mathematics. It had a limited memory, but could read control programs punched on 35mm film. Zuse followed with the V2 in 1938, and in 1941, the V3, which was partially funded by the German Air Ministry. The V3 had a relay-based memory and processor, and was destroyed during an air raid. After World War II, the computers were renamed Z1, Z2, and Z3 to avoid confusion with the V2 rockets.

Meanwhile, at Iowa State, another computer was born, called the Atanasoff-Berry, after Professor Atanasoff and his graduate student, Berry.

Professor Atanasoff was given a $7,000 grant to build the computer, which was called the "ABC" for short, and was completed in 1940. It was the first electronic computer, and was built using vacuum tubes. The legend is that Professor Atanasoff got the idea for the computer in 1937 while he was out for a drive.

At the same time, Howard Aiken was creating the MARK I automated calculator at Harvard, which he started in 1939. This project, done in conjunction with IBM, who paid $500,000 to fund it, was also called the Automatic Sequence Controlled Calculator. It was 51 feet long, weighed 5 tons, and had 750,000 parts. It was followed by the Selective Sequence Electronic Calculator. Both of these machines read their instructions from paper tape.

In 1943, Professor Brian Randell created the Colussus machine, which was used for breaking the German Enigma code during World War II. This computer was built with over 2,500 valves. It was a follow-on to an earlier code breaker called the Heath Robinson. ENIAC (Electronic Numerical Integrator And Calculator) was built in 1946 out of vacuum tubes at the University of Pennsylvania. It was programmed by plugging cables into sockets. It weighed 30 tons and used 150,000 watts of energy to drive the 17,468 vacuum tubes. It was followed in 1947 by the Harvard Mark II, the same computer in which Grace Hopper found a moth. In 1948, Alan Turing created a computer at Manchester University. Called the Manchester Mark I, it was the first machine that stored programs, a critical step towards today's computers. A group at Cambridge University followed, and a company called Ferrantis sold two copies of the Manchester computer, making it the first commercially sold computer.

The UNIVAC (Universal Automatic Computer) machine, which was as adept at processing text as numbers, came along in 1951.

Here are some others:

BINAC (1949)	**CADAC** (1952)	**APE** (1953)
Harvard MARK III (1949)	**ELECOM** (1952)	**AVIDAC** (1953)
SEAC (1950)	**MINIAC** (1953)	**OMIBAC** (1954)
SWAC (1950)	**MONROBOT** (1953)	**CUBA** (1954)
LEO (1951)	**FLAC** (1953)	**DYSEAC** (1954)
MANIAC (1952)	**GAMMA** (1953)	
	ALWAC (1953)	

There were also computers such as the Whirlwind, a 16-bit computer used for aircraft simulation, which later led to the SAGE air defense computers; and IBM computers such as the 650, 650-RAMAC, and 701.

Mainstream commercial computers followed with the seven giants: IBM, Univac, Burroughs, NCR, RCA, GE, and Honeywell. Of these, IBM still remains; Univac, Burroughs, and RCA are part of Unisys; NCR was purchased by AT&T; and GE was bought by Honeywell.

Birth of a Nation

Next came the personal computer, heralded in by the Altair. In this early era, which spanned the period from 1975-1977, there was no such thing as a standard, and the goal wasn't proliferation. Rather, the early market was a hobbyist market, in part an offshoot of the counterculture revolution, and most machines came as kits.

These early machines weren't particularly easy to use, and by today's standards didn't do too much, but they started an industry, and were the birthplace of giants Apple and Microsoft. Most of these machines were programmed by flipping switches. Here are some of the early machines.

1. **Apple I** — This kit computer, designed by Steven Wozniak while still at Hewlett-Packard, turned into the beginnings of Apple Computer.

2. **Electronic Products Micro 68.**

3. **HP 9100** — Of the machines listed here, this is the only one that wasn't a kit. Coming out in 1968, it was focused at the business market and cost $5,000.

4. **IMSAI 8080** — This was an imitation of the Altair design, also based on an 8080. IMSAI was an important early player, not only for helping popularize PCs, but because of the spin-offs, ComputerLand and MicroPro.

5. **IMSAI VDP-80** — A successor to the IMSAI 8080, it had a reputation for never working.

6. **MOS KIM-1** — This machine had 1K RAM; 2K ROM; 20 keys; a 6-digit, 7-segment display; a serial port; and a port for connection to an audio tape recorder. The microprocessor was a 6502. MOS was bought by Commodore in October 1976 and became the starting point for Commodore's PC business.

7. **Martin Research MIKE 2** — an 8008-based kit. Used a 20-key keypad for entering programs.

8. **Martin Research MIKE 3** — an 8080-based kit. Used a 20-key keypad for entering programs.

9. **MITS Altair 680b** — Appearing in 1976, it used a 6800 CPU and featured 17K of RAM. It used switches and panel lights for its input and output and was introduced to combat other 6800-based PCs, most notably the SWTP 6800. It never did well.

10. **MITS Altair 8800** — This was the first kit computer to be sold, and lead to the creation of the personal computer industry. You could get the kit for $439, which also gave you free membership in the Altair Users Club. One K of memory cost an extra $97. A serial card was another $119. And for $780 extra, you could get a terminal with a keyboard and a 32-character display. Tacking on BASIC ran another $350-$750.

11. **Polymorphic Systems Poly-88** — An 8080-based system originally called the Micro-Altair.

12. **Processor Technology Sol** — This computer was named to honor Les Solomon, the editor of *Popular Electronics* (the premiere computer hobbyist magazine of the time). It was, as well, a joke on the idea that it provided the wisdom of Solomon. It was created as part of a challenge from Les Solomon himself, who wanted to run a cover story on a terminal. Instead of creating a terminal, the engineers built a full 8080-based computer.

13. **RCA VP-111 hobby computer** — This was based on an 1802 microprocessor and came with 1K RAM. You programmed it with the CHIP-8 language.

14. **Scelbi-8B** — This featured the 8008 chip and 4K of RAM. It cost $849 assembled and tested.

15. **Sphere 1** — This computer was unique because it had a CRT built in.

16. **SWTP 6800** — Billed as "The Computer System You Have Been Waiting For," it featured a 6800 with 2K of RAM. The price for the starting kit was $450.

17. **Wave Mate Jupiter II** — another 6800-based machine, famous for delivering a complete system for under $1,000.

Did You Know?

The Blue Goose

MITS, which kicked off the personal computer industry with its MITS Altair computer, had a GM motor home, called the MITSmobile, that it used for promoting its products. The MITSmobile was also called the Blue Goose. MITS would drive it around the country, starting computer clubs. Bill Gates went on one of these tours. A competitor, Sphere, followed suit and created the Spheremobile.

An Early Letter from Bill

Bill Gates wrote one of the first letters complaining about personal computer magazine benchmarks. It would be the first of many letters vendors have sent regarding benchmarking techniques. In this case, though, the benchmarks weren't on a Microsoft product.

In the third issue of *Byte Magazine,* Bill Gates wrote in to comment on *Byte*'s evaluation of chips. He gave a strong vote for the 8080, ranking it over the IMP-16 and the 8008, saying, "I have spent the last three years programming microcomputers, most recently writing ALTAIR BASIC with Paul Allen and Monte Davidoff, and hope to share some of what I've learned with your readers." He criticized the benchmarking methods, and ended the letter with a correction: "PS: The program on page 54 of *Byte* #1 doesn't work since the dispatch table entries are three bytes long instead of two."

Rememberance of Things Past

While typing at your 120MHz Pentium with a multidisk, quad-speed CD-ROM drive; 64-bit graphics card; rumble seat speaker system; ISDN modem; and 64M of RAM; do you ever reminisce of times past? Fondly remember the simpler days when 16K was an unbelievable amount of memory? When keyboards were an unheard-of luxury?

A programmer at Microsoft did. After reading the book *Hackers*, Claus Giloi became excited about the enthusiasm of the early hobbyists, and decided to create a virtual Altair and IMSAI. He bought an 8080 reference manual at a used book store and used it to write an 8080 emulator. He used Bill Gates' original Altair, on display at Microsoft, as a model for his user interface. And then designed a Windows program to reproduce both computers (Figure 18-1). You program them by clicking on the switches, and read the output from the LEDs.

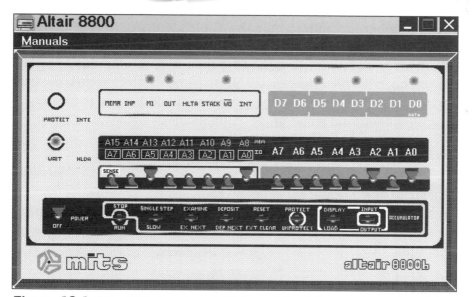

Figure 18-1 Claus' Windows-based Altair emulator fully reproduces the MITS Altair 8800b, complete with an 8080 emulator and LED output.

The World Changes

1977 was a great year, topped by two events that would irrevocably alter the computer industry: *Star Wars* and the Apple II came out. Both changed the outlook, the vocabulary, and the culture of a generation.

Pet rocks, the namesake of the Commodore PET, were the latest vogue. KC and the Sunshine Band topped the charts with "I'm Your Boogie Man," and even the theme song from *Rocky* was played over and over. *Saturday Night Fever* was a hit movie, and people actually wore bell-bottoms and platform shoes. Steve Miller and The Grateful Dead were popular. Hipper programmers listened to the mechanized sound of Kraftwerk, Rush's sci-fi rock, or even the Sex Pistols and the Ramones.

Along with this mix, the world of kit computers came to an end. Two friends, working out of a garage, created a machine that was to turn around the perception of personal computers; namely, the Apple II. The Apple II took the world by storm. All of a sudden, computers could be used by anyone. They were affordable, yet comparatively easy to use. You didn't need a soldering iron and you didn't need to enter programs by flipping switches. They had a catchy, approachable name. They had a friendly image. And they had fun software.

There were a number of computers in the Apple family, including the Lisa, which was a precursor to the Macintosh. Neither the Apple III nor the Lisa ever took off, being slightly mismatched for their time. Numerous Apple clones sprung up, with the Franklin Ace perhaps providing the first time a clone vendor gained strong market penetration. The following list shows the early Apple lineup, and some of the Apple clones.

Apple II	**Franklin Ace 100**
Apple IIc	**Orange**
Apple IIe	**Peach**
Apple III	**Pineapple**
Apple Lisa	**Pinecom**
Apple Lisa 2	**Wombat**
Computer and Peripheral Products — **Wildcat**	

Did You Know?

Captain Crunch

Captain Crunch, otherwise known as Richard Draper, was the champion of the phone phreaking movement. He also was an avid programmer and wrote an early word processor called EasyWrite. Some say he wrote this while in jail on phone phreaking charges. He wrote Easy Write because the word processor he wanted to use, Electric Pencil, wouldn't run on the Apple II.

IBM made a deal with Draper to offer EasyWrite as a word processor when it first shipped the IBM PC. It was a strange clash of cultures.

A Flash from the Past

One of the best selling Microsoft products in 1982 was the Premium Pack — a combination of its Apple Z-80 card, 16K memory board, and CP/M.

CoCo

The TRS-80 Color Computer was originally going to be called the TRS-90.

Meanwhile, in Gotham City

The introduction of the Apple II, while historically significant, didn't stop production of other computers. In fact, it was part of an incredible explosion of computer creativity. At the same time that the Apple II came out, Commodore released the Pet and Radio Shack released the TRS-80. In the four years that followed, hundreds of different computers came forth, from big names such as Hewlett-Packard and Atari, as well as small companies that released one machine before going under or mutating into different ventures.

It was a time of incompatibility. While most machines were based on the S-100 bus, used a Z80 for the processor, and ran CP/M, it was unlikely that a program designed for one machine would load, much less run, on another machine.

The 8086 and 6502 were also popular chips, and despite CP/M's overwhelming market share, there were plenty of other operating systems, including TurboDOS, Cromix, MP/M, Apple DOS, VersaDOS, HDOS, AMOS, OS65, NSDOS, TRSDOS, UCSD p-System, Pick, and CDOS.

Machines were sold preassembled, and the market started to shift to a business rather than hobbyist focus. Although Apple was a dominant market player, it was a giddy time filled with possibility. Here are some of the many machines from the time.

Adds Multivision

Alpha Micro AM-100

ALSPA AC-1 — This was an early portable, weighing 18 pounds. It used the Z80A and had 64K of RAM and an 8" floppy. It listed for $1,995.

Altos 586 — An 8086-based computer that ran Xenix, MS-DOS, Oasis, and Pick.

Altos 8000

Amperex GP 300

Atari 400

Atari 800

Basis 108 — This machine boasted both a 6502 and 8088. It came with 64K of RAM and could display 6-color graphics at 280 x 192.

BMC 20B

Bridge Computer Systems — This featured a 6 MHz Z80 and came with 256K of RAM.

Burroughs B20

Bytec Hyperion

California Computer 2210A

CCS Series 300

Challenger

CMS-16/UNX

Colonial Data SB-80/4

Commodore 64 — This and the two other Commodore computers listed here were favorites among home users and early programmers, especially given their low price tags. For example, the VIC-20 sold for under $300 when it came out.

Commodore Pet

Commodore VIC-20

CompuPro System 816

Computer Devices Dot

COSMAC ELF

Cromemco System One — This was an extremely popular computer, featuring a Z80A chip, 64K of RAM, 780K of disk storage via its floppies, and the CROMIX OS. It came in a 7" x 14" box, and sold for $3,995.

Custom Computer Systems ExecJr — Another lightweight machine, it had a Z80, 64K of RAM, dual 8" floppies, and weighed in at 30 pounds. All for $2,695.

Darius

Data General MPT/100

Data-Neve 8864

DEC Rainbow — The Rainbow featured Z80 and 8088 chips, and could run CP/M and MS-DOS. With 256K RAM, they started at $3,000. DEC thought it would own the market, but the systems never took off.

DECmate II — This was based on a 6120 processor, which used the PDP-8 instructions.

Delta Gold

Digital Group

ACE Discovery

Dual System 83 — This machine had an 8 MHz 68000, 256K of RAM, and ran Unix.

Dynabyte

Epson QX-10

Exxon 500

Fujitsu Micro 16s — This was another machine with both a Z80A and 8086, and was one of the early Japanese computers to hit the U.S. market.

Gavilan Computer Gavilan — a nine-pound 8088 portable with 80K of RAM. It listed for $3,995 in 1983. The president of the company used to be the president of Zilog.

Golden Computer International Sekon 64

Heath/Zenith Z-89 — This was another favorite, stemming from Heath Kit's early role as a provider of great electronics kits. It featured a 5.25" floppy, keyboard, two Z80s, and 48K of RAM.

Honeywell Microsystem 6/10

HP-65

HP-85 — This was a very popular micro-computer. (See Figure 18-2.)

HP-87

HP-150

Hyperion

Hyundai

IBC Cadet

IBM 5100 — This was one of the very early personal computers from IBM, predating the IBM PC.

IBM 5110

IBM CS-9000 — a 68000-based PC that came out after the IBM PC. This machine was focused more on lab work.

IBM System/23

ICL PC1

IMS SX — One of the ads for this computer ended with the line, "We'll tell you everything you ever wanted to know about SX."

Interact — This was an 8080-based machine, with 16K RAM, a keyboard, and a built-in 1500-bps cassette drive. It featured low-res color graphics, a tone generator, and Microsoft Basic.

Intersystems DPS 1

Intersystems PDS-80

Intertec HeadStart

Ithaca 525/800

JCS DCM*80

Kaypro — This was another very popular machine, famous for its portability.

LNW Research Corp LNW80

Lomas Data Products S100-PC

Figure 18-2 The HP-85 was a popular computer with a built-in display.

M*P*S The Computer For People Who Love Money — This has to be the all-time best name for a computer. It was a discount-priced computer billed as being made from the same parts as the pros. It featured a Z80, 64K of RAM, and a 7" amber display. Advertisements contained lines such as "Sure. The Computer For People Who Love Money won't do color graphics. But you're in business, not art school. And no, it's not IBM compatible..." All for $1,777.

Mercator MBS 4000

Micro Technology Unlimited MTU-130

MicroDaSys Inc MiniFrame — This featured two 68000 chips and one 6809, along with 256K of RAM.

Modula Computer Systems Lilith

Morrow Designs Decision I

NEC PC-8000

NEC/APC — This is one of the heavier entrants into computer history. It had a 2 MHz 8086, 8" floppies, 8-color graphics, and a whopping 256K of memory. It weighed close to 100 pounds, and also had a 40-pound 10M hard drive.

NNC Series 80

Non-Linear Systems Kaycomp II — This was an Osborne 1 clone, with a Z80 chip, two 5-1/4" floppies, and a 9" diagonal screen that displayed 80 columns. All for $1,795.

North Star Advantage 64K

North Star Floating Point

North Star Horizon II

Ohio Scientific Challenger I — Ohio Scientific was one of the early pioneers that bridged the gap between the kit computers and the commercial computers. Their top-end machine at the end of 1978 was the C3B. Featuring three processors, 48K of RAM, two 8" floppy drives, and a 74MB hard drive, it listed for $11,090. The Ohio Scientific is always dear to my heart, because it is where I cut my first BASIC code.

Ohio Scientific Challenger II

Ohio Scientific Challenger III

Ohio Scientific Challenger IV

Olivetti M20

Onyx 5001

Osborne 1 — This was a revolutionary machine at the time. It featured a Z80A, 64K RAM, Dual 100K floppies, and a 5" CRT. Its most notable feature was portability. It weighed 24 pounds, measured 9" x 20" x 13," and had a weatherproof case. It also came with a full bundle of software, including CP/M, WordStar, MailMerge, SuperCalc, Cbasic, and Mbasic. In 1982, it retailed for $1,795.

Osborne Vixen — This came out in late 1984, after Osborne had emerged from Chapter 11.

OSM Zems2 — OSM prided themselves on the machine's built-in, 20-minute, uninterruptable power supply.

Otrona Attache — This was another early Z80A-based portable, weighing 18 pounds.

Perkins-Elmer 7350

Personal Microcomputers PMC-80 — This was a TRS-80 clone.

Pronto Series 16 — an 80186-based machine.

Royal Business Machines Alphatronic Personal Computer

Quasar Data Products — Quasar billed this as providing the "best user-friendly implementation of a CP/M compatible operating system on the market."

Quay Corporation Quay 500

Sage Computer Technology Sage II

Sanyo 2000

Seattle Computer System 2

Sharp MZ-5600

Sinclair ZX81 — This was an all-time favorite computer, and was extremely popular in 1981. Selling for $99.95 in kit form

($149.95 assembled), it featured Extended BASIC, 1K of memory (expandable to 16K), and a hook-up for TV sets. Timex bought out Sinclair and turned the computer into the Timex Sinclair 1000.

Smoke Signal Chieftain — This ran OS-9 on a 6809.

Sorcerer

STM Pied Piper

Sunrise Systems C8/16

Superbrain II. Superbrain was another early leader. This machine featured a 24 x 80 12" display, two Z80 chips, and 64K of RAM.

Systems Group System 2800

Tano Dragon — Radio Shack Color Computer compatible

Tarbell Empire System

Technico 9900. Based on the TI 9900 chip, it featured 2K of RAM, 2K of ROM, and 2K of EPROMs.

Tecmar 86M — This featured an 8086, 512K of RAM, and two 8" floppies. It ran MP/M-86 and in 1982 sold for $7,595.

TEI System 48

Televideo TS 802

Texas Instruments Professional Computers

Texas Instruments TI 99/4A

Toshiba EW-1000

Toshiba T-200

TRS-80 Color Computer

TRS-80 Model I — These were another popular set of computers. I remember holing up in a closet in a school library to program one of these. The keyboard and cassette cables always fell out, so you needed to hold the cables in with one hand and program with the other.

TRS-80 Model II

Vector 2600

Vector 3005

Vector 5005

Vector MZ

Victor 9000

Visual 1050

Wang Professional

Wicat 68000 — This was a high-end machine at its time, featuring a 68000 processor, 256K RAM, and a 10MB hard drive, running the WICAT OS.

Wyse

Xerox 820

Xerox Alto

Xerox Star — Clearly the most influential computer per units sold, this was an incredibly innovative computer, featuring a mouse and graphical user interface. It never took off in the market. It debuted in 1981 for a mere $16,595.

Enter IBM

Apple dominated the computer world of 1981. It provided the first clear mass market leader. The IBM PC is what cemented the computer revolution and put the coffin lid on hundreds of incompatible computer vendors.

By the end of 1981, "Endless Love," the theme song from the horrible movie of the same name, topped the charts along with Kenny Loggins' "I Don't Need You." *The French Lieutenants' Woman* and *Body Heat* were shocking sensibilities. *Chariots of Fire,* with its synthesized Vangellis sound track won the Academy Award for best picture. Most programmers preferred *Raiders of the Lost Ark* or John Water's *Polyester.* The members of R.E.M. had been together a year and had created their first single, "Radio Free Europe."

Into this environment came the IBM PC, released in September 1981. The first IBM PC was a conservative machine, featuring an 8088, a monochrome screen, and Microsoft's DOS. *Byte's* first review of the IBM PC asserted

> For those of us who dislike giants, the IBM Personal Computer comes as a shock. I expected that the giant would stumble by overestimating or underestimating capabilities the pubic wants and stubbornly insisting on incompatibility with the rest of the microcomputer world.

> But IBM didn't stumble at all; instead, the giant jumped leagues in front of the competition … In fact, the only disappointment about the IBM Personal Computer is its dull name.

Amusingly, similar sentiments about IBM names still applied 14 years later, when reviewers preferred the code name Butterfly to the official name Thinkpad 701C.

While for a year after its release there were still vendors designing custom computers, that was soon to change. By the mid-eighties, just a few short years later, with the exception of Apple, most of the early computer vendors were gone or had shifted to producing IBM PC clones. And with this change came the meteoric rise of Microsoft.

The IBM PC had an open architecture, so not only could numerous cards be created for it, but so could numerous clones. The clone vendors mostly competed by providing cheaper computers, or variations to the IBM line, such as the Compaq Portable.

At first, most of the clones were pretty incompatible. Some software would run, and some wouldn't. Microsoft Flight Simulator, with its sophisticated graphics, was the ultimate compatibility test. If the computer would run this software, most people figured that it was sufficient to run most other software, too.

IBM followed the PC and XT with the AT in 1983. This featured an 80286, and like the earlier IBM models, was duplicated by the clone vendors. The one IBM computer that wasn't duplicated was the IBM PCjr, released in 1984. This computer, which IBM hoped would take over the home market, turned out to be an abysmal flop for many reasons, including the hard-to-use infrared chiclet keyboard.

Some of the early IBM PCs included

IBM PC — released at the end of 1981, the first models consisted of a 4.77 MHz 8088, 16K of RAM, 40K of ROM, a video/printer adapter, room for two 5-1/4" drives, and an audio cassette connection, for $1,565. With a 160K floppy, 64K of RAM, and a monitor, it upped to $3,005. And with two floppies, a CGA card, and a re-labeled Epson MX-80, the price came to $4,500.

IBM PC XT

IBM PCjr — Based on the 8088, this featured 64K of RAM, an infrared keyboard, two cartridge slots for games, a joystick, and a light pen. It cost $699 without a disk drive, and $1,269 with a disk drive and 128K of RAM. It was a major flop.

IBM AT

And here are some of the early IBM PC clones

ACT Apricot	**Osborne PC**
Advance 86	**Sanyo MBC550**
AMI-PC	**Seequa Chameleon**
Columbia Data Products	**Silver Fox**
Compaq Portable	**Sperry Personal Computer**
Corona PC	**Tandy 1000**
Corona Portable PC	**Tandy 2000**
Eagle PC	**Tava PC**
Handwell PC	**TeleVideo PC**
IBS PC 2000	**TeleVideo XT**
ITT XTRA	**Trios MicroMix 16**
Leading Edge PC	**Zenith Z-150**
Mindset	

Did You Know?

IBM 5100

The IBM 5100 was the first PC from IBM. It had a BASIC and APL interpreter. The hardware guys didn't think it needed a low-level language, such as Assembly, so the team wrote an Assembler using APL.

Store Struck

In 1982, a *Byte* columnist toured 165 computer stores counting what machines were sold. Of the 37 different computer brands he found, here are the top 14, showing the percentage of stores they were in. You can see the market starting to consolidate around Apple and IBM:

Computer	Percentage in Stores
Apple	73%
Atari	37%
IBM	23%
Commodore	22%
Vector Graphic	21%
Radio Shack	21%
Cromemco	18%
Texas Instruments	13%
North Star	11%
Dynabyte	11%
Data General	10%
DEC	9%
Zenith	9%
Altos	9%

Did You Know?

Camping Out

Tecmar was one of the early computer add-on vendors, and it supplied many of the hard drives and cards used by early IBM PC programmers. The company wanted to get a jump on the IBM PC market, so when the machines first came out, it had employees camp on the doorstep of the Sears Business Center in Chicago. Thus, it was able to buy the first two IBM PCs ever sold. As soon as the employees got the computers, they drove them back to Tecmar's headquarters in Ohio and ran them through analysis equipment to figure out how they worked.

What Came Next

By the end of the eighties, only two machines dominated: the IBM PC and its family of clones, and the Macintosh. Apple protected the Macintosh heavily, so only one clone really took off, the Taiwanese Akkord Jonathan. (Akkord went out of business and was sued by Apple, apparently in that order.)

Clone vendors invested great time and efforts in making their computers as compatible as possible with the IBM machines. As with the beginning of the eighties, numerous vendors showed up and disappeared. Of the early clone makers, Compaq and Dell are the main survivors.

A History of PC Bus Architecture

The bus is the part of the computer that is used to communicate between the motherboard (the main processor in a computer) and cards that are in the expansion slots; for example, the graphics card, cards for scanners, sound cards, and so forth. If you have a really fast expansion card, but the bus is slow, the computer won't be able to leverage the full capabilities of the card. So getting a fast, expandable bus architecture is important.

Most early machines used either unified motherboards (that is, there were no expansion slots) or the S-100 bus format. The S-100 format was that designed by MITS for the Altair. Thus, it was the first PC bus format. It was named for the bus's 100-line structure. MITS wanted to call it the Altair

315

bus, but competitors also used the bus format, referring to it as the MITS-IMSAI-Processor Tech-Polymorphic bus. This was quite a mouthful. On an airplane ride from San Francisco to a computer conference in Atlantic City, some key members of Cromemco and Processor Technology decided to simply call the bus the S-100, where S stood for "standard." The name stuck.

When IBM came out with the IBM PC in 1981, it introduced a new bus format. The bus architecture for the IBM PC family has changed much since then. Following are some of the key bus architecture changes in successive years. Each design was made with the idea of increasing throughput and performance.

1981

The IBM PC debuted with a bus that operated at 4.77 MHz and supported 8-bit cards in the expansion slots.

1983

The IBM AT came out, and wowed the world with its 6 MHz 80286 processor. Immediately, vendors provided ways to change the clock crystal to run the processor at 8 MHz, which the chip inherently supported. Clone vendors took advantage of this to gain an edge. The bus was a 16-bit bus, initially running at 6 MHz and then later increasing to 8 MHz. This is the ISA, or Industry Standard Architecture bus.

1987

IBM, hoping to release a better bus architecture, but in many eyes trying to kill off the clone business by establishing a proprietary bus architecture, released a new bus with the IBM PS/2, called the Micro Channel Architecture (MCA). The bus never took off, and without broad support from peripheral vendors, customers never fully realized the advantages it promised.

1988

Compaq, perhaps hoping to leverage the failure of MCA and its key position in the industry, released the 32-bit EISA (Extended Industry Standard Architecture) bus.

1992

Dell, with its XPS series, launched the VESA VL-bus. This bus was designed by a consortium of PC vendors; hence, its name, which stands for Video Electronics Standards Association.

1993

NEC launched the latest bus standard with their NEC Image P60. The PCI bus (peripheral component interconnect) is now found on most PC clones.

Did You Know?

Macintosh Floppies

The floppy disks on Macintosh computers store more data than those on PCs. They do this by varying the speed of the floppy motor depending upon the location of the disk head. As a result, they have the same bits-per-inch rate, no matter the track. The motor speed change follows the same pattern as the music diatonic scale.

It Even Does Windows

Windowing systems became popular, in concept at least, in 1983 through 1985. There was VisiCorp's VisiOn, whose name was an obvious pun on Vision. IBM was working on TopView. Digital Research had GEM. A small company called DSR, run by Nathan Myhrvold, had a TopView clone called Mondrian. The Macintosh would debut in 1984.

And in 1983, Microsoft announced Windows 1.0, along with a list of computers upon which it would run. The listing on the next page shows these early, ready-for-Windows computers. Windows would ship two years later, at the end of 1985.

This is a listing of computers from a 1983 article in *Byte* showing computers that were going to run Microsoft Windows 1.0. Of course, Windows itself didn't ship until two years later.

Apple IIe/Rana Drive System with 8086

Burroughs B20

Bytec Hyperion

Columbia Data Products MPC Portable

Compaq Portable

Computer Devices Dot

DEC Rainbow 100

Eagle PC

Hewlett-Packard 150

Honeywell Microsystem 6/10

IBM Personal Computer

Texas Instruments Professional Computer

Wang Professional Computer

Zenith Z-100

Great Quotes:

Incompatible Unix's

At the 1993 PC Expo, Bill Gates suggested that Windows NT would effectively knock out Unix. In fact, he went a step further, saying that Windows NT was in fact the same thing as Unix: "In a short time, it will be the most popular form of Unix ever. Windows NT will outsell those other incompatible versions of Unix."

Of course, while Windows NT certainly replaces the need for Unix in many cases, it and Unix are very different. Calling it the standard Unix, and the other, real versions of Unix incompatible, is pretty funny.

Do You Remember These Software Lines?

Just as there were tons of early computers, there were tons of early software packages. Some of the dominant early vendors were MicroPro, VisiCorp, Microsoft, and Digital Research. The following shows the software lineup of some of the most popular vendors in the early eighties. Most of these vendors have disappeared. Of the list shown here, only Microsoft and Broderbund have grown significantly since the early days.

Much of the software at the time was CP/M- and Apple-based. If you were using computers at the time, this list should bring back fond memories:

VisiCorp

VisiCalc

VisiDex

VisiPlot

VisiSchedule

VisiTerm

VisiTrend

VisiFile

Desktop/PLAN

Microsoft

Fortran

BASIC

Cobol

Z-80 Softcard

Typing Tutor

Olympic Decathalon

mu MATH/mu SIMP

mu LISP/mu STAR

MicroPro

WordStar

SuperSort

MailMerge

DataStar

SpellStar

CalcStar

Broderbund

Galaxy Wars

Alien Rain

Alien Typhoon

Apple Panic

Midnight Magic

Space Quarks

Sierra On Line

Screenwriter II

The General Manager

Beagle Brothers

Apple Mechanic

Beagle Bag

DOS Boss

Double Take

Pronto DOS

Utility City

Sirius Software

Space Eggs

Gorgon

Sneakers

Epoch

Beer Run

Hadron

Pulsar II

Epoch

This Microsoft ad from early 1980 shows its software line at the time.

Did You Know?

Spreadsheet Proliferation

VisiCalc was the first spreadsheet ever created. Three years after VisiCalc was introduced, there were over 24 different spreadsheets on the market.

Transcendentals

Originally, VisiCalc didn't have support for *transcendental functions* (mathematical functions such as sine and log). But a sneak preview write-up on VisiCalc praised it highly for its support of transcendentals. Therefore, it added them.

322

An Editor Is a Nerd's Best Friend

No matter what anyone does with a computer, at one point or another they've used an *editor*. In the early days, editors were relatively unsophisticated, designed to allow editing of system files and programs, and completely driven by keystroke commands. Today, editors have evolved into sophisticated programmers' editors, word processors, and desktop publishing systems. And unlike the early editors, most editors today allow the selection of commands from menus, use a mouse, and even display text with multiple fonts.

In the first days of editors, such things were unheard-of luxuries. To use the editor, the user needed to memorize a set of commands for navigating and editing files. Such commands became ingrained into daily life. And after spending a large amount of time learning such commands, most people became religious about their editor choice. So a person who was used to vi would only use vi, and would think Brief users were insane. People who memorized the WordPerfect keystrokes would resist moving to

Microsoft Word. In fact, if you ask a programmer about the first editor they ever used, they will fondly recount its various keystroke commands, even if they haven't touched the editor in 15 years. Likewise, people who haven't used WordPerfect for DOS in years can tell you what Shift+F7 does.

Of course, if you think line editors are somewhat clunky and hard to use, you must remember that before editors, everything was entered via switches, punched paper tapes, or decks of cards. So even though editors such as edlin were awkward, at least they were better than the alternatives.

There are hundreds of different word processors and editors, but certain ones stick out as important through computer history. The rest of this chapter looks at a couple of these editors and the commands they used.

TECO

With a name standing for "text editor character oriented," this was among the first computer editors, designed for the PDP-8. It was a buffer-oriented, line-at-a-time editor. So it could read a chunk of text from a file into a buffer, edit that buffer, write it out to disk, and read in another chunk to edit. It was hard to use, but very flexible. TECO was written and maintained by a group at DEC called the Moby Mungers.

Here are a few of the commands you would memorize when using TECO.

y$	Yank a page—that is, get a buffer from the file.
P	Go to a page.
w$	Write a page or file.
d$	Delete a line.

TECO's macro language in and of itself was flexible enough to use for programs. For example, the following TECO script will calculate an arbitrary number of digits of pi:

```
+0UN QN"E 20UN ' BUH BUV HK
QN< J BUQ QN*10/3UI
QI< \+2*10+(QQ*QI)UA B L K QI*2-1UJ QA/QJUQ
```

```
QA-(QQ*QJ)-2\ 10@I// -1%I >
QQ/10UT QH+QT+48UW QW-58"E 48UW %V ' QV"N QV^T '
QWUV QQ-(QT*10)UH >
QV^T @^A/
/
```

vi

On Unix, people undoubtedly used vi, as it shipped with all Unix computers. vi is still popular today, and versions are available on most PC platforms. It was, perhaps, the first full-screen editor, making it revolutionary for its ease of use. Because there were no such things as arrow keys, users needed to memorize a variety of keys for moving through the file. Once they had positioned the cursor, they would hit another command to change from command mode to editing. For example, if they wanted to change a word two lines above the cursor, they would hit "kk," hit "h" or "j" until they got to the word, hit "cw," and then hit the word. Recent versions of vi, much to my dismay, have added support for arrow keys and the mouse, so users no longer need to keep their fingers strategically poised over the movement keys.

Here are some of the vi commands.

h	Move the cursor left.
j	Move the cursor down.
k	Move the cursor up.
l	Move the cursor right.
yL	Copy from the cursor to the bottom of the screen.
dd	Delete a line.
.	Repeat the last command.
a	Append text (insert after cursor).
o	Insert a line.
cw	Change a word.
cfx	Change until the character x.
ZZ	Save the file and exit.

Nerd Humor:

Unix Tricks

Just as there used to be lists of things to do on your calculator to spell out words when you turned it upside down, there are also lists of Unix commands that return funny messages. Here are a few, showing the command to type at the $ or % prompt (depending upon which Unix shell you are running) and the computer's response:

```
$ cat "canned food"
cat: cannot open canned food

% ar m God
ar: God does not exist

% "How would you rate Quayle's incompetence?
Unmatched ".

% ^How did the sex change^ operation go?
Modifier failed.

% If I had a ( for every $ the Congress spent, what
would I have?
Too many ('s.

% sleep with me
bad character

% got a light?
No match.

% man: why did you get a divorce?
man:: Too many arguments.

% ^What is saccharine?
Bad substitute.

$ PATH=pretending! /usr/ucb/which sense
no sense in pretending!

$ drink <bottle; opener
bottle: cannot open
opener: not found

$ mkdir matter; cat >matter
matter: cannot create
```

326

edlin

Just as Unix included vi, DOS included edlin In its heyday, edlin was a frequently used and much cursed editor for modifying AUTOEXEC.BAT and CONFIG.SYS and writing batch files. Today, it is the subject of many jokes about the early days.

edlin has an amusing past. It was created by Seattle Computer Products — the same company Microsoft bought DOS from. It was only supposed to last for six months but ended up shipping with DOS 1.0. It remained the only built-in editor until DOS 5.0, when it was replaced by EDIT. (EDIT, by the way, is the editor portion of QuickBasic.)

edlin was a buffer-oriented, line-at-a-time editor. Users could load a file, use commands to switch to the line they wanted to edit, and then edit that particular line. If the file was too big to read into memory, they would read it in a chunk at a time.

Here are some of the edlin commands:

a	Read a portion of a file into memory.
c	Copy lines.
d	Delete lines.
e	Save and exit.
i	Insert lines.
L	Show a set of lines.
p	Show the next 23 lines.
q	Quit without saving.
s	Search for text.
w	Write to disk.

WordStar

For a time, WordStar was the ultimate in word processors, used everywhere. WordStar on DOS was a port from a CP/M version. It was awkward and ugly, but it sure beat edlin. Although it started as the king of word processors for the PC, it was rapidly eclipsed by an aggressive newcomer called WordPerfect. While WordPerfect was designed for DOS and the PC, WordStar held on to its earlier roots and eventually disappeared.

Amusingly, when Borland released its first set of products, Turbo Pascal and Sidekick, WordStar was the standard word processor. Because of this, Borland used the WordStar key commands for the editors in these products, so that users would have the familiar WordStar keystrokes available to them. The WordStar keystrokes are still part of Borland's products today. (They are no longer the default keystrokes, however. Instead, they are selected by choosing the "classic" keystroke option.) And in fact, more people at this point have been exposed to WordStar commands through Borland products than they ever were through WordStar itself.

Here are some of the frequently used commands from WordStar.

Ctrl+KB	Mark the beginning of a block.
Ctrl+KK	Mark the end of a block.
Ctrl+KC	Copy the block.
Ctrl+KV	Move the block.
Ctrl+QB	Move to the beginning of a block.
Ctrl+QC	Move to the end of the file.
Ctrl+QD	Move to the end of the line.
Ctrl+QR	Move to the top of the file.
Ctrl+KS	Save the file.
Ctrl+QA	Search and replace.
Ctrl+QY	Delete to the end of the line.

Brief

Along with vi, Brief rates as one of the most popular programmer's editors. Brief was originally created by a company called UnderWare. This company was bought out, and Brief eventually ended up at Borland, where its features are slowly moving into Borland's language products.

One of the key features of Brief was its macro language. Programmers could create their own custom macros that would format programs, substitute keystrokes (so they could type one letter, and the macro would fill in the rest of the word), compile programs, and perform any other operation you wanted. So Brief wasn't just an editor, it was a complete development environment. Users created hundreds of macros, and in fact, many Windows developers switch to a DOS screen to edit their programs, just so they can use Brief and their favorite Brief macros.

Here are a few of the Brief commands.

F6	Find and replace.
Alt+F6	Find and replace, going backwards.
Shift+F6	Repeat the last replace operation.
*	Undo.
Ctrl+K	Delete to the beginning of a line.
Ctrl+Backspace	Delete the word to the left of the cursor.
Alt+Backspace	Delete the word to the right of the cursor.
Alt+G	Go to a line.
Ctrl+Q[, Ctrl+Q]	Find a matching ({ < or [. (Useful for programmers.)
Ctrl+O+A	Opens a file, where the filename is the word that is under the cursor. (Useful for C and C++ programmers.)
Alt+C	Mark a column of text.
F8	Record a keystroke macro.

One of the most popular features of Brief was its ability to search for text using wild cards. Instead of looking for specific text, such as "Welcome to the asylum," users could search for text that matched a particular pattern. This is very similar to doing a DIR *.TXT to see all text files in a directory. This feature is called *regular expression matching*, and has a rich syntax of its own just for describing how to search for things.

Did You Know?

High Rollers

A number of people on Microsoft's OS/2 team (and thus, later on, the NT team) were avid gamblers. Their ring leader, Chuck Whitmer, created an extremely complex set of equations for modeling the way six-deck blackjack worked. From that, he and his group created a very sophisticated counting scheme. They would practice gambling late into the night, and make jaunts to casinos where they often played under false names.

They became extremely talented at the skill, and often received free airline tickets, fancy hotel rooms, and meals.

PCs for Guns

The Boston Computer Exchange started a program where it donates computers to schools in return for students' weapons. The type of computer donated depends on the type of weapon received. Several police stations have taken a similar approach.

Meanwhile, an ad in the Microsoft company classifieds offered to exchange a bulletproof vest for computer equipment.

Shoplifting

A ring of shoplifters stole $1.6 million in merchandise from Egghead between 1991 and 1993.

Racing Bulldozers

Bill Gates likes to drive fast. In the early days of Microsoft, he was known for racing his Porsche on back roads in Albuquerque. At one point he and another early Microsoftie, Chris Larson, snuck into a construction site, figured out how to drive the heavy equipment parked there, and then had a bulldozer race.

WordPerfect

WordPerfect, developed by Strategic Software International, later to become WordPerfect Corporation and now part of Novell, took over WordStar's position as the leading word processor. It redefined *easy-to-use*, with screens that popped up to show the various commands. WordPerfect still holds a strong position in the word processor market, led only by Microsoft Word for Windows.

WordPerfect uses the function keys, often modified by the Shift, Alt, and Ctrl keys, for its commands.

F1	Cancel.
F2	Search.
F4	Indent.
F6	Bold.
F7	Exit.
F10	Save.
Shift+F6	Center.
Shift+F7	Print a file.
Alt+F2	Replace.
Alt+F4	Mark a block of text.

Q: Why won't piranhas eat lawyers?

A: Professional courtesy.

Down by Law

While the computer industry isn't
always filled with professional courtesy, it is filled with lawyers. In the earliest days, when computers were still the realm of hobbyists, young, idealistic engineers and programmers dominated. As the computer industry grew, so did the number of lawyers and lawsuits.

Some lawsuits were just squabbles that grew into legal action. Others changed the industry. This chapter takes a look at some of the major and the insane lawsuits in the computer industry.

Look and Feel Back in Anger

Few suits captivated the industry more than the "look and feel" suits. These threatened to change the very fiber of the computer industry. Not suprisingly, there are two sides to the look and feel issues. (No, not the *look* side and the *feel* side.)

The first side is that of those filing the look and feel suits: computer companies spend inordinate amounts of time and capital creating products. In fact, a successful product can cost several million dollars to develop and market. During the development process, companies create a unique look and feel by which a product is identified. Apple, for example, prides itself on the intuitive user interface of the Macintosh family. If a company can't protect its look and feel, than all of its research and investment can be quickly ripped off by the competition.

Those being sued assert the other side of the issue. They maintain that the industry grows through innovation. In many cases, this innovation stems from taking a basic idea, one that perhaps is already on the market, and making it easier, more powerful, faster, or extending it in some unique fashion that benefits customers. Without the ability to innovate and improve, the industry would stagnate.

Sometimes, however, there are only so many ways to do something. This is easier to understand if you think of cars. In the United States, all cars have the steering wheel on the left, and the clutch is left of the accelerator. Suppose Ford sued Honda for having the same look and feel of the accelerator/clutch configuration. If it won, Honda might have to put accelerators to the left of clutches. People who switched back and forth between the two cars would probably cause a lot of accidents.

The potential for causing the analog of such accidents in software is what made so many people anxious about the results of the look and feel litigation.

The issue gathers further importance because there are standards that naturally emerge in the industry. When a product becomes an overwhelming success and dominates the market, it has certain advantages besides making a lot of money and having increased momentum. Dominant products have a large supporting network of books, trainers, consultants, courses, and programmers. If a company wants to introduce a product in the same category, in order to be successful, it needs to be compatible. This is the issue at stake with the Lotus vs. Borland, Paperback, and Santa Cruz Operation suits, as well as with the Ashton-Tate vs. Fox suit. How compatible can one be without infringing?

Technology Update

BYTE always searches far and wide for the latest in the technology of computing systems. This month in the hills of New Hampshire, we discovered an example of computer technology in the form of the first practical Touring Machine, shown here complete with a unary relocatable based operator (in IBM OS PL/1 parlance).

For those individuals having less than a passing acquaintance with computer science, the Turing Machine is a famous mathematical construction first formulated some decades ago by Alan Mathison Turing, and which can be shown to be logically equivalent to any digital computer implementation. A Turing Machine is to computing what a Carnot Cycle is to thermodynamics. (The fact that this particular Touring Machine implementation looks like a CarNot Cycle is purely incidental.) But Turing machines have been notoriously impractical in terms of everyday computer usage until this new product rolled into town.

This newly released virtual Touring Machine, version 27 chain level 1, incorporates numerous state of the art features which make it one of the better examples of the form. These features include:

1. SHIFT (micro instruction).
2. 10 speed clock controls.
3. 2 phase clock drive.
4. clock conditioner.
5. LCS (large cookie store).
6. global debugging mechanism.
7. flying head with head crash padding.
8. access arm.
9. audio output peripheral.
10. visual input scanner.
11. audio input scanner.
12. local debyking mechanism.
13. relocatable memory mapping software.
14. HLT (halt instruction).
15. system maintenance package.
16. competing access lockout feature.
17. nomadic road interfaces.
18. tape.
19. SHIFT (macro instruction).
20. EXCP (executing channel program).
21. sectored disk drive.
22. transmission links.
23. unallocated stowage.
24. machine environment (circa January 30 1976).

This excerpt from the April 1976 issue of *Byte* magazine is a classic example of nerd humor. It features numerous jokes on computer science and engineering terms, such as Turing Machines, Carnot Cycles, and various assembly language instructions.

If products could not be compatible with market leaders, or if companies couldn't naturally tend towards a standard, users would be unable to switch between products easily. This would lock a customer into a particular vendor's product line, making it difficult for users to work with products from different vendors. Of course, this is a wonderful thing for market leaders, who benefit if customers can't switch to competing, incompatible products.

Back to the Future

We'll begin our journey into look and feel issues with a very early case. MIS Press was one of the early computer trade book publishers. Its niche, at first, was providing manuals for software products. It would give a command-by-command tour of a product, essentially supplanting, though in some cases supplementing, the original product documentation. Some software companies disliked this, fearing that the manuals would make it far easier for people to pirate software. After all, most software at the time was too hard to use without a manual, and there was no such thing as on-line documentation on the PC. (There were still lots of copy protection schemes, though.) Small-time piraters wouldn't go to the expense of copying manuals. Somehow it felt much more unethical than lending a friend a floppy.

The MIS Press books, with titles such as *The Manual: dBASE III* and *The Manual: Lotus 1-2-3*, provided an easy way for users to get their hands on additional manuals. The manuals legitimately allowed customers to learn about products at home and while traveling, or to learn a product without having to buy it. They also made it possible for some people to use pirated software more easily.

Around 1985, Lotus sent MIS Press a cease and desist letter, claiming that giving a blow-by-blow rendition of each command violated copyright law. MIS agreed not to reprint the series, and then ran ads featuring scantily clad women whispering, "the book Lotus tried to ban."

An Apple a Day Keeps the Lawyers in Pay

This is perhaps the most famous look and feel lawsuit. In 1988, Apple sued Microsoft and Hewlett-Packard for copyright infringement of the Macintosh user interface. After seven years and millions of dollars, Apple

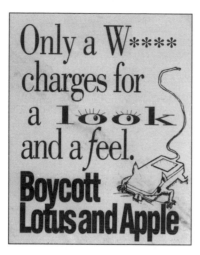

This sticker sums up the sentiments many programmers felt regarding the Lotus vs. Borland and the Apple vs. Microsoft look and feel lawsuits: innovate, don't litigate. I first saw this sticker on a Las Vegas phone pole at the 1990 or 1991 Comdex. It is by far the best industry sticker I've ever seen.

lost the suit and the Supreme Court rejected its appeal. The suit was one of the most publicized and controversial suits to shake the PC industry. At stake was the Microsoft empire and the ability of companies to build upon ideas of others.

Apple, as everyone knows, was the creator of the Macintosh. And the Macintosh's key appeal was the ease of its user interface. Its shipment marked the first time anyone, even someone who is completely computer illiterate, could sit down and be productive with a commercially available personal computer. Apple got many of its ideas from Xerox Parc, who in 1981 made a revolutionary machine called the Xerox Star. Among other things, the Star featured a mouse and a graphical user interface.

Microsoft also created a graphical user interface, called Microsoft Windows. In 1985, Microsoft negotiated rights to certain user interface design elements from Apple. Windows 1.0 and 2.0 didn't make dramatic inroads in the market, but Apple could see where things were going, and it realized its edge in the ease of use marketplace was now severely challenged. So, in March 1988, it reacted by suing Microsoft and Hewlett-Packard, the maker of New Wave, for copyright infringement of the Macintosh look and feel, claiming that it lost $4.5 billion in potential sales.

Apple's initial claims against Windows 2.03 were broadened in 1991 with the release of Windows 3.0, which it then added to the suit. Windows 3.0, of course, took off like a rocket, eventually becoming the dominant PC platform.

A long, bitter battle ensued. At its height, the lawsuit was the talk of every industry gathering. Windows software writers worried that it would destroy Windows, and thus their market. Apple supporters hoped it would rerstore the upper hand Apple once enjoyed. OS/2 supporters worried that if Apple won, it would next take on OS/2. Unix programmers worried that X/Windows and Motif would be next. And NeXT customers worried that NeXT would also be sued.

Apple claimed that its suit was critical to the ongoing health of the U.S. software industry. It argued that losing would threaten copyright protection of all software. Any vendor, domestic or international, would be able to copy software innovations. And since the U.S. was the leader in software development, that could put the whole U.S. software economy at risk.

Apple created illustrations showing similarities among the three products. Microsoft and Hewlett-Packard created illustrations showing how the products were extremely different. After all, with a flexible user interface, you can customize your interface in many ways.

In June 1993, U.S. District Judge Vaughn Walker ruled against Apple. Of the pieces Apple claimed were infringed, he ruled that at least 90 percent of the Windows elements were covered by Microsoft's license from Apple. And that two-thirds of the New Wave components were covered. He ruled that the remaining elements involved in the lawsuit could not be copyrighted, or were not original.

Apple appealed the ruling, and in September 1994 the appeals court agreed with the previous ruling, saying, "By virtue of the licensing agreement, Microsoft and Hewlett-Packard were entitled to use the vast majority of features that Apple claims were copied."

Great Quotes:

Foot the Bill

After Apple lost its look and feel lawsuit against HP and Microsoft, an HP spokesman said, "This is exactly what we had anticipated. The only thing left is to determine who pays for the legal fees."

As with many lawsuits, other parties got involved in the suit. Given that Apple copied a major portion of the Xerox Star interface, Xerox sued Apple for the same reasons that Apple sued Microsoft and Hewlett-Packard. It claimed that the Lisa and Macintosh Finder copied Xerox's work, and filed for $150 million in damages. After five of its six claims were rejected, the Xerox attorneys backed down. Analysts felt Xerox had a strong case, but because it waited so long to file suit, the statute of limitations had expired. Its earlier lack of interest in protecting its property rights prevented it from winning the case.

Great Quotes:

Dis'ing Xerox

Xerox had recently lost its look and feel suit against Apple because the statute of limitations had run out. Guy Kawasaki, formerly an evangelist at Apple, had this to say about Xerox at the Demo '92 trade show: "Xerox is incapable of turning a vision into a product. Xerox can't even sue you on time."

Don't Step in the Sheet

This is yet another lawsuit involving look and feel and copyright protection. Not only did the suit become the talk of the industry, but it also inflicted severe financial damage on several companies.

The first spreadsheet, VisiCalc, was created by Personal Software's Bob Frankston and Dan Bricklin. Lotus built an industry out of the idea, becoming the dominant spreadsheet vendor. With such market ownership, it provided a de facto standard for the commands to manipulate a spreadsheet.

Into this market climate, Borland introduced Quattro Pro in 1987 and followed with Quattro Pro 2.0 in November 1989. Quattro Pro was a blazingly fast spreadsheet that provided compatibility with Lotus 1-2-3 menu commands and macros. After all, in order to succeed, Borland needed to leverage existing user skills and knowledge. In addition to compatibility, Quattro Pro 2.0 had all types of innovative features, ran with less memory than Lotus required, and cost only $99.95 for existing Lotus customers.

In 1990, Lotus sued, saying that the look and feel of its product was illegally copied. It started by suing Paperback Software and Santa Cruz Operation (SCO).

Paperback Software was run by Adam Osborne, an early figure in the personal computer industry who, among other things, founded Osborne McGraw-Hill and created the Osborne computer. Paperback's goal was to create a line of inexpensive personal productivity applications, including a product called VP Planner. VP Planner was the product that got Paperback into trouble, as it used the same menu structure as Lotus 1-2-3.

Paperback lost the suit to Lotus, paying Lotus $500,000 and removing its VP Planner line of products from the market. This only worsened Paperback's financial troubles. Adam Osborne resigned, retired to Oregon, and disappeared from the personal computer industry. In a strange twist of fate, a company called WordTech bought the Paperback Software product line. Borland later bought WordTech, to use its database technology as the foundation for dBASE for Windows. Thus, Borland ended up sharing two aspects of the Lotus lawsuit.

Lotus also won a case against Mosaic's spreadsheet called Twin, which was a very close clone of Lotus 1-2-3. Mosaic pulled Twin from the market and shut down operations.

The SCO case was settled on June 17, 1991. SCO was given two months to remove its spreadsheet product, SCO Professional, from the market.

But the grand fireworks occurred during the suit of Borland, which started on July 2, 1990. Borland, hoping to have the trial in California rather than Boston, actually sued Lotus two days before Lotus sued Borland. The case was more complex than the other cases, as Borland provided an interface that was different than Lotus's by default, but provided a Lotus compatibility mode.

The Lotus-Borland case attracted much attention. As with the Apple-Microsoft suit, much more was at stake than menu compatibility of two spreadsheets. Lotus claimed its victory would give valuable protection to software vendors, allowing research and development dollars to pay off in market profits. Borland claimed the suit would eliminate software competition and suggested drastic consequences, such as Microsoft claiming copyright on the Windows API and then forcing a license fee on anyone who wanted to create a Windows program.

Definition:

API

API stands for *Application Programmer Interface*. Operating systems provide a layer between the users and the hardware. For example, in DOS you can use DIR to look at the files on a disk, rather than having to figure what signals need to be sent to the hard drive to get it to spin and how to interpret the data read into the disk memory buffer.

Operating systems also provide a set of calls that programmers can use to interact with the operating system. For example, DOS provides calls for reading and writing disk files. Windows 95 provides calls for creating windows, drawing bitmaps, and processing menu commands. Such calls are called APIs.

Richard Stallman, a famous software pioneer and a MacArthur fellowship recipient, was among the many developers strongly opposed to Lotus's position. In addition to being the head of the League for Programming Freedom, Richard is widely known as the president of the Free Software Foundation, a group that believes software should be free. Putting their lack-of-money where their mouth is, as it were, the Free Software Foundation creates large quantities of software, including GNU Unix, that they provide for free through a variety of mechanisms.

The League for Programming Freedom helped organize protests against the Lotus suit, with Richard Stallman saying, "If programmers can't implement the interfaces that people know, we are pretty much wasting our time developing software." He felt that "Lotus's victory will cut off meaningful competition and turn users into captives. No one should be allowed to monopolize user interfaces. It is against the public interest."

On August 2, 1990, the group held a protest. Starting at MIT, approximately 320 people walked to Lotus's nearby headquarters and gathered outside with signs carrying slogans such as, "Drop the Suit, We Have You Surrounded!" The protesters then chanted:

1-2-3-4
Kick that lawsuit out the door
5-6-7-8
Innovate, don't litigate
9-A-B-C
Interfaces should be free
D-E-F-O
Look and feel has got to go

Hex Numbering System

Why did the chant go from "9" to "A, B, C"? A programmer will immediately recognize that this is a hex number chant. The hex numbering system is one often used by programmers. In it, the numbers "0" through "9" represent "0" through "9." But "A" represents "10," "B" represents "11," and so on up to "F," which represents "15." This numbering system makes it easier to deal with the binary system used in computers.

Philippe Kahn commissioned this sweatshirt during the height of the Lotus vs. Borland look and feel lawsuit. A large man in a suit, clearly representing Lotus, bullies a programmer. Philippe paid a good chunk of change for full rights to the artwork, and had at one point planned to mail postcards with it to several million Borland customers.

On July 31, 1992, Lotus won the first round against Borland. To limit damages and any impact of an injunction, Borland removed all the compatibility macros and features in the current version of Quattro Pro. Then it quickly put the updated version into the channel.

The suit continued, and the July 1992 finding was confirmed by the Federal Court in August 1993. This led many to predict Borland's demise. Lotus was expected to ask for $100 million in damages, and Jim Manzi said he wanted to perform a "cashectomy" on Borland. And when Borland, at once gloriously trading at $82/share, fell to $7, it was an incredible takeover target. But the specter of the lawsuit allegedly scared off all suitors.

Great Quotes:

"We had the best technology, but you decided to beat us in court, and not compete in the marketplace. You privately told me several times to 'get out of the spreadsheet business,' and you boasted in the *Wall Street Journal* that you were going to perform a 'cashectomy' on Borland." — Philippe Kahn

Borland filed an appeal on December 13, 1993. One of its claims was that the judge who presided over the lower court seemed very biased towards Lotus. Many accused the judge of wanting Lotus to win so that there would be more jobs in his local Boston area. Once the case escalated, Borland's hopes rose. The new presiding judge, Judge Breyer, seemed to grasp the issues at hand, and also seemed to lean in Borland's favor. But, Judge Breyer ended up being appointed to the Supreme Court, and thus had to back away from the case. Once again, Borland's very survival seemed uncertain.

Lotus lost the appeal in March 1995, with the First U.S. Circuit Court of Appeals ruling that the elements Lotus said were infringed were inherently not copyrightable. Novell, which in March 1994 bought Quattro Pro for $110 million from the cash-starved Borland, immediately announced it would restore the Lotus 1-2-3 compatibility features. Borland breathed a sigh of relief, with Philippe Kahn saying, "This is a clear victory for consumers, computer programmers, and open systems, which will foster a more competitive software industry and promote innovation." The resolution, however, came long after Borland had suffered enormous troubles and damage in the market.

Paying for legal costs was an enormous burden. Not only did the suit consume the focus of lawyers and executives, but, as with so many suits, others joined in the fray. In this case, Borland's insurance carriers sued, hoping to avoid defense costs. Most importantly, they didn't want to pay damages to Lotus if Borland lost, which could have cost the insurers over 70 million dollars.

After Lotus lost, it immediately began preparations for taking the case to the Supreme Court. While most analysts believe that the Supreme Court will uphold the lower court ruling, the Supreme Court has not made its final decision at this time. Borland has contemplated suing Lotus to get Lotus to pay Borland's fees for five years of legal defense.

Do You Speaka My Language?

Now lets look at another defining lawsuit. Instead of dealing with the copyrightability of a product's look, this suit dealt with a different aspect of a user interaction — the copyrightability of the product's language. Ashton-Tate's dBASE grew from a simple program for tracking horse races to the leading PC database. And as such, it defined a standard language for creating database programs, the dBASE language. Many database companies, such as Fox and Clipper, sprung up by providing faster or broader database capabilities built on the dBASE standard.

Ashton-Tate sued Fox in November 1988, claiming that FoxBASE violated a copyright on the dBASE language. Fox claimed that the language was not copyrightable. And during a December 1990 hearing, a judge agreed. He ruled that the dBASE language was not copyrightable because it originated from a public domain program: JPLDIS from the Jet Propulsion Laboratory.

As with many cases, one suit leads to another. A week after the judge's ruling, a law firm filed a class action suit against Ashton-Tate on behalf of dBASE customers, saying that they had been overcharged through the Ashton-Tate licensing policy. After all, a product with public domain components clearly was worth less than one that had copyrighted components.

Ashton-Tate appealed the December 1990 decision, and the judge rescinded his earlier ruling. In November 1991, as part of Borland's purchase of Ashton-Tate, Borland agreed to drop its suit and to officially make the dBASE language public domain.

Clash of the Titans

The computer field is a fickle one. The leaders of one PC era, roughly an 18-month period, can quickly be supplanted by a more agile newcomer. WordStar dominated the word processor field, only to be toppled by WordPerfect. Hayes, the undisputed modem leader, ended up in Chapter 11, only to be bought by Boca Research. And database giants such as dBASE ended up eclipsed by Fox, Access, and Paradox.

Yet, despite the rapid turnover, some companies manage to gain incredible strongholds. Some say this results from a deep understanding of the market and extremely smart strategic investments. Others say it stems from monopolistic practices. Two cases clearly come to mind: the Federal Trade Commission's investigation of IBM, and the Department of Justice's investigation of Microsoft.

Did You Know?

The Required O.J. Reference

Judge Ito used an IBM ThinkPad 755c during the O.J. Simpson trial. A number of people, most likely competitors of IBM, called to complain that this was giving IBM free advertising. As a result, the IBM logo was removed from the computer, and the Sony logo was removed from the TV screens in the court room.

Red, White, and Blue Versus Blue

In the fifties, and for several decades thereafter, IBM had a stranglehold on the market. It had a reputation for rock solid technology and service. Employees and customers were said to bleed blue blood, and there was a popular saying, "No one gets fired for buying IBM."

In 1952, the Federal Trade Commission began an investigation of alleged monopolistic practices by IBM. This led to a 1956 consent decree that required IBM to keep its computer services businesses separate from its hardware and software businesses. Judge David Edelstein, who mandated the consent decree in 1956, stayed with the case for four decades, overseeing the 13-year antitrust case, and all other proceedings that followed.

IBM wanted Judge Edelstein removed from the case, arguing that "it is manifestly clear that a reasonable observer would question the judge's impartiality." Four attempts and 40 years later, IBM finally got Judge Edelstein removed from the case, with the hope that the removal would make it easier to overturn the 1956 decree. IBM argues that the 1956 restrictions prevent it from restructuring and returning to competitiveness in a market that has significantly changed.

Great Quotes:

Adam Osborne to IBM

Adam Osborne, maker of the Osborne computer, addressed an IBM future technology conference in the late seventies. This was during the height of the anti-trust suit. He said that the industry didn't care so much about whether IBM won or lost, because by the time the suit was over, IBM wouldn't matter. In many ways, his prediction was correct.

The Ongoing Saga of Billionaire Bill

Anytime a company becomes extraordinarily successful, it finds itself open to complaints of monopolistic and unfair trade practices. Microsoft is no exception. Having started from humble roots supplying BASIC interpreters for the early kit PCs, Microsoft grew to a multibillion-dollar company run by the richest man in the world. Along the way Microsoft made many enemies, created many jealous rivals, and shipped millions of copies of software.

The government investigated Microsoft for illegal practices, initiating a suit that ran over four and a half years, and in the process consumed over 14,000 hours of attorneys' time, 3,650 hours of economists' time, and involved interviews with hundreds of employees of Microsoft and its competitors. The legal process produced more than one million pages of documents.

The case dealt with the fundamental question of whether a company should be penalized for overwhelming success. In particular, was Microsoft's dominance the result of well-executed strategy, or was it the result of unfair activity? And consequently, were the financial hardships felt by competitors due to their own mistakes, or due to improper activities by Microsoft? In the Supreme Court ruling of U.S. v Grinnell Corporation, the Supreme Court stated that it is legal to obtain market dominance through "growth or development as a consequence of a superior product, business acumen, or historic accident."

Great Quotes:

The DOJ Case
When asked about Microsoft's market dominance during the Department of Justice investigation against Microsoft, a Microsoft lawyer said, "Microsoft concedes its products are popular."

The investigation was started by the Federal Trade Commission in June 1990 and acknowledged by Microsoft in March 1991. Among many areas investigated, the government was concerned with finding (1) if Microsoft's applications group had an unfair advantage over outside companies because of better communications with the systems group, (2) if Microsoft modified its systems software to prevent competitors' from working, and

(3) whether Microsoft used unfair licensing techniques to force all hardware vendors to ship Microsoft operating systems.

During this phase of the investigation, Microsoft often stated that there was a "Chinese wall" separating the systems group from the applications group. This wall would prevent unfair competition, and give outside companies the full amount of information that the inside groups had about systems software. Microsoft had an extensive evangelism program that it pointed to as proof of its information-sharing policies.

Industry opinions varied. Competing companies, which had felt the wrath of Microsoft, hoped the government would intervene, giving them much needed reprieve. Some even gave the government detailed suggestions on dividing Microsoft and on the types of license arrangements they would prefer.

Many companies were interviewed by the government or voluntarily supplied information relating to the case. Only in few cases were companies willing to indicate publicly that they were cooperating with the investigation, for fear that Microsoft would exact revenge. During this same period, numerous companies got together to form ABM groups (Anything But Microsoft). Such groups tried to make alternative standards to Microsoft's standards. For example, Microsoft had a mail API called MAPI. Other vendors created a competing standard called VIM. (Endorsed by several vendors including Lotus and Borland, this stood for Vendor Independent Mail, but was also called Vendors Ignore Microsoft.)

After years of investigation, the FTC voted on whether or not to charge Microsoft. In February 1993, its members came to a tie vote, deadlocked again in July, and in August they decided to drop the case. At that point, President Clinton's new assistant attorney general for the antitrust division, Anne Bingaman, decided to take up the case. Anne was determined to reverse the Reagan/Bush trend of being extremely lenient on big business, and saw the Microsoft investigation as a showcase. She took the case over from the FTC, bringing it into the Department of Justice (DOJ) territory. Once again lawyers trekked to competing companies, gathering and analyzing evidence.

And once again, vendors publicly complained about Microsoft activities that bothered them, hoping to leverage the continued scrutiny of the DOJ to force Microsoft's cooperation. For example, Microsoft put out a license agreement for Windows 95 that required vendors to affirm that developers working on Windows 95 would not also work on OpenDoc systems. When vendors raised a loud fuss, Microsoft backed down.

The DOJ was extremely frustrated. It needed to come to an agreement with Microsoft, so as to avoid endless litigation, but wanted to resolve issues it felt illegal. Some issues were easy to understand and document. Some of the issues that most upset competitors, however, were extremely complex, interwoven, and not easily solved.

After a marathon weekend session in July 1994, the DOJ and Microsoft reached an agreement. Microsoft would change certain practices. In particular, it would change the way it charged for copies of DOS and Windows, so that vendors paid only for units that they installed and shipped (rather than for each PC). Microsoft would also change its non-disclosure policies. Vendors who received beta copies of Microsoft operating systems would no longer be prevented from writing to competing platforms. Microsoft was happy, and the DOJ was happy. Attorney General Janet Reno concluded that the settlement "levels the playing field and opens the door for competition."

The government sent the resolution for review to Judge Stanley Sporkin. Judge Sporkin had a reputation for being extremely aggressive and outspoken. Competing vendors had the opportunity to make statements about the consent decree, and many filed complaints. For example, Lantec, which was busily involved in a suit against Novell, filed a complaint saying, "We do not believe that competition can exist where the company that controls a PC operating system's market is also in related secondary markets such as software applications."

A set of unnamed Microsoft competitors hired a Silicon Valley attorney named Gary Reback to present their case to Judge Sporkin. Reback provided the evidence from these companies, but did not identify the companies specifically, claiming that they were afraid of retaliation. Regarding Microsoft, Reback stated, "This is the most ruthlessly retaliatory company in the world." Despite the secrecy, it was widely known that Sun, Apple, and Sybase were among those funding Reback.

Judge Sporkin reviewed the case, and in an unexpected move, determined that it was not satisfactory, rejecting it on February 14, 1995. This was particularly surprising, as there may have been only one previous time when a

Several of the many Microsoft mugs.

"When you sell to small business, learn to speak their language. COBOL-80."

Ron Mayberry
Mayberry Systems, Inc., Belleville, Illinois

"It's amazing what a few key phrases will do for your sales record to small businesses. Words like "faster," "cheaper," and Microsoft's "COBOL-80."

I should know. I'm in the business of selling complete computer systems to one of the most demanding enterprises around: pharmacies. That means my programs have to solve the complex problems facing pharmacies today—the deluge of paperwork, regulations, and the need for immediate access to patient information.

I've sold a lot of minicomputer systems with programs written in DIBOL. Then I discovered microcomputers, and Microsoft's COBOL-80. Together, they're faster and less expensive than my old system, yet do all the same things. And more.

Like what? Like more flexibility and versatility. I use practically the whole range of COBOL-80 features, to speed inventory, billing, labeling, pricing, accounts receivable, patient profiles and

doctor lists. And I'll be using a lot of the same features to write a program for travel agents too.

Believe me, we checked them all, and only COBOL-80 had all the necessary LEVEL II features, plus the new CHAIN feature, program segmentation and formatted screen ACCEPT/DISPLAY.

The CHAIN feature impressed even a veteran programmer like me. With my menu-driven systems, I have total control over which program will execute

next. And it was great to find that COBOL-80's ACCEPT/DISPLAY statements give formatted screens that look the same as my old DIBOL screens. Yet with fewer lines of code.

With 300 different program modules, you can be sure I appreciate segmentation too. In one case, I collapsed seven segmented DIBOL programs into one segmented COBOL-80 program. Now I can organize my system according to program function rather than memory size.

My compile times? Incredible. Over 1,500 lines compile and link in just five minutes.

I know what you're thinking. 'Sounds great, but I wouldn't want to be in Mayberry's shoes when he translated all those DIBOL programs to COBOL-80.' Well, surprise. Since most DIBOL features translate into COBOL one-for-one, we converted the source code six times faster than originally scheduled.

So simply put, that's how Mayberry Systems Inc. learned for itself that COBOL-80 is one language that makes a lot of sense to small businesses.

In my opinion, COBOL-80 is first-class. And I thought you should know about it too."

COBOL-80 now supports Level II ANSI SORT/MERGE statements to interface with Microsoft's new sort facility, M/SORT.

COBOL-80 with documentation, $750.

Documentation purchased separately, $20.

M/SORT, $125.

MICROSOFT

10800 NE Eighth, Suite 819
Bellevue, WA 98004
206-455-8080   Telex 328945

Microsoft has come a long way from its nerdy early days focusing on
language products. You'd be hard-pressed to find Microsoft pushing COBOL as heavily as in this 1980 ad.

judge had rejected an antitrust consent decree. (In 1982, Judge Harold Greene forced the government to modify the agreement that led to the AT&T breakup.)

There was much speculation over Judge Sporkin's reasons for rejecting the settlement. Some said that it was the first time during the case that Bill Gates didn't get involved personally. Bill had been involved heavily with the FTC hearings and negotiated the decree with Anne Bingaman. Some said Sporkin felt frustrated with the DOJ's unwillingness to provide details of every aspect of its investigation and its lack of interest in a more comprehensive settlement. Others said Sporkin was strongly influenced by trade books such as *Hard Drive* and *Undocumented Windows 95* that described alleged nasty undertakings at Microsoft. (In fact, Judge Sporkin had to pay library overdue fines for *Hard Drive*.)

Judge Sporkin also focused on the issue of vaporware. In a 1987 self-review, Rob Dickerson, who worked in Microsoft's language group, wrote that one of the things he did deserving praise was orchestrate an announcement of QuickBasic timed to stymie Borland's upcoming release of Turbo Basic, the main competition. He stated, "My strategy involved a rapid product response to TurboB that could hold our position until QB4 hit the market."

The path by which the judge got this self-review is one twisted with irony. Rob Dickerson left Microsoft in late 1987 to join Borland, the competition. Microsoft sued Borland and Rob Dickerson, saying that he violated the non-compete clause of his employment contract. To prove that Rob knew Borland was the competition, Microsoft produced his self-review as evidence. Years later, Borland provided this document to the government during its investigation of Microsoft. Judge Sporkin then read it, calling it a "smoking gun."

Did You Know?

Banding against Microsoft

The Committee to Fight Microsoft Corp. is a federal Political Action Committee based in Florida. Their mission is to lobby to break up Microsoft. What ever happened to enjoying the sunshine?

As soon as Judge Sporkin criticized vaporware, many companies jumped to Microsoft's defense. After all, vaporware is an ingrained part of the industry, and holding it up as illegal would impact almost every other computer company. (See chapter 9, "Riding on the Vapor Trail.")

Judge Sporkin asked Anne Bingaman whether she thought Microsoft might agree to a more stringent set of terms. She replied, "Your honor, you don't have the power to do it." This certainly set the stage for Judge Sporkin to prove her wrong. In his ruling, he stated, "It is clear to this court that if it signs the decree presented to it, the message will be that Microsoft is so powerful that neither the market nor the Government is capable of dealing with all of its monopolistic practices. The attitude of Microsoft confirms these observations." He added further, "Microsoft, a rather new corporation, may not have matured to the position where it understands how it should act with respect to the public interest and the ethics of the marketplace. In this technological age, this nation's cutting-edge companies must guard against being captured by their own technology and becoming robotized."

In short, he felt that the agreement provided too few changes, too late in the game, and said, "Simply telling a defendant to go forth and sin no more does little or nothing to address the unfair advantage it has already gained."

His statements led to an uproar, partly because most thought the case was over, and partly because the various lawyers involved and the government lawyers felt that his ruling was inappropriate and overstepped legal boundaries. Both Microsoft and the DOJ appealed, with Janet Reno saying, "I think what the judge does is look at other practices that are not alleged in the complaint, and I think that's where we've got to draw the line." She also expressed her belief that Judge Sporkin was out of line in desiring further aspects prosecuted, saying, "Your honor, my statement to you is: I'm the prosecutor. You're the judge. I decide what makes out a winning case, and if I don't want to file it, nobody can make me file it." Judge Sporkin presented his own view of his role, when he sarcastically replied, "Can I use my own pen to sign the decree? I've got to play some role here."

Microsoft also spoke out against the Judge's suggestions that it engaged in unethical or illegal practices. Steve Ballmer said, "I feel so ethically clean." He conceded that Microsoft was very competitive, saying, "Yes, we are aggressive; yes, we are competitive. I didn't realize that was a sin."

While some companies complained, others supported Microsoft. For example, Charles Wang, the CEO of Computer Associates, said, "Justice should stay out of the business and let an American success story go on." Scott Cook, the chairman of Intuit, who falsely hoped Microsoft's planned acquisition of Intuit would not be opposed by the government, said, "Microsoft is a national asset."

The case then was sent to a three-judge appellate court review, where the judges rejected Sporkin's ruling and upheld the original agreement between the DOJ and Microsoft.

This aggressive, but simple t-shirt was created by Rob Dickerson, at the time part of Microsoft's languages group. Rob helped orchestrate a campaign against Borland's Turbo Basic. This very campaign would be called a "smoking gun" by Judge Sporkin during the Department of Justice investigation of Microsoft. Amusingly, shortly after creating this shirt, Rob switched companies and worked for Philippe Kahn at Borland. This limited edition t-shirt gained much fame and mystique in the industry, with many wondering if it's existence were really an urban myth.

At the same time that Rob Dickerson created the Delete Philippe t-shirt, Borland created its own competitive t-shirt. Brad Silverberg created this amusing Bill Gates bashing t-shirt. In a twist of fate, shortly after creating this shirt Brad left Borland to join Microsoft, where he is now the Vice President of Systems.

Patent Leather Shoes

Much of the legal activity in the computer field relates to patents. During the beginning of the personal computer industry, patent applications were relatively rare. Small companies couldn't afford the expense — it can take over five years to get a patent, and attorney's search and filing fees aren't cheap — and software companies didn't believe software could be patented.

This reluctance to apply for patents slowly changed in the seventies and strongly reversed in the eighties. While software itself cannot be patented, patents were issued that were broad enough to cover software. Here are some of the early patents that started to extend the patent boundaries. When you look at the dates, remember that the application process may have started years before the patent grant.

- A patent issued on October 5, 1971, includes a broad claim to a sorting method for sorting data records in a computer using a key.

- On May 26, 1981, S. Pal Asija received a patent for a data-retrieval program called SwiftAnswer. Some call this the first software patent.

- A patent issued on January 5, 1982, is for a logic code compiler.

- A patent issued February 24, 1987, is for data-entry screens.

- A patent issued January 10, 1987, includes a broad claim relating to a batch-file-processing method to improve application performance.

- A patent issued March 8, 1988, is for "A program for use in a word processing system including an operator display and operator input means."

The use of patents to protect software processes has skyrocketed. Certain companies lose money on their products year after year, only to have lucrative revenues from licensing their patents on their products. Big companies get as many patents as they can, not only to protect their technology investments, but also to shut down the competition or to use as bargaining chips.

Some of the top patent holders include

IBM	1,085
Toshiba	1,040
Canon Kabushiki Kaisha	1,038
Eastman Kodak	1,007
General Electric	932

One of the early software patent fights came from Paul Heckel, an engineer who created a product called Zoomracks. HyperCard, which Apple created long after Zoomracks, bore some resemblance to the earlier product. Heckel sued Apple, and they settled out of court.

Patent fights fill the papers every day. Some, such as the Intel versus AMD case, last for years. Others, such as Compton's multimedia patent, send shock waves through the industry. The reason patents get so much attention is that they impact every product developer. If developers inadvertently (or much worse, knowingly) infringe patents, their companies and products can be tied up in litigation for years, or they may need to pay expensive licensing fees. But if a broad patent is issued, it may be hard to avoid infringing it.

Compton's Takes on the World

The Compton's New Media patent case is one of the best examples of a broad patent case wreaking havoc in the computer industry. A seemingly mild-mannered side player, best known for its encyclopedia, Compton's New Media launched itself into the center of industry attention, quickly becoming one of the most hated computer companies.

Compton's New Media claimed to have a patent on the idea of multimedia, based on a patent it received on August 31, 1993, for a "Multimedia Search System Using A Plurality Of Entry Path Means Which Indicate Interrelatedness Of Information." After receiving the patent, Compton's issued a statement saying that anyone who planned to sell information in a multimedia format must pay a license fee to Compton's.

This struck a blow to the heart of the industry. Not only were CD-ROM developers, on-line services, games developers, and other interactive content vendors shocked, but the very existence of the software industry was challenged. This suit meant that Joe and Jane Nerd, sitting in their garage or basement, dreaming up the next generation killer product, might have to pay a licensing fee to a company they never really heard of, and who had nothing to do with them. The very thought of this dampened the entrepreneurial spirit that runs the edges of the industry. Needless to say, a grassroots protest — one might even say *flame war* — erupted quickly. Many companies challenged the patent. Eventually the patent was ruled too vague, and Compton's ended up with significant financial troubles.

A Story with Graphic Details

This is a story of a file format being introduced on an electronic forum as a potential standard, only to turn into a rat's nest years later when it had taken hold.

GIF (Graphics Interchange Format) is a standard file format for interchanging computer graphics pictures. It is a popular format for transmitting and posting graphics files on bulletin boards and other forums. (At one point, GIF was *the* method by which naughty pictures were transmitted electronically.) Many programs, such as Web browsers, provide the ability to read GIF files as well. In addition, there are hundreds of shareware programs and graphics applications that read GIFs.

CompuServe developed the GIF format in 1987 and encouraged its widespread adoption as a graphics format. Most people assumed that the GIF format, and the code to process it, was in the public domain. Unisys, however, had a 1985 patent on the compression scheme used in the GIF format, LZW (Lempel-Ziv-Walsh). Thus, Unisys pressed for royalty fees, claiming that any vendor that provided code for GIF encoding or decoding owed it money. When it went after the large vendors, such as Adobe, who licensed the technology for Photoshop, little was said. In fact, there wasn't really any publicity surrounding the action.

But then Unisys went after CompuServe and, after two years of negotiations, arranged licensing terms in June 1994. CompuServe, in turn, needed to pass on the royalty charges for software that supported GIFs, and that thus infringed Unisys's patent. On December 29, 1994, it posted a message stating that companies or individuals who created programs that could read or create GIF files had until January 10 to pay CompuServe royalties.

This was a huge shock. At the time there were over 40,000 pictures in GIF format on CompuServe, and many more on the Internet and other computer networks. As a result, many applications supported GIF, ranging from major applications such as Adobe Photoshop to popular shareware programs such as Paint Shop Pro. Requiring royalties could put many people out of business. For example, if you wrote a graphics manipulation program for fun that you posted for free on the Internet, and 50,000 people downloaded it, would you owe a huge amount of money to Unisys? If you only had to pay a few cents a copy, you could lose a lot of money fast. Even if you had to pay total fees of one dollar, the whole thought of having to pay a patent license fee for something that was supposed to be free contradicted the very idea of shareware. After all, on-line networks aren't just a transmission vehicle. They are a community and a way of life.

CompuServe claimed that the one-dollar, one-time fee, plus 1.5 percent of the software price, was passed directly to Unisys. Unisys, however, said that CompuServe was charging a higher royalty than Unisys was charging CompuServe.

A flame war ensued. In January 1995, Unisys began to back down, saying it wouldn't require licensing fees for noncommercial, nonprofit, GIF-based applications, and that it wouldn't press charges for inadvertent commercial use prior to 1995. Commercial products supporting GIF files, however, would owe royalties starting in 1995.

While this mollified some, there was much on-line flaming and movement to abandon GIF for other formats, such as JPEG. At the same time, CompuServe said it would develop a new graphics interchange format that would be royalty free, and asked for help from on-line denizens in designing what it called GIF24. Its chief technology officer furthered this by saying, "Having a graphic standard that requires the payment from licensees is seen as a big damper. We don't see it as a big revenue potential for anyone. We just see it as an annoyance." Many rejected CompuServe's efforts and the embers of distrust and anger still burn.

Cyrix is known for aggressive marketing and aggressive anti-Intel t-shirts, including this famous "So Sue Me" shirt. Intel did.

Have a Chip on Your Shoulder?

There is a saying that nothing is certain except death and taxes. In the computer industry, the adage is expanded: Nothing is ever certain, except death, taxes, and that Intel will be suing AMD.

The chip manufacturing business is extremely competitive, with Intel occupying the dominant position by far. Because of this, it sets a de facto standard for how PC chip sets behave. Other vendors, such as AMD and Cyrix, make a business out of providing clones of the Intel chips. If they can provide a cheaper or better version of the Pentium, for example, they can get millions of dollars by selling them to computer manufacturers trying to reduce the cost of their machines.

Companies often sue to protect their markets, especially if they believe trade secret theft, reverse engineering, or trademark infringement have occurred.

One of the best examples is that of Intel and AMD, who were involved in a string of lawsuits from 1982 to 1995. Many of these stemmed from different interpretations of a 1976 agreement between the two companies that states:

> INTEL grants to AMD a paid-up, non-exclusive, royalty-free
> license under all INTEL copyrights ... permitting AMD to make
> the following copies (and only the following copies):
>
> (a) To copy published INTEL instruction manuals and data
> sheets;
>
> (b) To copy microcodes contained in INTEL microcomputers
> and peripheral products sold by INTEL; and
>
> (c) To copy mnemonics published by INTEL in its manuals.

At the time of the agreement, Intel did not have microprocessors that used microcode, but later on, of course, chips did. And in particular, chips such as the 80386 were extremely reliant on microcode. AMD claimed this agreement gave it the right to create clones of Intel chips. Intel claimed it gave AMD the right to make copies, but not the right to sell those copies.

Intel introduced further complications by requesting that AMD drop promotion of the Z8000, which competed with the 8086. In return, it gave AMD the right to manufacture the 8086, 8088, 80186, and 80286 chips. But it didn't give AMD the rights to 80386 clones, which AMD wanted. The agreement between the two companies was a complex cross-licensing of technology, in which a point system was used to determine when one company had provided enough technology to warrant components from the other company. For example, if AMD gave Intel enough technology, it would be able to license the 386. Intel said AMD didn't have enough points to get rights for the 80386. AMD said Intel purposefully dragged its feet and violated the way in which points were given.

As with many lawsuits, what resulted wasn't a single suit relating to the 80386. Rather, a string of suits ensued. For example, Intel filed suit over 80C287 rights and lost the case based on the 1976 agreement. AMD sued Intel for antitrust activities and asked for $2.2 billion in damages. Intel sued AMD over 386 rights, claiming that AMD could not create the chip. AMD countered that it could, and that Intel was not holding up its side of the bargain.

And in yet another twist, Intel sued AMD over trademark protection for the name "386." AMD planned to call its 386 clone the "AMD 386." Intel believed that violated its trademark on the name "386" and sued prior to the AMD chip being announced. Eventually it was ruled that numbers cannot be trademarked, hence Intel changed its naming scheme. That's why the Pentium wasn't called the 586.

The suit over trademarking numbers is not nearly as interesting as how the suit occurred. Apparently, Intel suspected that AMD was planning to use "386" in its competing chip name, but had no evidence upon which to base a suit until the strange incident occurred involving Mike Webb. Mike Webb was an Intel field engineer who stayed in a Hilton hotel one night during a business trip. By coincidence, AMD's personal computer products marketing director was also named Mike Webb. And he happened to be staying in the same Hilton at the same time. Somehow, a package of materials in an interoffice envelope marked M. Webb was left at the hotel. The hotel staff shipped it to the Mike Webb who worked at Intel. They didn't realize it really was meant for the other Mike Webb. So when Intel's Mike Webb opened up the package, he saw that the cover page contained a trademarked name for a new chip called the AMD 386. This gave Intel the opportunity it was seeking to fire off another lawsuit.

AMD was given the right to sell 386s by an arbitrator in 1992. But an appeals court reversed that ruling in 1993. So Intel sued AMD for one billion dollars. The California Supreme Court then reversed the appeals court ruling at the end of 1994, once more giving AMD the right to create 80386s. As part of the settlement, AMD had to pay Intel 58 million dollars, but it did received a license for the 386 and 486 microcode. AMD also had to agree to limit the number of clones it created via outside production facilities. The total cost for all of this was over $100 million dollars in legal fees.

Just in case you think that wasn't enough, NEC and Intel also were in extended suits regarding 8086 and 8088 microcode. Intel sued NEC to prevent it from creating 8086 and 8088 chips. But a judge ruled that the NEC code didn't infringe on any of Intel's rights, so NEC sued Intel for unfair competition, saying that Intel prevented it from taking part in the success of the 8086 and 8088 market. In this case, the judge ruled that Intel lost its copyright to the 8086 and 8088 microcode, because it didn't require alternative vendors to include copyright notices on the chips. Current law, however, doesn't require this.

Meanwhile, Intel also sued ULSI, which was developing a 387 chip, saying that an engineer at ULSI took a copy of the 387 specification from Intel. The president of ULSI returned this document to Intel through its lawyers (who happened to be the same ones representing NEC in the NEC versus Intel lawsuit). The lawyers retained a copy, which they were to keep secret. Intel then sued the lawyers as well, saying that they allowed AMD attorneys and a consultant access to the document.

And just in case you thought the chip industry slacked off from keeping lawyers fully occupied, Intel and Cyrix also endured lengthy litigation, starting in 1990. Intel sued Cyrix for patent infringement. Cyrix sued Intel for unfair trade practices.

At the same time, Intel sued Cyrix over its Cyrix Instead advertising campaign. This campaign used a swirl similar to that used in the Intel Inside campaign. Instead of saying "Intel Inside," the Cyrix ads just said "Ditto." Cyrix claimed it was parody. Intel said it was trademark infringement. Cyrix stopped running the ad.

Great Quotes:

More Suits

After Intel countersued Cyrix, Cyrix cofounder Tom Brightman said, "We can only stand so much of Intel's bull."

You Are the Apple of My I-Frame

Apple developed QuickTime technology for displaying movies on PCs. It is available on both the Mac and Windows. Microsoft also has a video viewing technology, called Video for Windows. Many companies support both standards. Both QuickTime and Video for Windows support two different ways of displaying video. *Hardware playback* uses special graphics cards, such as the RealMotion card or Matrox Marvel card, which have chips on them just for playing video. Hardware playback gives the best quality and performance. The other approach, *software playback*, is inherently slower.

361

Engineers spend lots of time and use a myriad of tricks to improve software playback.

In 1992 Apple hired the San Francisco Canyon Company to help it accelerate QuickTime for Windows. Later, Intel hired Canyon to quicken a portion of Video for Windows. Intel then gave the code to Microsoft as part of a joint-development agreement.

In December 1994, Apple sued San Francisco Canyon Company for using code Apple owned for QuickTime. In particular, it said Canyon used the code in contract work for Microsoft and Intel in order to speed the performance of Video for Windows. In February 1995, Apple widened the suit to include Microsoft and Intel. Microsoft quickly removed the offending code, saying that it was irrelevant to the functioning of Video for Windows, and released a new cut, called Video for Windows 1.1e. Apple asked that any company who used the version of Video for Windows contact it immediately to join an amnesty program, which would then protect it from being sued by Apple. Canyon questioned Apple's involvement of Intel and Microsoft, with the company president saying, "Perhaps Apple is really interested in troubling Microsoft's life or Intel's life."

Meanwhile, Apple and Microsoft met to see if they could resolve the issue more amicably. That just heated things up, with Apple claiming Microsoft tried to bully it into dropping the lawsuit. In particular, it claimed Microsoft threatened to withdraw Apple from Windows 95 beta programs, and that Microsoft might even stop supporting the Macintosh. Of course, this was not what Microsoft wanted to emerge during the middle of its lawsuit hearing with Judge Sporkin.

Microsoft claimed that Apple grossly misinterpreted what happened, as noted by one of its vice presidents, Roger Heinen, a former member of Apple's QuickTime team. Heinen said, "When we walked out of that meeting, we had a dozen action items that we were planning to take up. But they must have walked out of that room and gone straight to their attorney's office." At the same time Apple asserted Microsoft pressured them, and stated, "They just don't have the right to extort."

Bill Gates then wrote a heated letter to Michael Spindler, saying he was upset with "the lack of candor and honesty Apple has shown in dealing with Microsoft during the last several months" and complained that Apple sued Microsoft rather than trying to work things out amicably. Bill also made the contents of the letter widely available. Spindler apparently returned the flames in a private letter to Bill.

Next, Microsoft filed a countersuit, claiming that Apple's suit was a deceptive business practice and part of a deliberate misinformation campaign against Video for Windows. As part of the campaign, it claimed Apple sent out a deceptive videotape showing Video for Windows with poor playback and other video problems. Further, Microsoft claimed Apple's amnesty program involved labeling Windows software with "Apple Multimedia Technology" stickers, and that Apple employees promoted the program on the Internet using false names. Brad Silverberg claimed Microsoft regretted filing the suit, but that "Apple continues to lie and mislead customers in the developer community. We feel an obligation to set the record straight."

Meanwhile, Anne Bingaman called Microsoft on a Saturday night to suggest that its behavior was being watched, and that it should reconsider withholding Apple from the Windows 95 beta program. Microsoft agreed, saying that it had planned to do so all along, and that in fact that a copy had been sent before Anne ever called.

As for the final resolution, well, that still awaits.

Great Quotes:

Kafka

Regarding Apple's accounting of a Microsoft and Apple meeting that led to an Apple lawsuit over code in Video for Windows, Roger Heinen, Senior Vice President at Microsoft and formerly head of the QuickTime team at Apple, said, "It's just as if I'm reading a story about an event I participated in, and it was as if I wasn't there. It's weird, almost Kafkaesque."

The Games People Play

You might think that the video game business is friendly. But as with any multibillion-dollar business, it is a viciously competitive one filled with lawsuits. Here are a few suits brought by game companies.

In 1988, Atari sued Nintendo, claiming that it engaged in monopolistic practices.

In January 1991, Macronix filed suit against Nintendo, saying that Nintendo purposefully changed its architecture so that other vendors' cartridges would not play on the Nintendo machines. Macronix sought $105 million in damages.

Coincidentally, in January 1991, Nintendo announced that it was dropping its policy of preventing developers who wrote for Nintendo from supplying its games to other platforms until two years had elapsed.

In November 1991, Sega sued Accolade, saying that software developers that created Sega titles should pay Sega a royalty. It also alleged that Accolade's games misled people into thinking they were produced for or licensed by Sega. During a stage of the suit, Sega forced Accolade to recall products, which may have cost Accolade ten million dollars in revenue. In May 1993, Sega and Accolade settled out of court.

In May 1992, Sega settled a suit with an inventor named Jan Coyle, paying him 43 million dollars for infringement of his invention that controlled video sprites via audio signals. Jan's suits against Nintendo and Atari were settled out of court. Jan filed his patent in 1975.

Atari sued Sega in October 1993 for patent infringement. In settlement in September 1994, Sega paid Atari 90 million dollars, and got 7.4 percent of Atari and rights to 70 Atari patents.

In 1995, Nintendo sued Samsung, the supplier of many of Nintendo's chips, saying it was supplying cartridge chips to companies who were making counterfeit copies of Donkey Kong. Nintendo first found counterfeit units in Argentina, where they were sold for as much as 50 percent less than legitimate copies. It then found counterfeit units throughout other Latin American countries, as well as in the Middle East and Asia. It analyzed the counterfeit units in its lab and found that they contained Samsung memory chips. Nintendo claimed it had been working with

Samsung to try to stop sales to counterfeiters, but that its patience wore thin.

Samsung countersued, saying that Nintendo defamed its character, and that it had made aggressive efforts to prevent counterfeit sales.

Prelude to a Kiss

In early 1990, Peter Norton Computing shipped a backup program that competed with Fifth Generation Systems' Fastback Plus. Fifth Generation sued, saying that Norton Backup violated copyrights and trade secrets. Norton Backup was created by a company called Quest Development. One of the Quest programmers had worked on Fastback. All types of allegations flew back and forth.

Symantec later bought Peter Norton Computing for 70 million dollars and the suit continued. Then, in 1993, Symantec bought Fifth Generation Systems as well, thus ending the suit.

Stacking It Up

Disk compression software allows more files to fit on a hard disk. In fact, sometimes you can double the capacity of a disk by using compression.

The Way Compression Works

Compression works by looking for common patterns and representing them in a compact way. For example, suppose you have a picture that has a black background. Much of the picture might then be composed of black dots followed by still more black dots. Let's say that part of the picture had 640 black dots in a row. That would take 640 bytes of memory. (Or more, depending on the graphics format.) You could compress this to three bytes by storing the number 640, followed by the color black, and having a program that could then expand those three bytes to 640 black dots.

Likewise, suppose that you have a chapter from a book. The combination "th" occurs very often in English text. For fun, count how many times it appears in this sidebar. (Yes, this one, not that one over there. Get the point?) Storing the letters "th" takes 16 bits, eight bits for each character. But, using certain compression schemes, you could store "th" using just one bit. That would give you a 16 to 1 compression ratio for every "th" encountered.

There are many different compression schemes used in software. Disk compression software typically provides 50–100 percent more disk space on a hard drive.

In September 1991, Digital Research's DR DOS 6.0 was the first PC OS to include compression software. Prior to that, disk compression software was a separately available product, creating a very healthy market for products such as Stacker, the leader in the market. Microsoft included disk compression software as part of DOS 6.0.

When Microsoft looked for compression software, it initially approached Stac. During negotiations, Microsoft allegedly threatened Stac, saying that if it didn't make a deal, Microsoft would essentially, though not intentionally, put Stac out of business. It furthered this by leaving a spreadsheet with Stac to prove its point. According to Stac, Microsoft wanted the disk compression technology royalty free. According to Microsoft, Stac wanted four million dollars per month compared to Microsoft's offer of one million dollars per month.

Stac broke off negotiations in April 1992, and when Microsoft went with a competing vendor, Stac sued Microsoft, saying that during the discussions Stac provided Microsoft with trade secrets. It further stated that Microsoft violated Stac's patents.

Great Quotes:

Gorilla
Regarding the Microsoft versus Stac suit, Gary Clow, President of Stac, said, "We are not going to sit by and let a 900-pound gorilla stomp all over our property rights."

Microsoft countersued Stac for reverse engineering, fraud, and patent violation, having bought prior rights patents after the suit began. (That is, they searched for a company owning a patent relating to Stac technology. They then bought that patent and sued Stac for patent infringement. It is a standard trick in patent battles.)

A high-visibility suit followed, with Stac awarded $120 million dollars in February 1994, and Microsoft awarded $13.6 million on Microsoft's countersuit. Microsoft appealed, and the companies settled out of court in July 1994, with Microsoft purchasing $39.9 million of Stac nonvoting convertible preferred stock (roughly 15 percent of Stac) and paying one million dollars per month for 43 months. In addition, the two companies agreed to cross-license their disk compression patents, and any related patents, for a five-year period.

Along the way, Stac licensed Stacker to IBM for inclusion in OS/2 2.1 overseas (in the U.S., IBM used DoubleSpace, the same compression used by Microsoft in DOS 6.0.) and to Novell for DOS 7.

During the suit, Stac ended up spending over eight million dollars in legal fees.

Boomerwang

Wang Laboratories is one of the older computer companies, having been founded by An Wang in 1951. In 1988, it had over three billion dollars in revenue, but by 1992 it had filed for bankruptcy protection.

In mid 1993, Wang sued Microsoft, claiming that OLE, a technology on which Microsoft was founding its future applications and operating systems, infringed Wang technology. Wang asked for an injunction against OLE and damages. In a separate suit, Wang sued Watermark Software, makers of OLE-based imaging tools.

In April 1995, Wang and Microsoft settled. Microsoft purchased 90 million dollars' worth of Wang convertible preferred stock and received a license to the Wang patents. Further, some of Wang's imaging controls would be incorporated into future releases of Microsoft operating systems, and the two companies agreed to cooperate on a variety of work-flow ventures.

More Patent Suits

Just in case you want more, here are some of the many other patent suits that have gone on in the computer industry.

In 1986, Prometheus Products and US Robotics sued Hayes Microcomputer Products to try to invalidate a modem patent relating to the Hayes AT standard. Hayes countersued, and also sued Everex and OmniTel in 1988. Numerous other companies then sued Hayes. Eventually, most companies settled out of court, paying Hayes licensing fees. In 1991, a jury awarded Hayes a $3.5 million settlement.

In 1986, Texas Instruments sued several companies for patent infringement, including Fujitsu Ltd., Hitachi Ltd., Matsushita Electrical Industrial Co., Mitsubishi Corporation, Samsung, and NEC Corp. Analysts projected TI would earn $280 million from the patent license fees from those companies in 1991 alone.

In 1988, Quantum Corporation sued Western Digital, saying Western Digital infringed Plus Hardcard patents. Two years later they settled, with Western Digital paying four million dollars. Quantum also won suits against Mountain Computer, Computer Memories, and NEC Information Systems.

In late 1991, Hayes went after Apple Computer, seeking one dollar per PowerBook sold, saying that the PowerBook modem violated a Hayes patent. Apple had chosen a chip set that it said avoided infringing the Hayes patent.

Great Quotes:

A Lawyer's Approach

After Hayes sued Apple regarding Apple's attempt to avoid a patent infringement case, a third-party developer said, "I told Apple [the approach they used] is obviously a fix thought up by a lawyer — not an engineer."

Hitachi sued Motorola in 1989, claiming the 68030 infringed patents on Hitachi's H-8. During the process, a judge almost halted shipments of the 68030, which would have stopped Macintosh production cold. Two years later, Motorola settled out of court.

In September 1990, Texas Instruments sued Dell for patent infringement. Dell countersued, accusing TI of fraud and unfair competition. They settled in March 1993, with Dell paying cash royalties to TI and with both companies cross-licensing patents. During the same time period, TI also sued Zenith Data Systems, Samsung, Daewoo, and Tandy Corporation. Tandy paid over five million dollars in royalties to TI, before filing a suit claiming that the patents were not valid and that the licensing fees were too high.

SmartCard International and Distributed Intelligence Access Systems fought for close to a year in 1990 regarding a patent, but concluded the matter with SmartCard licensing the patent.

In August 1993, Conner sued IBM for infringing five of its patents. IBM sued Conner Peripherals for infringing nine of its patents.

AST sued Texas Instruments for patent infringement in January 1994. TI countersued for patent infringement. Eventually, they settled with a cross-licensing agreement in which AST had to pay royalties to TI.

In November 1994, Data General sued IBM for infringing seven patents that Data General received during the Fountainhead project in the seventies, to create 32-bit minicomputers. This effort paralleled the Eagle project, which was featured in the book *The Soul of a New Machine*.

At the beginning of 1995, Apple and Electronics for Imaging Incorporated exchanged patent suits. Apple claimed that EFI infringed AppleTalk patents. EFI claimed that ColorSync infringed EFI's patents.

In early 1995, Creative Labs and Orchid Technology settled a pair of suits. Creative Labs had sued Orchid for patent infringement, and Orchid sued Creative Labs for restriction of trade.

In 1995, Checkfree received a patent on the process of deciding what payment method to use for paying bills electronically, and promptly sued National Payment Clearinghouse, a subsidiary of Intuit, for patent infringement. Intuit had a relationship for many years with Checkfree, which provided the bill-paying technology for Quicken, while National Payment had a relationship with Microsoft, to whom it provided bill-paying technology for Money. Then, in 1993, Intuit bought National Payment, after which this suit unfolded.

Did You Know?

Helpful Suggestions

The Lotus Ami Pro 2.0 spell checker doesn't recognize IBM (but probably will shortly, now that Lotus has been bought by IBM). Instead, it suggests "BIMBO." Likewise, the spell checker for Microsoft Mail suggests "penis" for Pentium.

It's All in a Name

Patents and copyrights aren't the only legal matters that companies take very seriously. After all, there are trademarks, too. Trademarks protect product names and slogans. This is very important. If a company spends a lot of money getting customers to recognize its product name, it doesn't want a competitor leveraging its efforts by bringing out a similarly named product.

For example, suppose there were Microsoft Windows and Novell Windows. Or Lotus 1-2-3 and Microsoft 1-2-3. Not only might consumers confuse the products, but they also might confuse the reputations of the different companies involved.

Before companies choose a product name, they usually go through a trademark name search. In this process, they determine whether the names they plan to use are already in use. If so, the company has three choices: find a new name, negotiate with the owner of a similar name, or risk it.

In some cases, the results can be rather amusing. For example, Lotus ran into a bit of a mess when it found "Lotus" was trademarked by a toilet paper company in France, Denmark, Australia, Spain, Columbia, Ireland, and Taiwan. Following are some name-mangling stories.

Noah's ARC

Originally, PKZIP was called PKARC. The creators of ARC went after PKWare, so the name changed to PKZIP.

370

We Don't Do Windows

Microsoft wanted to trademark the name "Windows" so it could receive the legal protection a trademark provides. To this end, Microsoft sent letters to numerous software companies that had the word "Windows" in their names or product names. The letters would typically offer a small amount of cash in return for selling the trademark, with a veiled threat if the company didn't comply. Most companies accepted Microsoft's terms. Other companies bargained for more cash or favors. Yet others harassed Microsoft so as to get maximum leverage from holding the trademarked name. For example, Figure 20-1 shows the bottom of a Borland ad from this period:

Borland C++ and ObjectWindows are trademarks of Borland International, Inc. Microsoft is a registered trademark of Microsoft Corporation. Windows is a descriptive term for systems that implement screen display windows on personal computers and workstations.

Figure 20-1 The fine print in Borland's ad is part of legal wrangling with Microsoft, to further the position that "Windows" is a generic term, not a trademarked term.

In another case, Microsoft wrote Scanrom Publications, makers of The First Electronic Jewish Bookshelf, saying that it needed to remove the word "Bookshelf," on which Microsoft had a 1990 trademark.

And Some More Protection Schemes

Microsoft is not the only company that aggressively protects its names. Novell is the maker of many networking products (as well as just about everything else). Network Communications Corporation also makes networking products.

Novell had a product named LANalyzer for Windows. NCC had a product named NCC LANalyzer. In the out-of-court agreement, NCC changed the name of its NCC LANalyzer product to LAN Network Probe, and paid an undisclosed amount to Novell.

WordPerfect also was involved in name suits. It forced a company called VersePerfect to change its name and also went after a company called TaxPerfect.

MicroHelp, one of the early creators of BASIC add-ons, is perhaps best known for its UnInstaller program, which removes Windows programs. MicroHelp sent threatening letters to some shareware vendors, in particular those for IYM (Uninstall for Windows) and Rosenthal (Uninstall), to protect the name. The companies replied that *uninstall* is a common term.

Scandals

Now it is time for some of the good stuff. Actually, not for the *really* good stuff, if you know what I mean. For the scoop on nerd sex, drugs, and rock and roll, you'll have to wait for my next book, *PC Roadkill '97*.

But even leaving out the stories of who top executives sleep with and whether or not anyone really tried those mushrooms in Super Mario Brothers, there are plenty of scandalous stories and lawsuits that relate.

The Strange Misadventures of Jim Brown

This case hit the industry on several levels. First, it involved trade secret violations during the hiring of a widely known industry executive. Second, it concerned email privacy. And third, it dealt with the ethics of the accused and the accusers' prosecuting tactics.

Gene Wang was the vice president of the languages marketing group at Borland International. He was known for his high energy, ability to turn situations around, competitive spirit, and marketing prowess. During a reorganization, a peer was appointed his new manager. Shortly thereafter, on September 1, 1992, Gene accepted a job as Vice President of Languages and Productivity Tools at Symantec, one of Borland's competitors.

After Gene left, Borland examined the mail left in his MCI sent mail folder and found several messages he had sent to Gordon Eubanks, the president of Symantec. Borland alleged that many of these messages contained trade secrets, including business plans, marketing plans, descriptions of unreleased products, and human resources and hiring information. Numerous detectives and the FBI were involved, and while searching the houses and offices of Gene and Gordon, they turned up more materials alleged to be trade secrets. Allegedly Gordon and Gene concocted a fake name, "Jim Brown," for discussing the information. Borland pressed civil charges for breach of contract and trade secret theft, and the Santa Cruz County district attorney pressed criminal charges.

A PR maelstrom swirled around the case. Borland claimed that the trade secret theft involved was extremely serious. Symantec claimed that Borland was harassing an ex-employee. Industry watchers expressed concern about whether two well-known and well-liked figures might end up in jail. If convicted, Gene and Gordon could be put in jail for up to six years and fined up to $210,000. Gordon Eubanks commented, "They want to put me and Gene in prison for years. This is a business dispute. Why aren't they pursuing a civil case? The whole thing makes no sense." Symantec also accused Borland of using the suit as a way to retain employees, saying, "We believe that this is an attempt by Borland to inhibit others from hiring Borland employees. This activity is clearly calculated to create publicity and harass."

Symantec challenged Borland to make the email public. That put Borland in an interesting trap. If the materials contained trade secrets, making them public could give valuable information to the competition. The information would no longer be secret, thus dramatically altering the court case. If it didn't make them public, Symantec could continue to hammer Borland in the press. Symantec also countersued, arguing that Borland put forth the lawsuit to lower the value of Symantec stock.

The case was unusual for a trade secret theft case in that the executives involved were well known and high-ranking, and that the email trail provided very clear evidence. Along the way, all types of strange twists occurred. Borland issued a restraining order to prevent the use of the materials by Symantec. This meant that Gene couldn't focus on language products, part of his original assignment, for some time. According to Gordon Eubanks, "We have an extremely sophisticated system in place to ensure that no aspect of the languages business is in front of Gene." This lasted only for a short while, with Gene then taking the helm of the languages business as well as productivity and scheduling tools.

Then Gene's administrative assistant, who left Borland to join him at Symantec, was caught at Borland copying data to floppy disks from her old computer. In another twist, it was revealed that Borland paid a consulting lawyer for the district attorney's office. Borland claimed that was because the county was broke and asked it for help funding the case. Symantec claimed it rendered the government's case tainted and biased.

The core of the suit revolved around what constitutes a trade secret, whether the trade secrets were adequately protected, and what damage release of the information would cause. Symantec didn't deny that it received the email. Instead, it claimed it didn't contain trade secrets, which are defined as "scientific and technical information." Symantec said, "We saw a lot of marketing information. We don't think it's considered scientific or technical information." Borland set about to prove otherwise.

The general reaction was to the further reaching ethical concerns about high profile executives and email privacy. Presently the case is still not resolved.

Sex: SCO harassment

Santa Cruz is a sleepy beach town lying ninety miles south of San Francisco. It is known for its strange mix of surfers, aging hippies, and computer yuppies. Not only do Neil Young and Santana live near Santa Cruz, but the offices of Borland, MetaWare, SCO, and start-ups such as Cool and Starfish are found there too.

Even though Santa Cruz is known for its liberalism and political correctness, that doesn't rub off on everyone in town. SCO, in particular, ran into several problems with sexual harassment cases. In the most famous incident, the president of the company was forced out. The suit started with one employee complaining that the president, co-founder, and CEO, Larry Michels, kissed her. Larry's first public statement was "Did it say I raped anybody? Did it say I pinned anybody down?" He was quickly fed canned statements by his lawyers and the PR department. Seven additional female employees and ex-employees followed with other allegations of harassment and discrimination. They claimed Larry groped and forcibly kissed them, and also exposed his genitals to them.

During the same year, the vice president of legal affairs settled a sexual harassment suit out of court.

As a result of the suit against Michels, SCO paid a combined $1.25 million settlement to the plaintiffs. Larry resigned in December 1992, to be replaced by his son, and in leaving, got a $354,000 departure bonus.

A Different Kind of Networking

An engineering student, Jeff Jackson, suggested his wife take a job with Novell to support their family while he finished school. Marie got a job as the secretary for a Novell executive. The 20-year-old Marie had an affair with a Novell supervisor and became pregnant by him. This led to the dissolution of the Jacksons's marriage. Marie later married the supervisor.

Jeff sued Novell, since in Utah you can sue a third party for activities that lead to the breakup of your marriage. The Utah Supreme Court, however, rejected Jeff's claim, saying, "It would be unreasonable to impose upon employers a duty to monitor romantic relationships among their employees to protect marital relations of which they may not even be aware."

Did You Know?

Did Bill Stop Opus?
A reader once wrote to the *Seattle Times* asking if it was true that the cartoon "Outland," written by Berkeley Breathed, ended because Breathed made fun of Bill Gates in the cartoon, and Bill put pressure on the paper. Actually, Breathed had decided to stop cartoon drawing after 15 years of doing so.

Bill Gates' Wedding

When Bill Gates got married on January 1, 1994, he wanted some privacy. After all, he knew there would be many people from the media trying to take photographs and cover the story. So he got married on the Hawaiian island Lanai, 90 percent of which is owned by Dole Food Company and its subsidiary, Lanai Company. Dole Food security guards kept reporters at bay. As a further precaution, Gates also rented all helicopters on nearby islands, so that no one could fly in and take aerial photographs. (Rumors that he rented all spy satellites as well are unfounded.) A Seattle television cameraman, Scott Rensberger, made it onto the island and filmed guards putting up a roadblock at a public beach near the Manele Bay golf club, where Gates was getting married. He was illegally arrested for trespassing and held for $1,500 bail. Gates' publicist said she'd drop charges if Scott immediately left the island, which he did. The incident led to a Hawaii attorney general's investigation, perhaps also related to longtime residents' complaints that Lanai Company had tried to limit public access to the island.

Scott sued Gates, Dole Food, and Lanai Company. Lanai and Dole planned to countersue, but that action was blocked by a Hawaiian judge. Scott won the case, saying, "You know, folks, I just took on two of the most powerful people in the world, and I won." As part of the settlement, Gates' publicist donated 40 computers to Lanai High School, $25,000 was given to Lanaians for Sensible Growth, and the reporter received letters of apology from Gates and the CEO of Dole Food.

It's Only Been Used a Few Times

In April 1995 Compaq sued Packard Bell, claiming that Packard Bell was shipping used parts in its PCs to enable the company to charge lower prices. Compaq said that Packard Bell even went as far as altering serial numbers in order to hide what it was doing. Compaq said it learned about Packard Bell's operations from former Packard Bell employees. Compaq also alleged false advertising, unfair competition, and deceptive trade practices. In an earlier suit, Compaq sued Packard Bell for patent infringement.

Packard Bell had just become the leading supplier of personal computers to the home market in 1994. It stated, "The complaint is totally without merit and specifically designed to stall Packard Bell's momentum in the marketplace."

I Know, It's Only Rock and Roll

Computer people, and engineers in general, are often musicians. Even if they are not, they often listen to music at loud volumes while working, sometimes in an effort to stay awake through the long hours. If they don't do this, many computer programmers wear the same ratty jeans and t-shirts that rock stars do. So there is clearly a correlation.

Sometimes, however, the music world and the computer world clash in court. One famous case, that of Bob Dylan suing Apple over the code name of a scripting language, is discussed in the chapter "Shh! It's a Secret Code Name." Here are two more.

Love Is All We Need

In 1981, Apple Corps Ltd., the record company started by the Beatles, and Apple Computer Incorporated, signed a secret agreement whereby Apple could use the name Apple for its computer business and thus avoid trademark concerns.

In 1989, multimedia began to take off, and Apple computers were used for creating and playing music. Apple Corps Ltd. then sued, saying that Apple violated its agreement, since it was now selling products used in creating music. In particular, Apple Corps Ltd. was concerned about MIDI support, CD support, and the sound chips in the Apple IIGS and Mac. Apple Corps asked for $250 million in damages.

In 1991 the two companies settled out of court, with Apple Computer paying close to $30 million in damages to Apple Corp. Just to make sure the suit didn't get lonely, Apple Computer's insurance companies sued Apple Computer as well, saying that Apple didn't adequately notify them of the lawsuit. The insurance companies claimed they were therefore not liable for the damages and defense fees Apple paid.

Great Quotes:

The Apple/Apple Suit
After settling a suit between Apple Records and Apple Computer, the Apple Records lawyer said, "It's been, as they say, a long and winding road."

Acid-Laced Toast

This is a classic example of cascading suits. Berkeley Systems created one of the best-selling pieces of software ever created, After Dark, which has sold over one million copies. After Dark is a screen saver package containing amusing animations that appear when a machine is left idle. After Dark provides screen savers ranging from Lissajous figures and away-from-my-desk messages to cats that scratch on the screen and Disney cartoons. But the most famous of the screen savers is the flying toasters. This is a set of winged toasters that fly across the screen. It is part of the first set of After Dark screen savers, and it is the image that graces the box cover and has come to symbolize the package and the company.

Delrina, most widely known for WinFax Pro, also makes a screen saver called the Opus N' Bill Screen Saver. For its debut, it featured an irreverent takeoff on the After Dark flying toasters screen saver, in which Opus (of "Bloom County" and "Outland" fame) walks across the screen and fires a shotgun at a flock of flying toasters. Appropriately, it called this screen saver Death Toasters.

While customers found the tongue-in-cheek humor amusing, After Dark did not, and consequently sued Delrina in September 1993. Delrina claimed that satire should be allowed, with Opus cartoonist Berkeley Breathed chipping in, "If David Letterman can depict the NBC peacock wearing men's boxer shorts, then Delrina should be able to plug a flying toaster with hot lead." Delrina settled out of court, and was forced to change its Death Toasters screen saver. The toasters now have helicopter blades instead of wings.

During the litigation process, in an attempt to show that Berkeley Systems didn't own the concept of flying toasters, Delrina stated that the whole set of flying toasters was based on the cover of the 1973 Jefferson Airplane album, *Thirty Seconds over Winterland*. Jefferson Airplane didn't find the coincidence particularly amusing, despite Berkeley Systems' claim that it hadn't seen the album cover at the time it designed its screen saver. So, in June 1994, Jefferson Airplane sued Berkeley Systems for copyright infringement, asking it to cease using the flying toasters.

Jefferson Airplane lost its case over a technicality. Copyright law in 1973 required a separate application for album covers, and Jefferson Airplane didn't apply at the time. In deference, though, if you use the flying toasters screen saver, just hum a few bars of "Crown of Creation."

We'd love to show you the album cover and screen saver in question, but apparently too much ill will still exists between these two companies. They refused us permission to show you the images. Check them out at a record store or computer screen near you.

Out of Line On-line

After a full day of work (or school) is over, what do computer people do? Play sports? Plant trees? Some do. But most head home and log on. The on-line world, CompuServe, Prodigy, AOL, BIX, CIX, MSN, the Internet, and home-brew bulletin board systems, is a world frequented by millions of people. Mostly, people exchange information, chat with friends, and fabricate stories for the sex forums, meanwhile tying up phone lines for hours and hours.

Sometimes, though, what people do on-line gets them in trouble. For the most part, on-line suits relate to distribution of bootleg software. After all, you can easily copy a commercial program to a bulletin board or an FTP site and let anyone download it. It's like lending someone your floppies on-line. Of course, that is highly illegal, because duplicating commercial software without paying for it violates copyright law.

Recently, though, more and more cases relate to what is said on-line. Posting a libelous message on-line can get you in big trouble. And you can be prosecuted anywhere that the message was read. Suing an individual for libel usually doesn't get one much money, unless, of course, you sue someone who is really rich. So, most suits go after the on-line providers, who have far more money.

The following stories of woe relate to on-line systems.

The Deadbeat BBS, Davy Jones Locker, And Other Sources of Booty

There are several cases where bulletin boards and Internet sites were used to post illegal software. For the most part, the activity is run by younger folks, but in one case such a system was run by a pair of grandparents. Once a system is found, it is typically shut down and the computer equipment is confiscated. If the charges are unjust, the accused's computer equipment still sits in a police locker until the trial is over, which is a bummer for those who depend upon computers for their livelihood.

One such bulletin board was the Deadbeat Bulletin Board, run by a seventeen-year-old out of Camden, New Jersey. Sixty Novell and Microsoft products were available on it to users for swap or charge. When the sysop (system operator) was caught, his bulletin board was shut down, his equipment was confiscated, and he was fined $25,000.

In a similar case in June 1992, the FBI raided a bulletin board in Massachusetts called the Davy Jones Locker. More than 200 copyrighted programs were found on the bulletin board, available for illegal copying. Products included those from AutoDesk, Borland International, Broderbund, Central Point System, Clarion Software, Fifth Generation, IBM, Intuit, Lotus, Micrografx, Microsoft, SPC, Symantec, and WordPerfect. The FBI seized the computers and the operator's business records.

Another case occurred in December 1994. In this instance, a federal judge
threw out a case against an MIT student who had been operating a secret
bulletin board on two MIT computers. According to the suit, the sites,
called the Cynosure, were among the largest hubs for transmitting boot-
legged software. The Cynosure was active from November 1993 until
January 1994. The student, who went by the names "Grimjack" or "John
Gaunt," didn't copy the software or profit from it, but rather organized the
sites and how software was added. Here, the government prosecuted
under criminal wire fraud laws. The judge ruled that while the student's
actions were irresponsible and may have violated civil laws, they were not
a criminal instance of wire fraud.

Even Uncle Sam Lands in Trouble

Not even the government itself is immune from on-line troubles. In one
case, the Judicial branch went after the White House. Before leaving office,
the Bush administration wanted to erase a variety of email messages and
phone logs that it considered unimportant. For some reason, though, even
though these records weren't important enough to save in the archives,
they were too private to leave in the White House for the next administration.

President Bush signed an agreement that would keep the files intact, but
make them his own private property, presumably for use in the Bush
Presidential Library he was establishing. This, however, contradicted a law
that was passed to prevent President Nixon from destroying the Watergate
tapes.

The White House was given an order to make secure backups of the
records, which were stored on 300 computer tapes. In June 1993, a U.S.
District Judge ruled that the White House had "dillydallied, done little and
delayed for the past five months rather than make serious efforts to comply" with an earlier order to preserve electronic records of email and
phone calls. The judge then threatened to impose fines ranging from
$50,000 to $200,000 per day.

For even more of a twist, the person Bush hired to transfer the files took a
job heading Bush's Presidential Library. This resulted in a civil lawsuit and
a criminal investigation.

I Just Read the Articles, Really

In 1992, *Playboy* sued an Oregon on-line service for copyright infringement, saying the company illegally scanned photos from *Playboy* and then sold the resulting GIF images. The on-line service countered that the users may have scanned and transmitted photographs, but that the on-line service itself never scanned images.

The tables turned somewhat in April 1994, when the National Writers' Union sued *Playboy* for electronic piracy. It claimed that *Playboy* put a 1967 *Playboy* interview with Fidel Castro on a CD-ROM without getting rights from the author. *Playboy* paid the writer $100 for putting the interview on CD, which the author thought was unfair. The author claimed that he did not give *Playboy* rights to distribute the article on CD-ROM, especially since CD-ROMs didn't exist when he wrote the article.

Church Trade Secrets

It's not only *Playboy* that is upset with postings on the Internet. In February 1995, the Church of Scientology sued Netcom and a BBS system when a former Church member posted messages critical of the church on those systems. The member posted what the Church claimed to be secret teachings. The Church claimed it had a copyright for the teachings and that, furthermore, the teachings were trade secrets.

While in and of itself the case was somewhat bizarre, it gained notoriety quickly for the way the Church tracked the person who posted the messages. The poster had used an anonymous Internet remailer, called anon.penet.fi. This system, run out of Finland, takes messages and resends them, but with an anonymous address. As a result, one can post and receive mail without having one's identity revealed. This is particularly nice for those who want to post critical messages, nude pictures of their boss, or any other anonymous messages.

The Church pressured the Finnish police into getting the sysop of anon.penet.fi to release records showing the original name of the sender. This sent shock waves through the Internet, as anonymous mailers are viewed as a sacrosanct service.

And One More Libel Case

In November 1994, an investment company, Stratton Oakmont, sued Prodigy Services Co. for $200 million. It claimed that subscriber messages on Prodigy's MoneyTalk forum contained inaccurate comments about Stratton Oakmont.

Prodigy currently scans the 75,000 daily messages posted on its service electronically. Messages containing profanity or racial slurs are bounced with automatic suggestions on how the comments can be reworded. Now if that isn't an opportunity for a hacker...

In May 1995, a judge ruled that since Prodigy actively edited messages on the forum, it was a publisher, not just a distributor, and thus could be liable.

Nerd Humor:

More License Agreements

One license agreement for Netinc's NetMenu product says:

"What Will Happen If You Violate This Agreement: You will be in very big trouble."

Remains of the Day

Could that be all there is? Of course not. But before you go away disappointed that I haven't listed every single lawsuit that has ever occurred in the computer industry, here are a few more.

The Start of Microsoft

Microsoft had a license agreement with MITS, where MITS paid Microsoft royalties on BASIC up to $180,000. MITS, of course, was the maker of the

MITS Altair, the first personal computer. At the time, BASIC was Microsoft's only product and Microsoft worked hand in hand with MITS. MITS restricted Microsoft from licensing BASIC to other vendors, and this held back many large opportunities for Microsoft. A company called Pertec bought MITS on May 22, 1977. They believed that they also were buying BASIC along with the company. Pertec sent lawyers after Microsoft, and the case went to arbitration. In the process, Pertec threatened to prevent any further Microsoft business if Microsoft didn't back down. These heavy-handed tactics against teenagers didn't go over so well, and in fact back-fired when they were used as proof of violating the contract Microsoft had with Altair. As a result, the arbitrator ruled that Microsoft had full rights to BASIC, and the rest is history.

What Do You Want for $45?

This is a story of why you should erase your hard drives before you sell computer equipment. In July 1990, Charles Hayes bought a Harris-Lanier computer system from government surplus. For a mere 45 dollars, he got quite a bargain: 13 computer terminals, two central memory units with 93 megabytes of memory, two cartridge module drives and nine printers. Normally, the government erases the files on computers before it sells them. But in this case, the computers were a little bit flaky, and the technician was unable to erase the data. He told the government this after the sale.

Unfortunately, the government had used the computer system to store information about FBI informants, witness protection programs, indictments, and employee information. The government then sued to have Hayes immediately return the system untouched and unexamined.

Bombs Away

Consultants always live on the edge, never knowing when clients will pay them. Getting paid on time is an even larger ordeal. Sometimes people are tempted to plant bombs in code. This doesn't mean an actual smoke-and-flaming-equipment bomb. (Even though computer equipment sometimes smokes, there is not in fact an operating system call to start such fires. There is, though, an Internet rumor about a utility for DOS called NOSMOKE.EXE, which puts out burning hardware.) Instead, a bomb is a piece of code that when activated shuts down a program. For example, a developer could plant a bomb that prevented anyone from using a product. Once the customer paid for the product, the company could deactivate the bomb. Placing code bombs is usually regarded as a bad thing to do.

Such cases actually happen. For example, in 1990 a company called Logisticon created software for use by Revlon Corporation. But the software it created contained a little more than Revlon expected. When Revlon refused to pay for the software, Logisticon set off a built-in logic bomb, rendering Revlon incapable of processing sales for three days. Needless to say, Revlon sued.

Give Me Back My Company

Mark Zachmann founded Z-Soft in 1983. Z-Soft was best known for a paint package called PC Paintbrush, which sold over three million copies. While PC Paintbrush, and in particular PC Paintbrush IV, was hot stuff in its time, it was later eclipsed by packages such as Photoshop and Fractal Paint.

Mark Zachmann sold Z-Soft in 1988 to Mediagenic, for a stock swap he thought would be worth four million dollars. Two years later, Mediagenic was floundering, and Mark's stock was worth less than $350,000. Mark sued Mediagenic, and dropped the suit after buying the company back for roughly $3.8 million.

Apple Shareholder Suits

In 1983, Apple made various statements about the upcoming Lisa computer. The Lisa, however, performed miserably in the market, leading in part to a $40 drop in Apple's share price. Investors sued in 1984, saying they were misled. They also claimed that, in 1982, Apple misled them regarding the prospects for the Twiggy drives, which were designed to be far faster than normal floppies, but never were shipped due to reliability problems. Damages were initially awarded, and then thrown out in appeal in 1991.

In 1989, shareholders sued Apple for securities violations, saying Apple didn't promptly disclose bad financial reports. A year later, Apple denied the allegations and settled for $5.65 million.

Jarndyce v Jarndyce

In Charles Dickens's novel *Bleak House*, a suit called Jarndyce v. Jarndyce lasts interminably, enriching no one but the lawyers. Such stories occur in the computer industry as well. In March 1989, Jasmine Technologies Inc. sued Rodime PLC and a variety of former Jasmine founders and executives, then at Rodime, for fraud, breach of contract, conspiracy, and RICO violations. Rodime countersued for breach of contract and asked for the $4.7 million that it said Jasmine owed.

A year later, Jasmine was in Chapter 11 and owed its lawyers $270,000, and Rodime had just climbed back from near bankruptcy. The two called off the suits, saying, "Basically, both parties agreed that it was silly to keep making the lawyers rich."

Repetitive Stress

Repetitive stress injury suits are increasing in frequency. Typing over and over again, as with any repetitive motion, can cause injuries including carpal tunnel syndrome and tendonitis. As more and more people spend all day and night working on keyboards, more and more people get these injuries. In fact, according to OSHA, 56 percent of work injuries in 1992 were repetitive stress injuries. Correspondingly, there have been a number of repetitive stress injury lawsuits. Keyboards even now come with tags warning that extended use can cause injury. (And significant extended use can cause drowsiness.)

In November 1994, a woman sued IBM, HP, and Microsoft, saying that while a clerk for DuPont, she used an IBM keyboard, an HP Vectra computer, and a Microsoft mouse, from which she got repetitive stress injuries.

In another case, Compaq won a lawsuit that office workers and journalists filed, saying that Compaq keyboards contributed to repetitive stress injuries. The jury ruled that Compaq was not obligated to warn users of the risk because it was not aware that the keyboards could cause injury. Likewise, Atex was sued for injuries relating to using its keyboards.

This type of lawsuit will continue. Meanwhile, ergonomic keyboards, once viewed as a bizarre phenomenon, are in vogue.

Despite its snappy copy, it is hard to believe that this ad is from 1984, not 1954. IBM provided a full range of products to supplement the IBM PC line. Here you can see an ad for their office furniture. It is unfortunate that ergonomic workstations haven't taken off in proportion to PC sales, as that would perhaps reduce the number of repetitive strain injuries.

Suit, Countersuit

After John Sculley left his position as CEO of Apple, he joined Spectrum Information Technologies. Shortly afterwards, he left, and sued Spectrum for ten million dollars, saying it failed to notify him about a pending SEC investigation. The stock price dropped 50 percent, and Spectrum returned suit, asking for $300 million for breach of contract.

Pop Torte

While this isn't exactly a computer suit, the link is interesting. Kellogg paid $2,400 to settle a 1995 lawsuit in which a customer said that a Kellogg's Pop-Tart, which he left for an extended period of time in his toaster, set fire to his kitchen. The lawyer in the case consulted humor columnist Dave Barry, who described how to ignite a pop tart in one of his columns. An assistant professor of Computer Science at Texas A&M reproduced Barry's experiment, and posted a lengthy discussion, complete with photographs, on the Web. You too can see exploding pop tarts at http://www.sci.tamucc.edu/~pmichaud/toast.

Less Weird Stuff

Weird Stuff is a famous computer store in the Silicon Valley area. It, like Fry's, is a staple of the Silicon Valley nerd community. There you can find just about anything. And most things that you will find are old, inexpensive, and probably should be in this book. One of the ways Weird Stuff got products was by buying them from "dumpster divers." These people look through the trash of computer companies, trying to find discarded software and hardware that might still have value.

At one point, two dumpster divers found 1,700 copies of NetWare 3.11 in a Novell subcontractor's trash bin. Weird Stuff bought them in 1992 and then tried to sell the whole set to a computer company for $500,000. When the purchasing company tried to verify the serial numbers, it found that Novell had no record for some of them. This alerted Novell to the sale, and Novell subsequently sued to stop the transaction in July 1993.

Good Rider on the Magic School Bus

Of course, not only is it interesting to read about suits, but it is also interesting to see what steps companies go through to avoid suits. Almost everything these days has a disclaimer on it. Software too is getting warning labels. For example, Microsoft sells a children's game called the Magic School Bus. In this game, children take an imaginary journey through the human body by driving a bus down someone's throat. Throughout, children learn about the different parts of a body, including a great multimedia scene in the stomach.

Before starting the tour, explorers receive several messages, most certainly placed by a legal team, reminding them not to try to drive a real bus through the human body. A narrator on a TV screen gives three reminders to kids, including:

> A school bus can enter someone's body and kids can go on a tour. True or false? That cannot happen in real life.

"To crash OS/2, you have to stay up night and day to build a terminator disk. Windows comes with that built in."

— James Cannavino, IBM

IBM heavily marketed the idea that OS/2 was crash-proof, and that it was therefore a far safer operating system to use than Microsoft Windows. In response, Microsoft allegedly pulled together a team to create and potentially propagate applications that would crash OS/2, to show that it was in fact not as stable and crashproof as IBM claimed.

Dirty Tricks

No chapter on lawyers would be

complete if not followed by a chapter on dirty tricks. Every industry has its hidden secrets. Car manufacturers have espionage campaigns. Cigarette manufacturers have more medical studies than can be believed. And it is probably safer not to wonder about the gambling industry. The software industry has its own unique flavor of dirty tricks. Here are a couple.

What's in It, Bricks?

MiniScribe Corp., a manufacturer of hard drives, was having financial difficulties and later filed for Chapter 11. It was under scrutiny by investors, and some officers wanted to make sure it could post a good quarter. Thus, to generate revenue they wanted to show a full warehouse of inventory ready to be shipped. Unfortunately, Miniscribe had very few hard drives, so Owen Taranta, former CFO, his wife and children, and some executives of

MiniScribe Corp. allegedly filled boxes with bricks, and thus the warehouse was filled with a number of boxes. If someone picked them up, they'd feel heavy enough to create the impression of hard drives inside.

This trick was caught by a new management team a year later. Some even say that a warehouse clerk accidentally shipped out some of the brick-filled boxes to customers.

I'm Jazzed

Allegedly, Lotus needed to ship Jazz by a particular date, but the product wasn't ready. So Lotus allegedly shipped out the manuals with a bunch of blank disks. When customers called up to complain, Lotus blamed the problem on the disk manufacturer, and then sent out the real disks. This bought Lotus a few days of extra development time.

We're Not Done If Lotus Runs

The DOS 2.0 team allegedly had this motto. They supposedly made sure that enough changes were made in DOS so that Lotus 1-2-3 would no longer run, giving Microsoft a bit of an edge over the competition.

Windows 3.11 and OS/2

IBM has two versions of OS/2. One includes built-in support for Windows programs, and one, called OS/2 for Windows, does not. OS/2 for Windows will run Windows programs, however, if Windows is installed on a machine. It simply starts up Windows itself and runs it within OS/2. This is not a simple trick. By doing this, IBM got around paying royalties to Microsoft for the copy of Windows code it previously was shipping with each copy of OS/2.

Making OS/2 run various versions of Windows is a long-term commitment. When Windows 3.11 came out, apparently it would no longer run under OS/2 for Windows. Allegedly, whatever stopped it from working had nothing to do with bug or performance fixes, so IBM customers claimed that Microsoft did this on purpose. Microsoft said it was purely accidental, and quickly released a patch that allowed the program to run under OS/2.

Microsoft's Performance-Tuning Diskette

Microsoft at one point sent a disk out to many of the registered Windows customers. This disk was called a "performance tuning disk." Running it would provide information on how to get Windows to perform better. In addition to whatever tuning advice the disk provided, it also checked to see if competing products, such as WordPerfect, were installed. If so, it suggested that the system would be optimized by replacing such products with Microsoft products.

In Electronic Disguise

On electronic forums, no one knows anyone's real identity. In fact, there is a popular cartoon that says "On the Internet, no one knows you are a dog." Thus, vendors often visit the forums of competitors in disguise and ask questions about upcoming products. Sometimes, they even start flames about bugs or policies.

At one point on a forum run by Will Zachmann, a "disgruntled IBM customer" claimed OS/2 was causing his company numerous problems. Will, being a big OS/2 fan, traced the origin of the "customer," and found out that he used a Microsoft credit card to pay for the account.

More Warehouse Troubles

MediaVision grew dramatically, expanded, and then went into Chapter 11 after growing too rapidly and having numerous financial troubles. Investigators found that it seemed to have two sets of books, one for what was really going on and one for investors. Apparently, it also had a secret warehouse containing returned merchandise. That way, the books would show only what the company sent out, without subtracting large returns. The president of the company was also investigated for buying his girlfriend presents using company funds. The CFO, CEO, COO, VP of Sales and other officers resigned and new management took over.

Great Quotes: The Spirit of Competition

Take an Aspirin

"When I read about TrueType and PostScript in the same sentence, I get sick." John Warnock, President of Adobe, makers of PostScript. TrueType is a competing solution from Microsoft.

OLE

"It's crazy. It doesn't work. It's not a serious contender, and frankly I don't worry about it." John Warnock, President of Adobe.

Jobs on NT

"It's Microsoft's second attempt at a Unix wannabe. It's better plumbing for Windows. You're still stuck with the worst development environment." Steve Jobs.

Dis'ing Xerox, Part II

"It doesn't matter how great the computer is if nobody buys it. Xerox proved that." Chris Espinosa, a member of the original Macintosh team.

Look Out, Bill

Regarding how he felt about upcoming competition from Microsoft Network, Ted Leonsis, the President of America Online commented that watching Jerry Seinfeld with his kid is what takes him away from exploring on-line systems: "So I fear Jerry Seinfeld more than I fear Bill Gates."

How Much for a 28.8?

In a conference discussing on-line services, Scott Kurnit, Executive Vice President of Prodigy Services, said this regarding Microsoft Network:

"Letting Microsoft handle all the billing is somewhere between drug-dealing and suicide."

Gotta Beat Those Guys

Regarding NextStep's prospects as compared with the Taligent OS, Steve Jobs said, "We should be able to beat Taligent, or we are just incompetent."

OS/2 Sucks

In an internal 1991 memo, Bill Gates criticized IBM's OS/2 2.0, saying it was "a poor product with poor Windows functionality."

Scope/2

"OS/2 is good technically. It just has bad breath." Mike Maples, Senior Vice President at Microsoft.

Competing with Microsoft

"Competing with Microsoft is like putting your head in a vice and squeezing it as hard as you can." — Anonymous

"Bill is not a nasty guy to compete with." Gordon Eubanks.

"Doing a good job isn't illegal." Esther Dyson.

"I wish he'd get married and have a couple of kids so he couldn't work as many hours as he does." Pete Peterson, executive vice president of WordPerfect at the time.

The IBM Purchase of Lotus

"It's pretty remarkable how senior management at Lotus could totally erode and mismanage a major franchise and still walk away with tens of millions." David Readerman, Montgomery Securities.

Benchmarks

Customers often want to know how fast a product performs. So magazines and other industry analysts create benchmarks to measure product performance. Once a benchmark is released, vendors often optimize their products for the particular benchmark. Numerous database tools and compilers are known to have code in them that specifically checks to see if certain benchmarks are being run. The tools then generate code that answers the benchmark problem, lightning fast. Of course, the speed of processing the benchmark program has no relation to how a slightly different version of the same program would run. The tools win the benchmarks, but don't perform as fast as expected when customers use them in the real world.

How do benchmarks work? Suppose, as a contrived example, that a magazine uses the factorial function as a way to benchmark a math chip's speed. The factorial function returns n*(n-1)*(n-2) ... 2*1. So, 3! is 3*2*1. A chip (or compiler) could check for this type of operation, and then use a look-up table. It could build in the answers for a number of factorials (e.g., 10!, 20!, 40!, etc.). If asked what 41! is, it would just find 41*40!, and look up 40! from its table. That would save it 40 multiplications, making it far faster than a competing chip or compiler. Of course, this solution would show that the factorial function is fast, but would not deal with other typical problems encountered by real-world customers.

Virus Patrol

PKZIP is a very popular program for compressing and uncompressing files and is made by a company called PKWARE, Inc. A shareware version is distributed on many bulletin boards. The most recent version, for example, is called PKZ204G.EXE. Those who regularly use PKZIP know to look out for new versions, so as to have the latest and greatest in software compression.

Someone posted a file called PKZ300B.EXE on numerous forums. From its name, one would have thought that this was a new version of PKZIP, and many innocently downloaded and ran it. It turned out to be a virus, and had absolutely nothing to do with PKWARE.

Did You Know?

Did It Happen?

The computer HAL from the movie *2001* was supposed to go on-line in January 1992.

Computers on the Silver Screen

Having taken a look at some of the events in computer history, let's see how these are reflected in the movies. There are tons of movies these days that feature computers. In fact, it is hard to find a movie taking place in the current time that doesn't have computers in it. For some reason, though, the computers in many of these movies insist on outputting characters one at a time, with teletype noises in the background. The same exact low-res screens often turn into high-end workstations by the end of the movie. This, of course, disgusts the nerds in the audience.

On the other hand, there is nothing like offbeat humor, hot special effects, or a hip reference to technology to get a computer-enthusiast audience cheering. It is no wonder that *Buckaroo Bonzai* and *Circuitry Man* are among computer hackers' favorites.

Here are some of the classic computer movie moments.

Desk Set

This 1957 movie starring Spencer Tracy and Katherine Hepburn was one of the first movies featuring computers. Tracy interjects a computer named Emmy into Hepburn's research department, creating the potential for many human researchers losing their jobs. After being asked a complex question about Watusis and Corfu, the computer blows up.

2001

This classic movie from 1968 is filled with computer scenes of the HAL 9000, a futuristic computer that talks, reasons, and struggles with conflicting programming. Most computer programmers I know are saddened when HAL becomes dismantled. The name HAL, of course, happens to be made of the letters preceding each of the letters in IBM. Quotes from and references to HAL permeate the computer culture.

THX-1138

In George Lucas's first film, a citizen named THX 1138 and his lover LUH 3417 battle robot police and a central computer system after they dare to fall in love. 1971.

Soylent Green

This 1973 flick features some of the first virtual reality scenes, where those who are about to die get to view movies showing natural scenes that have long since been destroyed by civilization.

Dark Star

A computer lover's cult classic, this 1974 film was John Carpenter's first. The crew of a spaceship flies through space blowing up planets. One of the bombs becomes stuck, thus endangering the ship. The bombs are run by AI computers, and the crew and bomb engage in a philosophical debate about perception to convince the bomb it never really got the command to explode. The bomb thinks for a moment and stops the countdown. In the ending scene, the bomb says, "Let there be light," and then it explodes.

Three Days of the Condor

The bad guys shoot up a perfectly fine PDP-8, along with Robert Redford's boss, girlfriend, associates, and anything else that moves. 1975.

Demon Seed

In this 1977 horror movie, a computer determines to take over the world. Amusingly enough, this was the same year that the Apple II came out.

Star Trek

In the first *Star Trek* movie, created in 1979, one of the displays on the bridge shows futuristic patterns that somehow relate to running a starship. These patterns are actually running on a Radio Shack TRS-80.

Tron

In a movie that set new ground for the quantity of computer graphics in a film, a character is somehow scanned into a computer and sets off trying to battle the master control program that is killing free programs everywhere. While the movie isn't exactly tops, it is a must-see for computer nerds. 1982.

War Games

In this 1983 movie, a high school senior played by Matthew Broderick hacks into a Defense Department war game simulator using an IMSAI computer in his bedroom. Donating the computer for the movie was one of the last things IMSAI did before going out of business.

Electric Dreams

In this cutesy Bud Cort movie from 1984, a single guy buys a computer. He accidentally drops it, endowing the computer with extra intelligence. The computer proceeds to help him win the heart of the girl upstairs, but then it becomes jealous. It ends up spreading out into the global electronic community.

Terminator

When the *Terminator* walks around in this 1984 classic, text flashes before his eyes with targeting information, linguistic information, and more. In one scene, a screen of code flashes before his eyes, which is theoretically something relating to his internal programming. The code is some 6502 code, written with the Lisa assembler. Thus, the terminator was being run by the same chip as the Apple II.

Jumpin' Jack Flash

From the terminal she uses at the bank, Whoopie Goldberg intercepts and decodes a message from a trapped spy. Bank terminals often get cross-wired with an Eastern European exercise program, through some miracle of electronics. I guess if you have enough wire running through a bank, it somehow becomes unshielded enough to act as a giant antenna. Otherwise, cross-continental TV broadcasts probably wouldn't show up on a bank terminal. 1986.

Star Trek IV

Having arrived in twentieth century San Francisco, Scottie goes to a construction company to try to design transparent aluminum. He attempts to construct a wall for the whale they are trying to transport to the Earth of the future. The construction company has a Macintosh. Scottie talks to the computer, which of course doesn't do anything. The engineer hands him the mouse, but Scottie treats it as a microphone. It's a great scene, frequently relived for nerd comic relief everywhere. Once Scottie gets hold of the machine, it somehow goes through many chemical calculations that would never be able to run on the Mac, but look fine as the series of bitmaps that they are. 1986.

Wayne's World 2

Dana Carvey, the comedian of "Saturday Night Live" fame, has a brother famous to nerds. Brad was a coinventor of the Video Toaster, and hence Dana wears a Video Toaster t-shirt in this movie. 1993.

Jurassic Park

In a scene where they are desperately trying to escape the dinosaurs, one of the characters runs to an X Windows workstation, looks at it, and says, "Unix. I know this." Which seems a little bit unlikely, but thrills the programmers in the audience of this 1993 hit.

True Lies

In the crucial opening scene, the spy played by Arnold Schwarzenegger sneaks into the office of an Arab businessman, slaps a box with blinking lights on the back of the machine, and boots up Arabic Windows. Tense moments follow as a hacker waiting in a van then tries to decode an access code or encryption of some sort so he can download files. Why he didn't just download the files and figure out how to decode them later is beyond me, since DOS and Windows don't have a security system. 1994.

Forrest Gump

In one scene in this 1994 movie, Forrest claims that his financial worries are over because he has invested in a fruit company. The company is Apple Computer.

"You are seeing a computer industry milestone—a RISC-based Windows Solitaire game."

— Bill Gates, Microsoft

These words set the stage when Microsoft showed Windows NT running on a RISC machine for the first time.

In the Beginning

You've read about the early computers, and how they changed in sizes from rooms filled with vacuum tubes to the machines we know and love today. Now it is time to see how these companies started. We'll first look at the origins of the chip makers. Then, we'll examine the origins of some key hardware and software vendors, as well as some magazines.

Chip Makers

The computer revolution never would have occurred if it hadn't been for integrated circuits, commonly called *chips*. Most chip manufacturers are headquarted in California, south of San Francisco in an area appropriately known as Silicon Valley.

The success of the chip business is in many ways an accident. The first microprocessors were not built with computers in mind. The 6502, which formed the heart of the Apple II, was designed for controlling traffic lights.

The 4004, which turned into the 8008, 8080, 8086, and today the Pentium, was designed for a custom calculator — and it almost never saw the light of day. In fact, Robert Noyce, the head of Intel, projected that the main market for microprocessors would be watches.

Let's take a look at the start of two important players in the chip market: Intel and Chips and Technologies.

Did You Know?

What a Withdrawal

Robert Noyce was one of the founders of Intel, and he became extremely wealthy as a result of his efforts. He allegedly once stood in a long line at his bank and, when he got to the teller, calmly withdrew $1.3 million from his account so that he could buy a Lear jet.

Intel

Robert Noyce was one of the founders of Fairchild Semiconductor. In 1968, Noyce left that company because he couldn't get the owners to grant stock options to all employees instead of just the managers. He and some partners immediately created Intel. The first microprocessor, the 4004, was created in 1969. It was designed as a general solution to making calculators. The name came from the number of transistors that would be needed to provide the same functionality as the chip.

What isn't widely known is that all of this almost didn't happen. In fact, Noyce allegedly almost ended up a pig farmer.

Noyce was a brilliant student in electrical engineering. When pledging a fraternity, he and several other frat pledges were given an initiation assignment of stealing a variety of things. Noyce was given the task of stealing a pig from a local pig farmer. He was an honest guy, but decided to do it anyway. After he successfully stole the pig and brought it back to the frat house, he felt guilty. So he went to the farmer and confessed what he had done. The farmer was very upset and, instead of thanking Noyce for his honesty and asking for restitution, he pressed charges and tried to get Noyce thrown out of school.

Noyce's physics professor managed to convince the farmer that it would be OK if Noyce stayed in school, but only under strict supervision. If the farmer had had his way, personal computers might never have been invented.

Chips and Technologies

The computer industry is a close-knit one, with many ties among companies. For example, Gordon Eubanks of Symantec used to work at Digital Research. Adam Osborne used to work at Intel, as did Apple's Mike Markkula. Chips and Technologies is no exception.

Gordon Campbell was the head of marketing at Intel. He thought EEPROMs were the coolest thing, but Intel didn't share his enthusiasm. Sensing a market opportunity, he left Intel and raised $30 million of venture capital, forming SEEQ Technologies. He later got sacked by the venture-capital firm, leaving with $2 million in stock. (In case you aren't up on all of the industry acronyms, EEPROMs are *electrically erasable programmable read-only memory;* essentially, chips that can contain

Moore's Law

Moore's Law is a famous law created by Gordon Moore, one of the cofounders of Intel. It says that the number of transistors that can fit on a chip will double every eighteen months. Essentially, that means the power of a computer will double every eighteen months. Apparently, Moore was on his way to give a talk to the employees, but he hadn't prepared beforehand. Nonetheless, he still needed to give a talk on the future of the computer industry. So he invented Moore's Law, since it described what had happened at Intel during the previous eighteen months. The engineers at Intel have been struggling ever since to make sure it stays true.

programs, such as BASIC or BIOS and have two important properties. They retain the programs when the power is turned off, but unlike normal ROMs, which are created once and could never be changed, these can be erased and reprogrammed.)

Campbell and a real estate developer then pulled together $1.5 million, and they formed a new company to design tools for creating custom PC chips, called Chips and Technologies. The company ran out of money before bringing products to market, so Campbell chipped in some of his own money and borrowed money from the CFO to make payroll. Out of money once again, he searched for backers but could find none. Fortuitously, he ran into Kay Nishi, Microsoft's representative in Japan, who helped him line up $1.5 million from Japanese investors. That was enough to get the first product out the door, a set of five chips that replaced 63 chips used in the IBM PC. This let IBM clone vendors save an incredible amount of money and effort when making PCs, and Chips and Technologies not only helped drive the flood of PC clones and the ensuing price wars, but became a great success.

The Hardware Vendors

The computer revolution was feuled not only by chips, but also by the enterprising individuals who combined these chips into affordable computers. Many of the early companies have long since disappeared, but their influence and spin-offs remain in what has grown from garages into a multibillion-dollar industry.

MITS

The computer that kicked off the personal computer industry was the MITS Altair. MITS, which stood for Micro Instrumentation Telemetry Systems, was originally an electronics store. Its owner, Ed Roberts, sold model airplane radio transmitters out of a garage in Albuquerque, New Mexico. When business got good enough, he moved out of the garage into a space formerly occupied by a restaurant called The Enchanted Sandwich Shop. Roberts left the sign up, and it certainly set the atmosphere for the various computer engineers and followers who would soon troop there.

But MITS didn't jump from selling airplane transmitters to selling computers. That was a fluke of the market. MITS had been selling calculator kits. But, by the mid-seventies, the calculator business was dominated by the large chip makers. For example, in early 1974, a MITS calculator kit cost $99.95. A preassembled calculator from Texas Instruments cost less than $50. It was clear who would win in the market. Ed Roberts decided to sell kit computers instead.

Fortunately for Roberts, *Popular Electronics,* a widely read magazine among electronics enthusiasts, was looking to write about a kit computer. It knew of two such kits. One was Ed Roberts' kit. Based on an 8080, it sounded like a great machine, but so far it was only an idea. The other was an 8008-based machine called the Mark-8. It wasn't as powerful as the 8086-based machine, but it existed. It looked like the Mark-8 was going to win out. But, just before *Popular Electronics* had to make its decision, an issue of the competing magazine *Radio Electronics* came out, covering the Mark-8. Now the choice was easier; *Popular Electronics* would cover the MITS computer so as to upstage *Radio Electronics.*

This put Roberts under intense pressure. After all, he now had very little time to turn his idea into a real machine. He was $300,000 in debt and needed $65,000 to finish the machine. He went back to the bank for more money, sure it would turn him down. Instead, the bank gave him the money, figuring that he would go under, but at least he could pay off some of his debt in the process if it funded him a little further. Roberts now had enough money to pull the computer together. With no time to spare, he created one and sent it to *Popular Electronics* by Railway Express, ready for the review. For some reason, though, the computer never arrived. There was no time to create a new one, so *Popular Electronics* shot an empty box with lights and switches on the front panel, figuring that by the time the magazine hit the stands, the computer would be ready. That fake cover was the very one that set Paul Allen and Bill Gates off to the desert to found Microsoft.

MITS had a hard time coming up with a name for its new computer. Its technical writer, David Bunnel, who would go on to found *PC Magazine,* was in charge of coming up with the name. His top candidate, "Little Brother," wasn't too promising. Neither was PE-8, a tribute to *Popular Electronics.*

Les Solomon, the editor of *Popular Electronics,* wanted a more exciting name for the product and for his cover story. He turned to his twelve-year-old daughter for help in finding a name. Since she was watching "Star Trek," he asked what the name of the computer on the show was. Of course, she answered "computer." That didn't seem like a great name, so she suggested Altair, which was the place where the Enterprise was going on that evening's episode.

The MITS Altair made the January 1975 cover of *Popular Electronics,* and instead of the hundred or so orders that the bank expected, thousands flooded in.

Eventually, MITS ran into financial and management troubles, and it was bought by a company named Pertec in May 1977. The Altair disappeared shortly thereafter, washed over by the oncoming wave of the Apple II. Ed Roberts changed careers, moving to Georgia to become a small town doctor.

Did You Know?

1974
The 8080 came out in 1974, as did the Xerox Alto.

Parasitic Engineering

Parasitic Engineering was an early computer company that provided add-on boards for the MITS Altair. The name was chosen after Ed Roberts, the president of MITS, referred to add-on companies as parasites. After all, he felt MITS should get all the revenue from add-on products.

Parasitic Engineering was founded by Howard Fulmer. Fulmer had thought about calling the company Symbiotic Engineering instead of Parasitic

Engineering, again because of Roberts' remark, but wanted to avoid any confusion with the Symbionese Liberation Army.

IMSAI

IMSAI was another of the first personal computer companies. Its computer competed with, and eventually outsold, the MITS Altair. The company was started by Bill Millard, who had worked as an IBM salesman and as a MIS manager for the city of San Francisco. While most companies at the time were created by engineers who built computers and then found a demand for them, Millard built a sales-oriented organization.

Millard's original goal was to run a consulting business, helping businesses select and configure computer systems. One of the company's first jobs was to pull together a system for handling accounting at a New Mexico car dealership. Millard then figured that he could resell the system to a number of other car dealers across the country. But MITS wouldn't give him a discount on the Altairs. Frustrated but not discouraged, Millard decided to build his own computer. He hired an engineer to analyze the Altair and build a computer for IMSAI. This turned into the IMSAI 8080, and the company began to grow.

Almost everyone whom IMSAI hired had gone through EST (Erhardt Sensitivity Training), which was in vogue in California at the time. The company focused on goals and "making miracles." Engineering backgrounds were less important than attitude, and in contrast to the "nerd" culture at Microsoft, employees included a vitamin salesman and a Uriah Heep roadie. During IMSAI's heyday, it was approached by numerous investors, including Charles Tandy from Radio Shack. IMSAI turned them all down. Business was booming. Who needed outside money?

Unfortunately, the management style didn't allow focusing on problems, and the company had several, including manufacturing problems, poor forecasting, poor documentation, poor customer support, and flaky machines. One machine, the VDP-80, was rushed to market and was almost unusable when released. Because the financing structure required a steady base of future sales to fund current expenses, IMSAI ended up with heavy financial troubles, and after massive layoffs in October 1978, it folded.

Along the way, the director of marketing left to form MicroPro, and the director of sales left to form ComputerLand.

Cromemco

Cromemco was another of the early computer leaders. It started as an add-on company for the MITS Altair, and originally planned to connect a digital camera, called the Cyclops, to the Altair. The founders had lived in the Crothers Memorial Hall dormitory at Stanford's Graduate School, and they shortened this name to create the company name. The company's first product was a video display card for the Altair.

Cromemco was a market leader for many years. The Cromemco has long since disappeared, done in by the incredible success of the IBM PC.

Osborne Computer Company

Adam Osborne wrote the technical manual for the 4004 chip for Intel. In fact, he wrote the 8080 manual that Paul Allen and Bill Gates read to figure out how to create an 8080 emulator when they started Microsoft. Osborne's first book outside of Intel, *An Introduction to Microcomputers*, was included by IMSAI with every computer it sold. This led to the start of a publishing company now known as Osborne-McGraw Hill.

Osborne also created the Osborne Computer Company, which in April 1981 released the Osborne 1, the first successful portable business computer. The Osborne 1 was designed so that it could fit under an airplane seat. It was unique in that it included a bundle of software including CP/M, CBASIC, Microsoft BASIC, SuperCalc, and WordStar. Osborne gave shares of stock in the company to the software suppliers in return for bargain prices.

Unfortunately, Osborne Computer Company went bankrupt. Osborne went on to found Paperback Software, a maker of desktop business applications including a spreadsheet with a menu structure similar to that of Lotus 1-2-3. That company too went out of business, following a lawsuit lost to Lotus. Osborne retired to Oregon, where he lives today, reportedly in ill health.

Hewlett-Packard

Hewlett-Packard was formed in 1939 with a $538 loan. The two founders, William Hewlett and David Packard, worked out of their garage in Palo Alto, California. The company's first product was an oscillator, and its first customer was Walt Disney Co.

Radio Shack

Tandy started as a leather business in 1927. The venture was quite successful, and in 1962 Tandy bought a set of nine mail order stores called Radio Shack. Radio Shack became a popular hangout for youthful circuit builders, myself included.

Some of the engineers at Radio Shack were fascinated with the early computers and decided that they should build their own. Radio Shack's management didn't approve, so the engineers kept the project under cover. In December 1976 the project became official, with the mandate to create the computer as inexpensively as possible so that Radio Shack could sell it for $199. As a result, the engineers skimped wherever possible. For example, the first machine lacked lowercase letters just to save $1.50 on parts. It is no wonder, then, that many early users had to type with one hand while holding the keyboard jack into the back of the machine with the other.

The TRS-80 was announced in August 1977 and sold for $399. Radio Shack figured it would be lucky if it sold 3,000 units in the first year, but by the end of September, it had already sold 10,000 of them. The TRS-80 Model II came out in May 1979. These machines were somewhat affectionately called the "Trash 80s." Eventually, Radio Shack switched to creating IBM PC clones, and is a minor player in the computer business today.

Did You Know?

Lisa
The Lisa computer, from Apple, officially stood for "large integrated software architecture," but rumor says it was really named after Steve Jobs's daughter. Steve was not married to his daughter's mother, and allegedly even denied being the father until forced to take a blood test.

Woz's First
The first computer Steve Wozniak used was a PDP-8.

Apple

Steve Jobs, Steve Wozniak, and Mike Markkula were the founders of Apple Computer. The two Steves were the creators of the company, having had a few business adventures together beforehand. Mike joined them to provide financing and much-needed management experience, changing the company from a group of friends creating some kits for a hobby to an incredible success story.

Stephen Wozniak created his first computer in 1971. He called it the Cream Soda Computer, because he and a friend had been up all night drinking cream soda while creating it. It went up in a cloud of smoke when they demonstrated it to the press.

This didn't discourage Steve, and a year later he formed an informal technology company with Steve Jobs. It didn't sell computers. Rather, Jobs and Wozniak were very interested in *phone phreaking*. This is the use of electronic devices to avoid paying for phone calls. There are all types of devices for this purpose, ranging from ones that emit special tones to get free long-distance wires, to ones that simulate the sound of coins dropping into a pay phone. The company created a phone-hacking device called the *blue box*, and sold it to friends and to others at college. Through this interest, Jobs and Wozniak met the most famous phone phreaker, Captain Crunch. Captain Crunch's real name was John Draper; he got his nickname after discovering that a whistle from Captain Crunch cereal emitted a tone that, when whistled into a telephone receiver, would give free access to a long-distance line.

Captain Crunch would later work at Apple to design a telephony card for the Apple II. Not only could the card automatically dial phone numbers, but it had phone-phreaking capabilities as well. Needless to say, Apple never shipped it. Captain Crunch also wrote the word processor that IBM marketed along with the first IBM PC.

Wozniak left Berkeley, where he was studying, to work at HP. Jobs left Reed College to work at Atari. Jobs and Wozniak had another informal business at that point as well. Wozniak had designed a Pong game, called Breakout, that used one third of the chips most implementations did. Nolan Bushnell challenged Wozniak to get it to under 40 chips, offering $700 if he got it to under 50 chips, and $1,000 if he got it to under 40 chips. Four days later, Wozniak delivered a 44 chip design. (One of Wozniak's designs also displayed "Oh Sh*t" instead of "Game Over" when the player lost.)

Did You Know?

What a Tour!

The first two chains to carry IBM PCs were the Sears Business Centers and ComputerLand. Both carried other brands as well. When Sears executives visited Atari, they were given quite a tour by Atari's president, Nolan Bushnell. He put them in cardboard boxes and ran them through the production line.

Wozniak designed the Apple I while he was still working at HP. He had read the first issue of *Byte* and was interested in computers, but couldn't afford to buy one. He initially designed a 68000-based computer, but the chips were too expensive, so he switched to a 6502, which cost $25. The computer featured 8K of RAM, and a video and keyboard connector.

Wozniak and Jobs then gave out schematics for the computer at the Homebrew Computer Club, the extremely influential first computer club. Jobs thought they could make some money by selling the circuit boards at the club in kit form. It would cost them $1,000 to get the board silk-screened, and $20 to have each board created. If they sold the boards to 50 people at $50 each, they would break even. They decided to go for it, funding their venture by selling their most-prized possessions. In this case, Jobs sold his van, and Wozniak his two HP calculators.

Prior to starting the business, Wozniak checked with HP to see if it wanted the design, since after all, he had created it while working at HP. HP said it wasn't interested in the hobby market and signed a release form.

Jobs and Wozniak's plans were altered when a local computer store, the Byte Shop, ordered 50 units. The hitch was, it wanted the full units pre-assembled. Jobs and Wozniak got a 30-day loan from a bank for $20,000, borrowed $5,000 from a friend and a relative, and pulled together a bunch of friends to assemble the machines. Thus was born the Apple I, which was the first Apple computer. It sold for $666. Over the next ten months, they sold 125 of them. And in March 1976, they created the formal Apple partnership. A partner that owned 10 percent then sold out for $800, because he thought Apple was going to go broke. So much for his instant retirement plans.

Wozniak then designed the Apple II, which enhanced many aspects of the Apple I, but was still designed based on what was cheap at the time. Jobs made sure that the case had a professional, approachable look rather than the hobbyist look that most computers had at the time.

Some friends put Jobs and Wozniak in touch with Mike Markkula, who had been the marketing manager for memory chips at Intel before retiring in his mid-thirties. He was extremely excited about Apple's prospects and joined the company, pitching in $91,000 of seed money for his share in it.

Apple marketed the Apple II aggressively, taking glitzy ads out in *Playboy* as well as computer magazines. The Apple II became a hit, penetrating the home and business market. The rest is history.

Did You Know?

Ross Perot
Ross Perot, the founder of Electronic Data Systems (EDS) and a presidential candidate during the 1992 election, was at one point a very successful IBM salesperson.

CTR
IBM used to be called Computing-Tabulating-Recording. It changed its name in 1924.

IBM PC

IBM had thought about getting into the PC business for several years, and had a number of PC projects. All were killed because they were infeasible due to technical, marketing, or general political requirements. But IBM still wanted to be in the business. The group leader, Bill Lowe, was a risk taker. He chose a maverick, Don Estridge, to lead the group. Estridge refused. He didn't want to be part of another failed PC venture at IBM. But Lowe really wanted him to lead the group, so asked him what it would take. Estridge laid out four demands.

1. The IBM sales force wouldn't sell the computer; it would add another $500 to the price to support the company's infrastructure.

2. The team would not be located in IBM's regular building in Boca Raton.

3. No executives would visit the team.

4. There would be no IBM tie-lines into the offices.

Lowe agreed to the terms, and thus the PC team, code-named Acorn, was born. Estridge would later be offered over a million dollars to work at Apple, which he refused. He died in 1985 in an airplane crash in Dallas.

This is a very early IBM PC shirt. Apple successfully penetrated the education market. As a result, students would use Apple II's when studying and then would go on to recommend them to businesses. IBM countered with an aggressive student discount program and a university campus marketing program. This shirt, which features the front of an original IBM PC on the front and the back of the PC on the back, dates from the early eighties, shortly after the IBM PC was introduced.

Compaq

In the summer of 1981, three guys from Texas Instruments, Rod Canion, Jim Harris, and Bill Murto, sat around a table in the House of Pies restaurant in Houston, Texas. They decided they wanted to form a company, but couldn't decide whether they should create a Mexican restaurant, build hard drives, create a device for finding lost car keys, or, just maybe, start a computer company. They ended up choosing the latter and sketched out a company plan on the back of a paper placemat. They decided to make a computer that would be 100 percent IBM-compatible, and for an added edge, portable. Of course, *portable* in this case meant a little bigger than most of today's tower systems, and heavy enough to throw out someone's back.

The Compaq computer, which came out at the end of 1982, took off wildly. During the first year, the company sold 47,000 computers, pulling in $111 million. Not only was the Compaq 100 percent IBM-compatible, making it attractive to IBM dealers, but Compaq also gave dealers a 36 percent margin rather than the 33 percent that IBM gave. Compaq also hired away a guy named Sparky Sparks from IBM to set up its dealer network. Sparky had earlier done the same thing for the IBM PC.

And Speaking of Compaq

Ben Rosen, a venture capitalist who has funded many of the most influential and successful computer companies, was discussing what he had seen at a trade show with one of his partners.

"Got anything, Ben?"

"Well, I have a guy who has created a spreadsheet and needs some money to market it. Only thing is, he's not quite sure if he wants to continue with it, or if he is going to go visit his yogi in India, or if he just wants to teach meditation. How about you?"

"Well, I met with some folks who say they want to make a clone of an IBM PC. They are real energetic."

"How did their designs look?"

"They didn't have any, and they don't really know much about hardware. But they drew a picture of what the box might look like on the back of an envelope."

Ben decided to fund both companies on a lark. The spreadsheet company was Lotus. The hardware company was Compaq.

Great Quotes:

The Upgrade Market

"Perhaps the most under-appreciated of all developments is the fact that the computer industry sells a device that now requires replacement every three years." Michael Dell.

Dell

Although Michael Dell's first job was working in a Chinese restaurant, he became very interested in computers in junior high school, where his math teacher had a teletype. If he stayed after school, he could use it. This led to a job writing copy protection software when he was 15 years old.

Three years later, he was a student at the University of Texas when he started a thriving gray market business. He would buy machines from dealers who had bought far more IBM PCs than they possibly could sell (so as to get the best discount), and then he would resell them. He was making $30,000 a month at this business when he decided to drop out and form a company making IBM PC clones. This was Dell Computer Corporation, one of the leading PC vendors today.

Sun Microsystems

DARPA, part of the U.S. military, wanted to use Xerox Alto workstations for a project. Sensing that it had a captive audience, Xerox planned to charge a very high price. DARPA balked and looked for computers elsewhere. It came across a generic 68000-based computer that had been designed by a German graduate student at Stanford named Andy Bechtolscheim. The computer was named SUN, which stood for Stanford University Network.

Bechtolscheim looked for someone to build the computer for DARPA. Stanford wouldn't, since, after all, it was a university. 3COM wasn't interested. Bechtolscheim then approached IBM. He had heard that IBM liked formal presentations, so he borrowed a tuxedo from the school's drama department so that he could dress formally. Wearing that and a pair of tennis shoes, he presented his proposal to IBM, which also rejected him. Rather than give up, he decided to form his own company, and together with two other graduate students, Vinod Khosla and Scott McNealy, and Bill Joy, who had worked on Unix at Berkeley, he formed Sun Microsystems.

Great Quotes:

Market Share

"My job is to get a fair share of the software applications market, and to me that's 100 percent." Mike Maples.

Software Companies

Now that you have learned about how some of the major hardware companies formed, lets take a look at the software companies. While hardware companies often require major funding — for creating circuit boards, building manufacturing facilities, and maintaining inventory — software companies do not. A typical software startup requires a good idea; hard-working, heavily caffeinated programmers; and some good computers.

Microsoft

Bill Gates was a computer fanatic from the time he first put his hands on a computer in high school. While still in high school in 1972, he and his buddy Paul Allen formed a company called Traf-O-Data. It created a 8008-based machine for tracking traffic which didn't do particularly well. But Gates and Allen became increasingly involved with a variety of early computer ventures in the Seattle area and soon were widely known. TRW gave them both job offers, and Allen left college to work there, while Gates got a temporary leave from high school for the job. Eventually, Allen switched to Honeywell Inc., and Bill went back to school.

In January 1975, while Gates was a freshman at Harvard, Allen bought the famous *Popular Electronics* issue that featured the MITS Altair. Both men were mesmerized, and they called Ed Roberts, the President of MITS, saying that they had a BASIC that would run on the Altair. Skeptical, Roberts said he would buy the first BASIC that anyone showed him actually running on the Altair.

Allen and Gates switched into high gear. They bought Adam Osborne's 8080 book and built an 8080 emulator on Harvard's PDP-10. Six weeks and many all-nighters later, Allen flew to Albuquerque, where MITS was located; entered the program, switch-throw by switch-throw; and lo and behold, the first time it actually hit Altair hardware, it worked.

MITS went for it, and offered Allen the position of Director of Software. Gates dropped out of Harvard, moved to Albuquerque, and formed Microsoft.

For the first two years, a restrictive licensing agreement held back Microsoft — its arrangment with MITS prevented it from licensing its BASIC to other computer vendors. When MITS was bought by Pertec, Gates and Allen were free of the restrictions, and Microsoft rapidly grew.

Did You Know?

NSF

The BASIC language was developed in 1964 by two Dartmouth professors. They were funded by a grant from the National Science Foundation. BASIC was an instant hit in the programming community.

At first Microsoft focused on computer languages, starting with BASIC and then branching out to other languages, and eventually end-user applications as well. It wasn't until IBM asked Microsoft to do an operating system that Microsoft entered what was to turn into an extremely lucrative and critical business.

In 1980 IBM approached Microsoft, asking it to supply BASIC for the upcoming, top secret IBM PC. IBM brought along with it a typical IBM NDA, which was extremely restrictive. Bill Gates, Paul Allen, and Steve

Ballmer dressed in jackets and ties, took a deep breath, and signed. So as not to discuss any trade secrets per the NDA, they simply took IBM on tour of Microsoft, which at the time employed 50 people.

In later business discussions, IBM asked Microsoft about providing an operating system for the PC. Microsoft suggested that IBM contact Gary Kildall, the maker of CP/M. When IBM arrived, Kildall was out flying (some say he was flying recreationally, but Kildall says he was on a business trip). Kildall's wife, a cofounder of the company, was blown away by IBM's incredibly restrictive NDAs and refused to sign. So IBM trooped back to Microsoft, and Microsoft agreed to supply DOS.

At the time, Microsoft didn't have an operating system, but figured that creating one would benefit sales of its language products. Microsoft had no idea that DOS would grow into one of the most important revenue generators for the company.

Microsoft bought the operating system from a nearby company called Seattle Computer Products. This company had developed an operating system for its 8086 boards, because it was tired of waiting for Digital Research to release a 16-bit version of CP/M. Seattle Computer called its operating system QDOS — or Quick and Dirty OS, since it was pulled together in only two man months by an engineer named Tim Patterson. (Patterson now works at Microsoft.)

Seattle Computer Products also created edlin, which was supposed to be replaced in six months by a better editor. QDOS 1.14 is what turned into IBM PC-DOS 1.0, and QDOS 1.24 is what turned into IBM PC-DOS 1.1.

Microsoft first bought a license, and then, closer to the time of the IBM PC launch, paid $50,000 for all rights to QDOS. (In 1986, Seattle Computer Products sued Microsoft for $60 million over some of the terms in their agreement. They ended up settling for $925,000.) Two weeks later, IBM announced the IBM PC.

Until the very day that the IBM PC shipped, Gates was panicked that IBM might drop the IBM PC project, and that Microsoft would thus have wasted a lot of time and energy pulling together DOS. Of course, as everyone knows, the IBM PC did ship. And in fact, shortly thereafter, IBM sent a thank you letter to Microsoft for all its hard work. The letter said "Dear Vendor ... You've done a fine job."

Did You Know?

Sweating It Out

When Microsoft worked on DOS for the first IBM PC, IBM made Microsoft maintain very tight security. The beta of the IBM hardware had to be kept in a secret, windowless room. It was a very small, unventilated room, and the temperature would get over 100 degrees at various times. Needless to say, whoever was programming inside got very sweaty.

A Merger That Never Happened

At one point during the late seventies, Microsoft considered merging with Digital Research, the makers of CP/M.

The Boat Launch

DOS 5.0 was launched on a five-hour boat cruise around New York City. Dave Brubeck provided the music. The boat was nicknamed DOS Boat.

In yet another pun, Microsoft released a CD with Brubeck's music, called *Take Five*, to go along with the event.

Digital Research

Gary Kildall got a Ph.D. from the University of Washington, and then went to the Naval Post Graduate School in Monterey, California, where he taught computer science. On a lark, he bought a 4004 chip, hoping to make a program to compute navigational triangles, since his father ran a navigation school in Seattle. This experience led to a contracting job with Intel, where he wrote a PL/1 compiler for the 4004. In order to get that to work, he wrote a small operating system, using the PDP-10 emulator at Intel. This operating system, which closely followed the TOPS-10 OS from the PDP-10, later turned into CP/M.

A friend of Kildall's thought the 4004 would be a great platform for a horoscope kiosk. They designed one, and it made its way into a few locations in the San Francisco area. This was the first commercial use of parts of CP/M. The machine, however, had complicated controls, and the horoscope printouts often jammed, leading to customer frustration and a failed venture.

Meanwhile, Kildall continued working with Intel. Consulting for Intel was fun, but involved a long drive. Since he preferred to work in Monterey, which was a far more beautiful place than the Intel office, he decided to put together a machine, so he could work from home rather than have to use the chip emulator at Intel. He scammed a used floppy disk drive from Shugart (in fact, not only was it used, it was from a continuous-use torture test) and, with a friend's hand-built disk controller, linked it to an Intellec-8.

Kildall designed CP/M for this machine. In order to make it easier to port to other machines, he split CP/M into two layers. The BIOS layer, a term still in use today, provided the hardware interface layer.

IMSAI contacted Kildall about licensing CP/M, which he did for $25,000. This legitimized his business, and he then formed Intergalactic Digital Research, quickly to be shortened to Digital Research. CP/M took off, and Kildall made millions.

Digital Research was purchased by Novell, and Kildall went on to do community fund-raisers for kids with AIDS in Austin, Texas. He apparently ran into trouble with drinking, and he died in 1994 after hitting his head on a pinball machine in a club in Monterey, California.

Symantec

Gordon Eubanks was in the Navy. He enjoyed working on nuclear submarines, and when given a chance to get a graduate degree at the Naval Post Graduate School in Monterey, California, he jumped at the opportunity. Hearing that Gary Kildall's course was the hardest, he immediately signed up for it. Kildall became Eubanks' graduate thesis advisor and suggested that Eubanks continue Kildall's work on a BASIC interpreter. Eubanks did exactly that, placing the resulting program in the public domain. After graduating, he went to work for Kildall, heading up the computer languages group at Digital Research.

Two programmers, Keith Parsons and Alan Cooper, approached Eubanks regarding his BASIC. The three got together over a period of several all-nighters and updated the version of BASIC to a version called CBASIC, which they planned to sell through their company, Structured System Group. Eubanks was hoping to make $10,000, because he wanted to buy a house in Hawaii.

In addition to selling CBASIC, Structured System Group was the first distributor of CP/M, and it also sold a general ledger program for the unheard-of price of $995. Structured System Group sold many units, with Parsons' girlfriend taking orders while sunbathing nude in the back yard.

Later on, Cooper created a product code named Ruby that was picked up by Microsoft and turned into the foundation for Visual Basic.

For Eubanks, CBASIC lead to a company called Compiler Systems, which lead to Symantec Corp. Symantec is extremely successful today, with products in a broad range of categories. Symantec has acquired many companies, including Think, Central Point, Fifth Generation, Norton Computing, and Delrina.

Software Arts

In the late 1970s, Dan Bricklin was worried about his career as a programmer. He figured that programming was getting so easy that soon anyone could do it, and as a result, he would be out of a job. So he decided to go to the Harvard Business School. While there, he wanted to write a program to help him with his homework problems. His professors had demonstrated a method that some companies used — filling huge blackboards with rows and columns and recalculating numeric relationships through tedious hand calculations. He decided to use this method for his computer program and, over a weekend in early 1978, wrote a demo in BASIC.

Bricklin hooked up with a buddy of his from MIT, Bob Frankston, to turn his idea into a commercial product; together the two formed a company called Software Arts. Dan Fylstra, a Harvard Business School graduate who had worked with Frankston on a previous project, pulled together a marketing agreement for the company. His company, Personal Software, would market the product, and pay Software Arts a 37.5 percent royalty on retail copies and a 50 percent royalty on products sold directly. At the time, Personal Software was selling various games, including one of the first games, Micro Chess. The proceeds from Micro Chess are what provided the marketing dollars for VisiCalc. Personal Software was also the first company to market Zork. But that is a later story.

Bricklin did a lot of the design work, and Frankston did the coding. He wrote the program on an Apple II emulator that was running on a Multix machine, using the graveyard shift (from midnight to 8 A.M.) so as to save money.

Coincidentally, there was another group using machine cycles at the same time. A group of programmers in France was using the same machine to create an ADA compiler. Of course, the graveyard shift for Frankston was prime time for the programmers in France.

Originally, Frankston wanted the program to only use 16K of memory, but, chagrinned, he admits it required 32K instead. That's a far cry less than the megabytes used by spreadsheets today.

While eating breakfast after one of these all-night programming shifts, Frankston came up with the product name, VisiCalc, short for *visible calculator*. It was the first spreadsheet and one of the most important products for the Apple II, launching the personal computer into the world of business.

Bricklin now runs a small software company. Frankston works at Microsoft.

Did You Know?

Easier Than Getting a Printer

Bob Frankston was one of the authors of the first spreadsheet program, VisiCalc. VisiCalc was marketed by a company called Personal Software, which later turned into VisiCorp. Frankston had worked with Personal Software prior to writing VisiCalc. In this earlier encounter, he ported a bridge program to a TRS-80 Model I. He didn't have a printer, so when he wanted to look at program listings, he would take Polaroid pictures of the computer screen.

Borland

After moving to the United States, Philippe Kahn worked as a consultant for Adam Osborne. Two days before he was going to receive his first paycheck, Osborne Computer Company folded, and Kahn went without pay.

When Kahn started Borland, he had no money. He and the early employees worked out of two rooms on top of a garage in Scotts Valley, California. He had trouble getting anyone to carry his software, because he didn't have a green card, and venture capitalists wouldn't invest in the company, so he decided to gamble on placing an advertisement. The only trouble was, he didn't have any money to pay for the ad.

He called up *Byte,* the premier computer magazine, and tried to get credit. A *Byte* representative came out to the office to see whether Borland was real. Kahn and his crew invited everyone they knew to come over so that they could "populate the office and look professional." They drew up a flip chart with an extensive media plan, showing how they were going to advertise in all magazines except for *Byte.* Then, in the middle of the meeting, Kahn was given a message from Epson calling to arrange a big deal. The "message" was fake and planned in advance.

While Kahn was out of the office, the *Byte* representative was left alone with the flip chart, which he examined. Kahn and the others watched him through a small hole that was in the wall. When the *Byte* rep saw that *Byte* magazine wasn't in the plans, he called *Byte* headquarters and arranged for credit. Borland then ran its first ad, for Turbo Pascal, and became an overnight success. You can see a copy of this ad in the chapter, "Oh Please, Mr. Ad Man."

This is a very funny board game produced by Lotus as a gift for its employees. The playing cards are filled with interesting Lotus trivia. Some examples are

- Willie Nelson calls product support to fix his 1-2-3.

- "Metro" is the name of a large department store in Germany, Switzerland, and Austria. Legal says we can't use it for the product name in these countries.

- Metro code-named Tradewind while Tradewind simultaneously code-named Casino.

- Import mega-salami and pickles from New York for Mitch's going away party.

- When I type "open the pod bay doors, Hal," Lotus' HAL responds with "I can't do that."

- QA discovers an obscene error message just before shipping 1-2-3 for the PC Jr.

- Lotus acquires GCI, the same company whose founder invented contact lenses for chickens.

- "Spencer for Hire" TV series scene filmed in Jim Manzi's office.

Lotus

Mitch Kapor was a well-rounded guy. Before starting a software company, he was a graduate student, a disc jockey, a Transcendental Meditation teacher, and a mental ward counselor. He pawned his stereo to buy an Apple II computer, and on it wrote a VisiCalc add-on called VisiPlot/VisiTrend. Personal Software — the marketers of VisiCalc — carried it, and then bought it for $1.2 million. Kapor ended up working at Personal Software for five months. In a strange twist of fate, Kapor bought Personal Software in 1985.

Kapor took half of the money that he got from the VisiPlot sale and created 1-2-3 for the IBM PC. It was based on a spreadsheet program written for the Data General minicomputers by a guy named Jonathan Sachs. Lotus 1-2-3 had a spreadheet, graphics, and a word processor, making the three parts of the product that lead to its 1-2-3 name. The word processor, however, was a pain to write, so the company dropped it in favor of a simple data manager.

Kapor then raised $3 million in venture capital and hired McKinsey & Co. to help run the business. It spent $1 million on the January 1983 rollout of Lotus 1-2-3, and after the first year, had $53 million in revenue. A year after that, it sold $157 million in software and had 700 employees. One of the McKinsey consultants, Jim Manzi, took over as president.

Lotus had a number of struggles after the success of 1-2-3. Its follow-on products, Symphony and Jazz, were big flops. In 1984, Microsoft offered to buy Lotus, but the negotiations failed due to what some said was a clash of egos, with Manzi talking Kapor out of the deal.

Mitch Kapor resigned from Lotus in July 1986 and is now an investor in several computer companies and very active with the Electronic Freedom Foundation. IBM purchased Lotus for over $3.5 billion in 1995.

Adobe

John Warnock was a graduate student in mathematics at the University of Utah. He worked in the computer center, creating a program for registering students for classes, to help support his family while he went to school. By chance, another graduate student working on a computer graphics problem was talking with Warnock about a difficult problem relating to drawing objects in front of other objects on a computer. Warnock came up with an elegant, hidden-surface algorithm that got him instant attention in the computer science community and led to his switching majors.

After receiving his graduate degree, Warnock went to work for Xerox PARC, where, along with a guy named Martin Newell, he created a graphics language called JaM. (JaM stood for John and Martin, of course.) JaM turned into something called Interpress. Xerox wasn't interested in turning Interpress into a product, so after two years, Warnock left, formed a company called Adobe Systems Inc. with a fellow Xerox worker named Chuck Geshcke, and turned Interpress into PostScript. The name "Adobe" came from a creek that ran outside Warnock's garden in Los Altos, California.

Ashton-Tate

Wayne Ratliff worked at Martin-Marietta. At his job, he used a public domain database system called JPLDIS, which came from the Jet Propulsion Laboratory. Ratliff decided to make a PC version of JPLDIS so he could track horse races. He enhanced the JPLDIS design in a number of ways, including adding a query-by-form type interface.

But Ratliff didn't have the time to keep working full-time and market this product, called Vulcan. So he sold the marketing rights to George Tate, with the hopes that he might earn $100,000. Tate renamed the product dBASE II and from it built Ashton-Tate. (There was no Ashton, but Tate figured Ashton-Tate sounded sophisticated, whereas Ratliff-Tate did not.) dBASE became one of the best-selling database products, and Ratliff ended up making millions.

George Tate died of a cocaine-induced heart attack in 1983, and Ed Esber, who had just been hired away from VisiCorp, took over as the president. Esber was forced out in early 1990, and Borland ended up buying Ashton-Tate for $440 million in 1991.

Novell

Novell started off as Novell Data Systems, a maker of CP/M computers. Its machines had a bad reputation, and business was going poorly, so it

In 1981 business at MicroPro was booming. WordStar was the hottest word processor around. And the company needed to expand its empire, as shown in this ad that could just as easily have run in the back of a *Batman* comic book. The world knew little of Microsoft and IBM's impending announcement about the IBM PC.

decided to branch into a new area. In September 1981, it hired three contractors, who formed a company called SuperSet, to create software that could link computers together so that they could share a hard drive. This was important technology for the time, because hard drives were extremely expensive. SuperSet's technology allowed computers to share and lock directories and files on the server computer. The company created a computer to provide this technology, called the Novell Data Management Computer, which shipped in November 1981. SuperSet then moved its solution to the IBM PC.

Meanwhile, Novell Data Systems went broke. The only part the venture-backers thought worthy to salvage was SuperSet's IBM PC work. SuperSet continued this for two years while the rest of the company was broken apart. Novell restarted in 1983, concentrating solely on software. In order to grow the market, it sold network cards and workstations at cost, making a few dealers unhappy in the process. Today, Novell is one of the five largest software companies.

MicroPro

Seymour Rubenstein started his career as a technical writer. He then became a programmer for a military defense firm, and he later drifted West to work for a small computer company founded by Bill Millard. That folded, and after a variety of other stints, Rubenstein worked for Millard again, at IMSAI. He started as a product marketing manager and quickly moved to become the Director of Marketing.

Rubenstein was known as a champion deal-maker. Two of his triumphs at IMSAI were deals with Digital Research and with Gordon Eubanks. Rubenstein negotiated a flat-fee license for CP/M from Digital Research for $25,000. Reportedly, after making the deal he told Kildall, "If you continue this practice, you are not going to make nearly as much money as you are entitled to." Rubenstein got an unlimited license for Gordon Eubanks' BASIC in exchange for a computer, disk drives, a printer, and some technical support. He was also known as one of the few people ever to out-negotiate Bill Gates.

Rubenstein left IMSAI to form MicroPro in late 1978. Its first two products were SuperSort and WordMaster. In 1979, the company released WordStar, which would become the dominant word processor for a time, and for a while, MicroPro became the largest software company.

WordStar gained a reputation for not keeping up with the times. MicroPro resisted making a native implementation for the IBM PC, instead relying on its CP/M port. By the time MicroPro overhauled its flagship product, WordPerfect had taken over the market. Seymour Rubenstein resigned in 1983, only to return as a consultant six years later.

MicroPro renamed itself to WordStar International and bought ZSoft in 1993. With mounting losses, it merged with SoftKey Software Products Inc. and Spinnaker Software Corporation in early 1994. The combined company turned into SoftKey International.

ComputerLand

ComputerLand started in September 1976 as a sales franchise for IMSAI. The first store opened in Hayward, California, in November 1976, and the first franchise store opened in February 1977 in Morristown, New Jersey. ComputerLand was originally called Computer Shack, but after a threat from Radio Shack, changed its name.

ComputerLand became a dominant computer chain, but later ran into some financial troubles. In 1994, Merisel bought the franchise and distribution portions of ComputerLand for close to $100 million.

Merisel

Speaking of Merisel, Softsel Computer Products Inc. was an early distributor of software. It started with two guys, Bob Leff and David Wagman, selling computer adventure games out of the back of their station wagon. Later, the company merged with MicroAmerica to turn into Merisel, one of the largest software and hardware distributors today.

Electric Pencil

One of the earliest word processors was called the Electric Pencil. It was written by Michael Shrayer, who previously had worked as a camera operator and at other film-related jobs, including a stint on "Candid Camera."

Heading west to get out of the East Coast rat race, Shrayer ended up in the ballooning California computer scene. He created an editor called Extended Software Package 1, based on public domain software shipped by Processor Technology. Hobbyists bought enough copies that Shrayer could live off the revenue, and he extended it into a product called the Electric Pencil. Over the lifetime of the product, Shrayer created 78 different versions for the various platforms that Electric Pencil supported. Shrayer closed the company after shipping 250,000 copies of the product.

Peachtree Software

At the end of 1975, a couple of folks who met at the Georgia Tech graduate school got together to form a business. They were excited about the birth of the personal computer, and they formed an Altair dealership called Computersystem Center. Business was sometimes slow, so they programmed in their idle time, writing several business accounting packages. Soon they formed a network for distributing software called the Altair Software Distribution Company. After MITS was bought by Pertec, they decided that the company needed a new name. Based in Georgia, they went with an old standby. If you've ever been to Georgia, you know that almost everything has the word *peachtree* in it, one way or another. Thus, they changed the company's name to Peachtree Software.

Peachtree is still around today, selling business and accounting software, though with the emergence of Lotus 1-2-3, Excel, and Quicken, the product no longer retains the market position it once had.

ButtonWare

Jim Button worked at IBM for 18 years. On his own he decided to write a simple database program called PC File. Rather than forming a large company, Button decided to let anyone try it out and distribute it. If the person liked it, Button asked for $10 in return, relying on the general honesty of the software consumer. This approach was in stark contrast to the plethora of copy protection schemes popular at the time. Button had hoped to earn enough money to buy a new computer. Instead, he ended up making $490,000 in 1983 alone, and he left his job at IBM to form ButtonWare, one of the first shareware companies.

Oracle

Oracle was founded in 1977 by Ed Oates, Bruce Scott, Robert Miner, and Larry Ellison. The company's original name was Software Development Labs.

Did You Know?

A Translation Issue
The popular video game Donkey Kong never has a donkey in it. Instead, there is a large ape that looks like King Kong. That's because the game was going to be called Monkey Kong, but the name was mistranslated.

InfoCom

In 1977, the game Adventure became wildly popular on the ARPAnet. It was a public domain program written by Willie Crowther and Don Woods, and it was heavily inspired by Dungeons and Dragons, a fantasy role-playing game still popular among programmers.

Adventure spawned several PC adventure games, including many from Scott Adams, a Microsoft version written by Gordon Letwin, and games such as Leather Goddesses of Phobos, Leisure Suit Larry, King's Quest, and hundreds of shareware adventures.

After solving Adventure (through using a debugger to cheat and find the final clue), a group of programmers from the Dynamic Modeling Group at MIT — Marc Blank, Dave Lebling, Tim Anderson, and Bruce Daniels — got together to write their own adventure. Blank was on a break from medical school, Anderson had just completed his Master's degree, and Daniels was working on a Ph.D. They were all looking forward to some fun hacking.

Thus they began writing Zork. It was a common practice among the group to name unfinished programs "zork." This was a hacker word meaning "total destruction." So, the group named the software "zork," figuring they would change the name later. They wrote it on a DEC system-10 using a language called MDL, which came from a language called MUDDLE, which came from a language that was (and still is) very popular at MIT, LISP.

Once they finished the game, they changed the name, as they planned, to Dungeon. But, the company that made Dungeons and Dragons didn't think too highly of that and sent a threatening letter from their lawyers. Even though the programmers thought they could use the word *Dungeon*, they decided to avoid the legal hassle and changed the name to Zork.

In 1979, the group incorporated, forming InfcoCom. According to Anderson, it wasn't pulled together to sell Zork. Rather, it was to give MIT students a place to go after graduating. InfoCom started with $11,500 in the bank. It was enough to buy some limited equipment, but not enough to pay anyone, so everyone accepted IOUs instead of paychecks.

Once it had a PC version available, InfoCom sought a distributor. Microsoft already had an adventure game and thus wasn't interested, so InfoCom contacted Personal Software, distributors of VisiCalc. Personal Software took InfoCom on and assigned a marketing guy named Mitch Kapor to promote the company. Kapor, of course, later moved on to found Lotus.

The first PC versions of Zork came out in December 1980, for the TRS-80 and the Apple II. Personal Software sold 1,500 copies of the TRS-80 version and 6,000 copies of the Apple version in the first nine months.

With the success of VisiCalc, Personal Software decided to focus on business applications rather than games, so InfoCom got the distribution rights back and promoted Zork itself.

Did You Know?

Addresses and Numbers

Many computer companies have computer related addresses or phone numbers. For example:

The last four digits of Microsoft's phone number are 8080.

The last four digits of PC Connection's phone number are 8088.

The last four digits of *Win Tech Journal*'s phone number are 0386.

The last four digits of Travelling Software's phone number are 8088.

There are plenty of computer-related street names as well.

The road around Microsoft's campus is called Disk Drive.

Seagate also has a road named Disk Drive.

Microsoft has a lake named after Bill Gates' email address: Lake BillG. This is pronounced Lake Bilge.

Apple's headquarters are at 1 Infinite Loop.

Delta Products Inc. was located at 15392 Assembly Lane.

MPS Distributors, Inc. was located at 1105 Terminal Way.

Magazines

How does one keep on top of the latest developments in the computer industry? By reading the trade magazines, of course. Today, computer magazines grace the counters of every airport bookstore. Glitzy ads rival those in *Elle* and *Cosmopolitan*. (Well, almost.) But this wasn't always the case. Computer magazines started out as hobbyist newsletters. Many have come and gone, but some of the very first still remain. Let's take a look at the humble origins of some of today's giants.

Dr. Dobbs

One of the very first computer newsletters published was the nonprofit *People's Computer Company* newsletter. This was a true offshoot of the sixties countercultural movement, with a mission to educate people about computers. It had a statement: "Computers are mostly used against people instead of for people ... used to control people instead of to free them ... time to change all that ... we need a People's Computer Company." It was a sentimentality widely felt among the early computer hobbyists and designers.

After receiving many requests to cover Tiny BASIC, *People's Computer Company* decided to do a special three-issue magazine just focusing on that. The writers who kicked that off were Dennis Allison and Bob Albrecht. They shortened their names (taking the "D" from Dennis and the "ob" from Bob) to create *Dr. Dobb's Journal of Tiny BASIC Calisthenics & Orthodontia.* It was a hit and continued well beyond the first three issues. The name was later broadened to *Dr. Dobb's Journal of Computer Calisthenics & Orthodontia,* and finally shortened to the simpler *Dr. Dobb's Journal.* Today, *Dr. Dobb's* is one of the largest-circulation computer magazines, known for its focus on programming issues.

PC Magazine

Among many things, David Bunnel was the head of documentation at MITS, and he also organized the Altair newsletter. After leaving MITS, Bunnel started numerous magazines, including the incredibly successful *PC Magazine.*

Byte

Wayne Green was the publisher of a ham radio magazine called *73.* His magazine was growing, so he decided to computerize the operation. But before doing so, he figured he had better brush up on computer technology. He found very little topical information, so he decided to start a magazine, calling it *Byte.* The first issue came out in 1975.

Unfortunately for Green, he had run into some legal trouble and had been convicted of tax evasion, so his lawyers advised him to keep *Byte* separate from *73* until the various cases were resolved. Therefore, Green set his ex-wife up as the owner and office manager. After the first issue, his ex-wife, her new husband, and the editor ousted Green. In 1979, they sold the magazine to McGraw-Hill.

Though it no longer holds its former place as *the* computer magazine, *Byte* remains a widely read and popular magazine today.

Boston Computer Society

It's not a magazine, but what the heck. The Boston Computer Society was founded in 1976 by Jonathan Rotenberg, who was 13 years old at the time. Today, the Boston Computer Society is one of the largest and most influential computer users' groups.

Did You Know?

It's a Mad, Mad World

Donald Knuth is a very famous computer scientist. He was the creator of TeX, an early document layout system, which he used to get high-quality, computer-generated pages for his books. He also wrote what is regarded as one of the fundamental books on computer algorithms. He is particularly famous for his discussions of sorting techniques.

His first publication, though perhaps more widely read, was not as academic. He wrote an article, "The Potrszebie System of Weights and Measures," that appeared in the June 1957 *Mad* magazine.

Memories of the Way We Were

Kids today have it easy. Back in the old days, we used to walk for miles just to see a computer. Through the snow. And keyboards? Bah. We used switches. And we liked it.

Thing is, though, it's all true. These are only a few of the hardships one endured in the early days of computers. With the number of transistors on a chip doubling every 18 months, and storage and peripheral devices dropping in price on a monotonic downward spiral, it is no wonder that machines today are dramatically different from those of four, let alone 20, years ago. As a conclusion to our tour through the underworld of computing, let's take a dash through some of the antiquated activities of the earlier days.

Driving for Miles to Talk about Computers

In the early days, not many people knew about computers. The Homebrew Computer Club, which started in 1975, was the first computer club. It was followed by several others, including the Boston Computer Society, which was founded in 1977, and trade shows such as the West Coast Computer Faire, which also started in 1977. As computers became more and more affordable, more and more people were involved with them. Still, by the mid-eighties, it was rare to accidentally run into people who knew about computers, and thus computer people hung out at users' groups, trade shows, and even computer stores, just to chat about the latest developments and admire the latest in hardware.

That's changed. It is hard to go anywhere, whether to a movie theater, restaurant, or on a hike in the wilderness without running into someone talking about computers. And with more widespread use of computers, such conversations wander farther from the technical truth, occasionally causing one to cringe. I know many people from companies such as Microsoft and Apple who don't mention where they work at parties just to avoid the questions, "What should I buy?" or "Can you help me get my computer to work?" — questions that used to lead to hours of pure pleasure.

Paper and Cassette Tapes

CD-ROMs are fast becoming standard on most new computers. But during the first five years of personal computers, input devices were far more primitive. Early computers, such as the Altair, used switches for entering programs, and LED lights for showing output. The MIKE used an innovative hex pad for entering programs. And once the power was turned off, all of one's data and programs went away. So, if users wanted to use Microsoft BASIC on the Altair, they had to type (well, switch-flip) the 4K program in by hand. Then they could enter their own programs. Once they turned off the machine, all would be lost.

Microcomputers were quickly augmented with cassette and paper tape inputs (Figure 24-1). Users could buy software, such as Microsoft BASIC and the subLogic Flight Simulator, on rolls of paper tape. The TRS-80, Apple II, and IBM PC all came with cassette interfaces. Of course, for kicks, we'd put rock and roll tapes, typically Pink Floyd, into the cassette decks to see what would come out, either as programs or as data.

By the early eighties, almost all computers came with floppy drives. Of course, at first floppies from one machine usually couldn't be read on machines with the same size drives from other vendors.

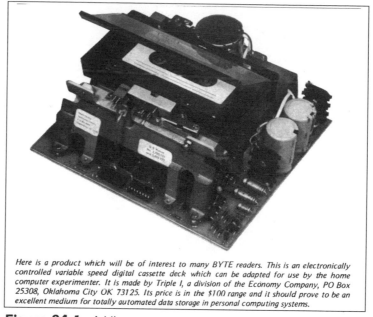

Here is a product which will be of interest to many BYTE readers. This is an electronically controlled variable speed digital cassette deck which can be adapted for use by the home computer experimenter. It is made by Triple I, a division of the Economy Company, PO Box 25308, Oklahoma City OK 73125. Its price is in the $100 range and it should prove to be an excellent medium for totally automated data storage in personal computing systems.

Figure 24-1: Adding a cassette to your computer meant saving much time typing in hex programs.

Flippin' the Floppy

At first, floppy drives used only one side of the floppy. Floppy disks were expensive, at least for hobbyists. It was a well-known fact that by flipping over a floppy disk and cutting a notch in just the right place, one could use the other side of the disk, thereby doubling the amount of data that could fit on a single disk. This was usually called "double-siding" a diskette.

Of course, there were risks to this. If users put the hole in the wrong place, the intervening plastic would still appear to be a write-protect, so they'd need to punch a hole again. If they completely screwed it up, they could punch a hole through the magnetic media, destroying disks. And there were plenty of warnings about the flip side of disks not being guaranteed, or of having data bleed through, thereby destroying what was stored on both sides.

All one really needed to double-side diskettes was a hole-punch or a pair of scissors (Figure 24-2). Several companies, though, introduced special tools for punching the right size hole at the correct place.

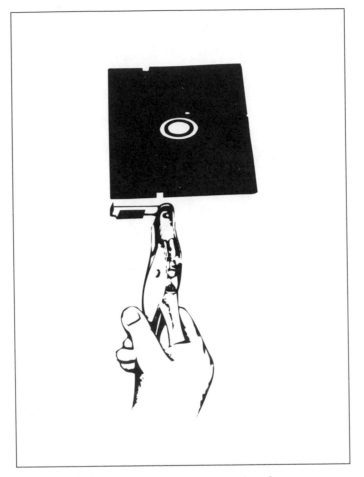

Figure 24-2: One of the many approaches for using both sides of floppy disks.

Not All Floppies Were Created Equal

In the early days of floppies, one engaged in much debate over the merits of different brands of floppy disks. Magazines were filled with ads describing why their brands would guarantee safety. There were Maxell, Memorex, Verbatim, Elephant, IBM, Dysan, and many more brands. Of course, if someone lost data using a particular brand of floppy, news would travel quickly through the grapevine, and groups would quickly switch their allegiances to what was believed to be a more reliable brand.

Colorful Language

Another popular debate was over whether green screens or amber screens were better. After all, if users were going to stare at a screen all day long, they wanted to make sure that they had the best possible monitor. While the popular opinion was that amber was better, the only clear answer was that both beat connecting the computer to a TV screen.

Basic Maintenance

Keeping a computer running used to be a major undertaking requiring regular maintenance. By this, I don't mean backing up on a regular basis or cleaning dust off the monitor.

Many peripheral cards, especially on the Apple II computers, built up crud along the connecting pins, especially when there was high humidity. So, typically once a day during the summer, a user would pop off the top, take out the cards, and clean the edges off with an eraser. Likewise, the integrated circuits used to pop out, causing all types of good fun. A user would open the top and press the chips down every week or so to keep things running smoothly. This was particularly the case for the first 90,000 Apple IIIs manufactured, since the assembling machines didn't insert all of the chips far enough. One approach to reseating the chips was to drop the machine from a one-foot height.

And, of course, moving parts fared worse. On a regular basis, one needed to tune floppy drives. For many drives, such as those on the Apple II, this was done by turning the drive upside down. There were a series of black and white lines on a cardboard disk underneath the motor. A screw nearby, (a *trim pot*, to be exact), adjusted the speed of the motor. A user would turn it until the lines would stop looking like a blur. At the correct frequency, the pattern would stabilize.

Let's not even talk about card-punch machines.

Pining for a Printer

Printers were relatively expensive in the early days, especially if a user wanted to match the quality of the daisy-wheel typewriters that were so popular at the time. There were numerous solutions to this problem, including mechanical devices that one could put on top of an electric typewriter to punch the keys (Figure 24-3). Later on, many typewriters came with built-in ports so that they could be connected to computers . Eventually, the price of printers came down so dramatically that no one would think of switching to a typewriter to get the best output quality.

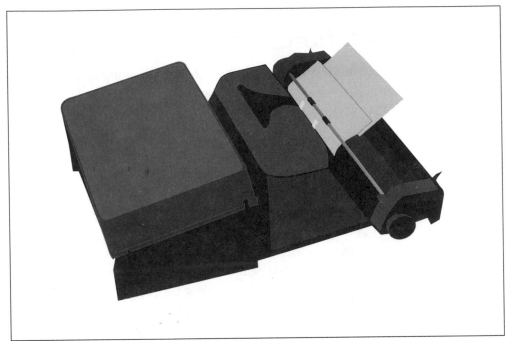

Figure 24-3: Several devices were designed for connecting computers to typewriters. Some, such as the one illustrated here, consisted of boxes filled with relays that would sit on top of the typewriter. The relays would fire, striking the keys on the typewriter, like a pair of electric hands. Some electric typewriters added interface ports, and provided devices for connecting the typewriter interface to the computer serial port.

Punching the Clock

At first, computers didn't come with built-in clocks. So every time users turned on their computers, they needed to type in the time. This was just part of getting ready for a day of computing. If they forgot the step — or just skipped it, as many of us did, — the time stamps on files would be all across the map.

Users could add a system clock if they wanted, with boards such as those from AST gaining much attention.

Those Wonderful Modems

Connecting to the Internet was not as easy as it is now. Most modems ran at 300 baud, (that is, 96 times slower than a 28.8 modem). Getting a clean connection was difficult. Not only were modems not nearly as tolerant of line noise, but to make a call, a user would dial the number manually using a normal phone. Then the phone receiver would be jammed into a pair of squishy cups containing a speaker and microphone for connecting the phone to the computer (Figure 24-4).

Figure 24-4: An early modem ad, featuring squishy cups for the phone handset.

I'm Dreaming of Hard Drives

In the early days, hard drives were a luxury, a heavy, slow, and incredibly expensive luxury. A 5MB hard drive cost more in 1981 than a fully loaded Pentium, with a 1GB drive in 1995.

Learning to Park

Of course, once users got a hard drive, they needed to take care of it. One of the most critical steps with the early hard drives was parking the heads. To do so, a user ran special system software that would move the heads off of the data area. If a user failed to do so and then moved the computer, the hard disk head could bounce, hit the disk surface, and destroy data or even the whole disk. This was called a *head crash* and lead to much paranoia every time a computer was moved. Eventually, hard drives automatically parked their heads on power down, eliminating this critical activity.

Revvin' Up the Z

Before Apple and IBM redefined the industry with the success of the Apple II and the IBM PC, the Z80 was the most popular chip for computers. And with it, CP/M was the most popular operating system and had the widest software base. If you wanted to run CP/M programs on your Apple II or IBM PC, you would have had to get an add-in card with a Z80 chip on it.

One of the most popular add-in cards came from Microsoft (Figure 24-5). In fact, the SoftCard was one of Microsoft's most successful products at the time. Similar cards were available for adding Z80 chips to IBM PCs.

Figure 24-5: Microsoft, which would base its fortune on the success of DOS, is here extolling the benefits of adding CP/M capabilities to an Apple II via the Microsoft SoftCard.

It is amazing what lugging portable computers through airports will do for you. After this piece of direct mail went out, one programmer wrote me to tell me his wife hung it on the refrigerator to prove that even nerds could have muscles.

So Long and Thanks For All the Fish

So there you have it. The last 20 years of computing technology have been remarkable ones. The industry has grown from a few hackers working out of garages to a multibillion-dollar, glitzy industry, with hackers still working out of garages. Although the technology today blows away the dinosaurs of the late seventies, much of the industry spirit stays the same, showing up in the pranks, hacks, and late-night activities of a bunch of nerds just wanting to have fun and make some money.

I hope you've had fun reading this book, and have learned a little bit more about how the remarkable computer industry operates. Remember, next time you pull an office prank, send a photo to me. And never keep your back turned for too long. In the words of Richard Stallman, "Happy hacking."

Index

C

Z

ALSO NEW FROM IDG BOOKS

"Alan Cooper is a software god... This is a landmark book."—Stewart Alsop, Executive Vice President of InfoWorld Publishing

ABOUT FACE
THE ESSENTIALS OF
USER INTERFACE DESIGN

ALAN COOPER

"Father of Visual Basic"
Microsoft Windows® Pioneer Award Honoree

Foreword by Andrew Singer

COVERS WINDOWS 95

No Matter How Cool Your Interface Is,
Less of It Would Be Better

Rethink Windows Interface Design.

About Face: The Essentials of User Interface Design
by Alan Cooper

ISBN: 1-56884-322-4
$29.99 US/$39.99 Canada

To Order, Call 800-762-2974

IDG BOOKS WORLDWIDE

Order Center: **(800) 762-2974** *(8 a.m.–6 p.m., EST, weekdays)*

5/8/95

Quantity	ISBN	Title	Price	Total

Shipping & Handling Charges

	Description	First book	Each additional book	Total
Domestic	Normal	$4.50	$1.50	$
	Two Day Air	$8.50	$2.50	$
	Overnight	$18.00	$3.00	$
International	Surface	$8.00	$8.00	$
	Airmail	$16.00	$16.00	$
	DHL Air	$17.00	$17.00	$

*For large quantities call for shipping & handling charges.
**Prices are subject to change without notice.

Ship to:

Name _____

Company _____

Address _____

City/State/Zip _____

Daytime Phone _____

Payment: □ Check to IDG Books (US Funds Only)

□ VISA   □ MasterCard   □ American Express

Card # _____ Expires _____

Signature _____

Subtotal _____

CA residents add
applicable sales tax _____

IN, MA, and MD
residents add
5% sales tax _____

IL residents add
6.25% sales tax _____

RI residents add
7% sales tax _____

TX residents add
8.25% sales tax _____

Shipping _____

Total _____

Please send this order form to:

IDG Books Worldwide
7260 Shadeland Station, Suite 100
Indianapolis, IN 46256

*Allow up to 3 weeks for delivery.
Thank you!*